Advertising
to
Children

The American Academy
of Advertising

In 1957, Dr. Harry Hepner (Syracuse University) presented the idea of an organization for advertising educators to Robert Feemster, advertising director for *The Wall Street Journal* and chairman of the Advertising Federation of America. Feemster agreed such an organization would be a good idea and asked Dr. J. Leroy Thompson, first director of the Dow Jones Educational Service Bureau, to invite teachers to attend the 1958 Dallas AFA conventions.

Attending that first 1958 Dallas meeting were:

Donald Davis (Pennsylvania State University)
Jerry Drake (Southern Methodist University)
Milton Gross (University of Missouri)
Harry Hepner (Syracuse University)
Donald G. Hileman (Southern Illinois University)
Frank McCabe (Providence, R.I.)
Royal H. Ray (Florida State University)
Billy L. Ross (University of Houston)
J. Leroy Thompson (Dow Jones Educational Service Bureau)

Hepner explained that there was no organization servicing advertising teachers in business and journalism schools. Gross and Drake, active in the national professional advertising fraternity, Alpha Delta Sigma, did not join the Academy at the beginning. The others decided to proceed with the framework of an organization and named interim officers. At Hepner's recommendation, academy titles were used for the officers: Hepner as National Dean; Ross as National Associate Dean; George T. Clark, New York University, as National Registrar; and McCabe as National Bursar. The first year was devoted to increasing membership and developing a structure. The second national meeting was held in Minneapolis, June 7-10, 1959. The interim officers were elected to continue in their positions for a one-year term.

During the 1960-1961 year, membership grew from 123 to 241. The Academy established relation with the Associations of National Advertisers, Association of Industrial Advertisers, and the American Association of Advertising Agencies.

Today, the Academy has over 600 members. The Executive committee of the Academy, which meets twice a year, consists of a President, President-Elect, Vice President, Secretary, Treasurer, Past President, and Executive Secretary; the nationally elected President of the Academy annually appoints over 60 members to approximately 11 committees. The Academy maintains relationships with many advertising-related associations, including INAME and the Accreditation Council for Education in Journalism and Mass Communication.

Objectives

The Academy is established as a professional organization for teachers in advertising and for industry professions who wish to contribute to the development of advertising education.

The general objectives of the Academy shall be:

- ✧ To provide an organization through which all persons interested in advertising education may coordinate their efforts to advance academic and professional advertising.

⋄ To assume leadership, especially in academic circles, for an objective and realistic appraisal of the functions and responsibilities of advertising in modern society.

⋄ To strive for increased recognition by both educators and industry professionals of the value of and need for professional education programs for advertising.

⋄ To stimulate research in advertising, especially research about professional educational programs for advertising.

⋄ To develop closer liaison with academic disciplines with which advertising is concerned, not only in such primary fields as business administration, communications, journalism, and public relations, but also in the behavioral sciences, humanities, and other liberal arts areas.

⋄ To encourage closer cooperation among teachers of advertising for the development and better use of teaching materials and methods, for the expansion of recruiting programs, and for sponsorship of scholarships and internships, in order to attract and to develop talent for the field of advertising.

⋄ To develop closer liaison with the many organizations associated with the advertising industry.

Academy Website

The American Academy of Advertising maintains a website, available via Internet, to assist Academy members in keeping current with the Academy.

The Academy Website is at: http://Advertising.Utexas.Edu/AAA

This website contains listing of all Academy committees, Constitution, By-Laws, etc.

Website manager is Joe Bob Hester, Texas Tech University.

Advertising to Children

Concepts and Controversies

M. Carole Macklin
Les Carlson

Editors

SAGE Publications
International Educational and Professional Publisher
Thousand Oaks   London   New Delhi

For information:

SAGE Publications, Inc.
2455 Teller Road
Thousand Oaks, California 91320
E-mail: order@sagepub.com

SAGE Publications Ltd.
6 Bonhill Street
London EC2A 4PU
United Kingdom

SAGE Publications India Pvt. Ltd.
M-32 Market
Greater Kailash I
New Delhi 110 048 India

Printed in the United States of America

Library of Congress Cataloging-in-Publication Data

Main entry under title:

Advertising to children: Concepts and controversies /
    edited by M. Carole Macklin and Les Carlson.
        p.   cm.
    Includes bibliographical references and index.
    ISBN 0-7619-1284-3 (cloth; acid-free paper)
    ISBN 0-7619-1285-1 (pbk; acid-free paper)
    1. Television advertising and children—United States.
    2. Advertising and children—United States. I. Macklin, M. Carole.
    II. Carlson, Les.
    HQ784.T4 A29 1999
    302.23′45′083—dc21   99-6231

00   01   02   03   04   05   7   6   5   4   3   2

Acquiring Editor:	Harry Briggs
Editorial Assistant:	Mary Ann Vail
Production Editor:	Wendy Westgate
Editorial Assistant:	Nevair Kabakian
Typesetter/Designer:	Marion Warren
Indexer:	Jean Casalegno
Cover Designer:	Ravi Balasuriya

Contents

Introduction

Πdvertising to children is a topic that has consistently stirred debate over the past 25 years. Numerous reasons explain the keen interest. First, the extent of children's understanding of advertising messages is unclear. Second, some fear that children may not comprehend the persuasive aspects of advertising; therefore, children are unable to defend against messages. Such concerns have been exaggerated, perhaps, by the increase in spending to capture the children's market. It has been estimated that U.S. television advertising directed to children cost $894 million during 1996 (Crowe 1997). Advertisers have been willing to spend large amounts because they realize that the children's market is huge. McNeal (1998) estimated that children under 14 years spent $24 billion in direct purchases and influenced family spending by another $188 billion during 1997. Obviously, marketers wish to learn whether their money is well spent in approaching this market. Moreover, parents, educators, and concerned others want to learn how effective communication directed to children really is.

Our purpose is not to present a review of the vast number of research studies published in the past few decades. Such reviews are available (e.g., Young 1990). Rather, we wish to present cutting-edge research on topics of current debate, such as cigarette advertising, plus address children's advertising more broadly. Our goal is to present state-of-the art research that addresses the following: what children know and think about advertising; how advertising works with children; what issues are in the forefront of societal and public policy thinking. Moreover, we look to the future as we present what leading advertisers and academicians believe are topics ripe for research.

In the first section of the book, we include works that examine children as an advertising audience in the following ways: what they know and think about advertising, how they view television, and how they derive meaning from messages. We are pleased to begin our collection of chapters with one by Deborah Roedder John. As a leading researcher over the past 20 years, she reviews the research literature on different-aged children's knowledge, understanding, and feelings about advertising. Her chapter will help the reader understand why children of different ages hold varied views of advertising. In Chapter 2, Tamara Mangleburg and Terry Bristol increase our understanding of children's skepticism toward advertising. They offer us a socialization explanation, focusing on how skepticism is learned through interaction with parents, peers, and television. Robert Abelman and David Atkin help the reader gain a better grasp on children's viewing motives and viewing patterns in the third chapter. Not only do these authors profile the child television viewing audience, they also identify three distinctive viewer archetypes. In the fourth chapter, Cindy Dell Clark provides us with a holistic perspective on children and advertising. She argues that children actively construct meaning when viewing advertising by using the processes of personal and cultural symbolism. Thus, the reader gains a fuller understanding of the dynamic interaction between the child and the ad.

In Part II, we present primary research that assesses societal impact and concern. Alison Alexander, Louise M. Benjamin, Keisha Hoerrner, and Darrell Roe contribute to our understanding of children's advertising before it became a fashionable research topic. In Chapter 5, they examine commercials from the 1950s in programs aimed at the child market. Their content analysis shows marked distinctions from commercials in modern decades. In Chapter 6, Ann Walsh, Russell Laczniak, and Les Carlson increase the reader's understanding of how parents view children's television. More specifically, they segment mothers according to their parental styles. Then they examine how the particular segments view various options regarding the regulation of children's television. Darrel Muehling and Richard Kolbe continue the regulatory theme with a specific examination of advertising disclosures. In our seventh chapter, they find fine-print disclosures to audiences to be different between prime-time and Saturday morning viewing times. Mary Martin, James Gentry, and Ronald Hill also present differences, this time between girls and boys when reacting to magazine ads. In Chapter 8, they assess adolescent girls' and boys' evaluation of ads and brands that use physically attractive models as endorsers. Girls, but not boys, with poor body images seem affected most by ads with physically attractive models. In the last chapter of this second part (Chapter 9), Bonnie Reece, Nora Rifon, and Kimberly Rodriguez continue with the human body theme. Their content analysis of food ads shows that ads targeted to children contain some nutrition information. However, their work shows that even greater emphasis is placed on other themes (such as taste and excitement) that may ultimately affect children's health.

In Part III, we include recent and basic research on today's two hot buttons: smoking and alcohol. Chapter 10 presents work by Laura Peracchio and David Luna regarding the discouragement of smoking initiation among children. Public policy makers will be particularly interested in how these researchers use a youth attitude assessment to develop an analogy-based advertising campaign with the purpose of discouraging smoking initiation. In the eleventh chapter, Barbara Phillips and Liza Stavchansky contribute to our further understanding of underage smoking by studying cigarette characters (Joe Camel and the Marlboro cowboy). They report that while these characters do send positively identified messages, junior high students were more skeptical and more negative toward these characters than some advertising critics might believe. Richard Fox, Dean Krugman, James Fletcher, and Paul Fischer use eye tracking to monitor how young people view print ads for cigarettes and for beer. As they bring the third part of the book to a close (Chapter 12), these researchers express concern for the one-third of the sample who did not look at the cautionary statement to "think when you drink" and the almost 25% who never fixated on the warning message on the cigarette ad. Their work suggests that we may have to pay careful attention to the communication power of various warnings.

Our final section of the book, Part IV, provides wonderful challenges for the reader. We are proud to present the insights of leading advertisers and academicians as to what they see as future topics for our research.

Christine Wright-Isak raises three important issues in Chapter 13: how we accumulate information about children, how we develop safeguards for children about their participation in new technologies, and how appropriately advertisers are communicating with children about brands and products. Carole Walters challenges us in the fourteenth chapter to improve our understanding of how children respond to information via the Internet. She highlights children's apparent ability to multitask, an ability whose impact we little understand. Another leading academician of long standing, Marvin Goldberg, points out in the fifteenth chapter that we have often failed to contrast effects between younger and older children. For example, the literature on cigarettes and youth typically focuses on 13- to 18-year-olds while neglecting to examine younger children (2- to 12-year-olds). Finally, in Chapter 16, Jeffrey Stoltman presents us with a broad view of a number of topics and approaches that are needed to further our understanding of children and advertising. For example, he points out that we know little about the short- and long-term effects of children's exposure to communication intended for adult audiences.

We hope that after reading this book your interest in the topic of children and advertising will be stimulated. We thank all of the authors for their insightful and informative contributions. It is our sincerest hope that this book will spur additional high-caliber work in children's advertising.

References

Crowe, Bill (1997), "Advertisers See Big Buys in Little Eyes," *Broadcasting & Cable*, 28 (July), 47-48.

McNeal, James U. (1998), "Tapping the Three Kids' Markets," *American Demographics*, 20 (April), 37-41.

Young, Brian M. (1990), *Television Advertising and Children*, New York: Oxford University Press.

PART
I

In Search of What Children Know
and Think About Advertising and
How Advertising Works

Through the Eyes of a Child

———

Children's Knowledge and Understanding of Advertising

DEBORAH ROEDDER JOHN

Early interest in the area of children's advertising was ignited, in large part, by questions about children's knowledge and understanding of television advertising. Beginning in the early 1970s, arguments emerged that advertising to children was inherently "unfair," based on theories developed by child psychologists and exploratory research conducted by consumer researchers that revealed young children to have little understanding of the persuasive intent of advertising, viewing it as informative, truthful, and entertaining (e.g., Blatt, Spencer, and Ward 1972; Ward, Reale, and Levinson 1972). A rancorous public policy debate ensued, culminating in a 1978 Federal Trade Commission trade rule proposal to ban television advertising to young children under the age of eight. At the heart of these debates were questions about children's knowledge and beliefs about advertising, as well as assessments of the age at which children attain an "adultlike" understanding of advertising messages and their intent.

3

Although debate over banning television advertising to children dissipated with the defeat of the FTC's trade rule proposal in early 1980, interest in the topic of children's knowledge and understanding of advertising continues to this day. One important reason for its longevity is the fact that concerns about misleading or unfair advertising to children continue to emerge over time. Just as the dust was settling on the debates about banning advertising to children, new debates were forming on issues ranging from "program-length" commercials for action figures and toys connected with television programs such as *Teenage Mutant Ninja Turtles* to advertisements for cigarettes and alcohol that appealed to children through the use of cartoon characters such as Joe Camel. These debates continue today, with an even greater need to understand more about what children know about advertising and what they infer from advertising messages.

Further, an unprecedented amount of marketing attention is being directed toward the ever-expanding and lucrative children's market. With a combination of allowances, earnings, and gifts, children 14 and under spent an estimated $24 billion in direct purchases and influenced another $188 billion in family purchases in 1997 (McNeal 1998). Advertising has been increasingly called upon to communicate with this market, reflected in a 50% increase in advertising in child-directed media from 1993 to 1996 alone (Leonhardt 1997). Beyond commitments in dollar terms, marketers are realizing they need to be more attuned to this market and possess a better understanding of what children and adolescents know about advertising, what they trust and mistrust, and what appeals to them most.

Although a large body of findings has accumulated over more than 25 years of research, few attempts have been made to summarize this literature in a comprehensive manner. Several efforts were made to summarize portions of the literature in the late 1970s and early 1980s (e.g., Meringoff and Lesser 1980; Resnik, Stern, and Alberty 1979; Sheikh, Prasad, and Rao 1975), with more recent reviews appearing less frequently and almost a decade ago (Raju and Lonial 1990; Young 1990). During this time, researchers have challenged and qualified some previous findings and, perhaps more important, have proceeded to look at new questions that take us beyond basic questions of children's knowledge of advertising intent, deception, and truthfulness.

In light of these observations, the purpose of this chapter is to review what we know about children's knowledge and understanding of advertising. To do so, we summarize academic research from the past 25 years on the topic, accessing findings from a diverse set of journals and books written by scholars in marketing, journalism, speech and communication, and child psychology. We cover topics such as children's ability to distinguish commercials from television programs, children's understanding of advertising's persuasive intent, children's ability to recognize bias and deception in advertising, children's beliefs about the truthfulness of advertising, children's knowledge of advertising tactics and appeals, and children's use of cognitive defenses against advertising. Absent from the review are several topics related to advertising and children, such as parental views about advertising to children, effectiveness of specific ad executions and appeals (e.g., commercial repetition, rap music), advertising's long-run effects on choice and consumption, and content analyses of children's television commercials. The focus is on what children know about advertising in general, and how they use this knowledge in response to advertising messages.

The review is structured around major steps or building blocks of advertising knowledge, such as the ability to distinguish commercials from programs and the ability to understand advertising's persuasive intent. These steps are discussed in the order in which they emerge in the developmental sequence from preschool to adolescence. For example, the ability to distinguish commercials from programs emerges first, followed by the knowledge that advertising has a persuasive intent. These topics are, therefore, discussed in this order to underscore the sequence of development as children become more knowledgeable about advertising. The chapter concludes with a discussion of what factors underlie this sequence of development and what topics remain for future research.

Distinguishing Commercials From Programs

As children move into and through their preschool years, they learn to identify television commercials and distinguish them from other forms of programming. By the age of five, almost all children have acquired the ability to pick out commercials from regular television programming

(Blosser and Roberts 1985; Butter et al. 1981; Levin, Petros, and Petrella 1982; Palmer and McDowell 1979; Stephens and Stutts 1982; Stutts, Vance, and Hudleson 1981). In some cases, a substantial percentage of even three- and four-year-olds have been shown to discriminate commercials above chance levels (Butter et al. 1981; Levin, Petros, and Petrella 1982).

A study by Eliot Butter and his colleagues illustrates findings in this area. Preschool children, aged four and five years, were shown videotapes of the *Captain Kangaroo* program, edited to include four 30-second commercials between program segments. Separators were placed between the commercial and program segments, consisting, for example, of a voice saying that, "The Captain will return after this message." Separators are commonly employed in television programming aimed at children, especially Saturday morning cartoons and shows such as *Captain Kangaroo*. While viewing the tape, children were instructed to tell the experimenter "when a commercial comes on." Children were also asked at approximately 10 to 15 seconds into each program segment, "Is this part of the 'Captain Kangaroo' show?" In addition to these direct assessments, children were also asked open-ended questions, such as, "Why do they put commercials on television?" and "What is the difference between a commercial and the 'Captain Kangaroo' show?"

Using this methodology, Butter et al. (1981) reported that 70% of the four-year-olds and 90% of the five-year-olds identified all four commercials. Older children identified significantly more commercials, yet even four-year-olds were able to distinguish commercials from programs at an above-chance level. However, the ability to identify commercials did not necessarily translate into an understanding of the "true" difference between commercials and programs (entertainment vs. selling intent). Ninety percent of the younger children could not explain the difference between commercials and programs, even though discriminating the two was relatively easy. Other studies have reported similar findings, noting that children of this age usually describe the difference between commercials and programs using simple perceptual cues, such as "commercials are short" (Palmer and McDowell 1979; Ward 1972). Thus, as Butter et al. (1981, p. 56) conclude, "young children may know they are watching something different than a program but do not know that the intent of what they are watching is to invite purchase of a product or service."

Understanding Advertising's Persuasive Intent

An understanding of advertising intent usually emerges by the time most children are seven to eight years old (Bever, Smith, Bengen, and Johnson 1975; Blosser and Roberts 1985; Robertson and Rossiter 1974; Rubin 1974; Ward, Wackman, and Wartella 1977). Although children can discriminate commercials from programs by the time they are five years old, as noted earlier, it takes a few more years before children expand their knowledge base to include an understanding of advertising's persuasive intent. Prior to this, young children tend to view advertising as a form of entertainment (e.g., "commercials are funny") or as a form of unbiased information (e.g., "commercials tell you about things you can buy"). Quite abruptly, around the age of 7 or 8 years, children begin to see the persuasive intent of commercials, coming to terms with the fact that advertisers are "trying to get people to buy something."

These developmental patterns are well documented by Robertson and Rossiter (1974) in one of the earliest and most influential studies on the topic. First-, third-, and fifth-grade boys were interviewed and asked a series of open-ended questions to assess whether they recognized the assistive (informational) intent and persuasive (selling) intent of advertising. For example, children were asked questions such as, "Why are commercials shown on television?" and "What do commercials try to get you to do?" To understand the emergence of both types of intent, several potential antecedents of attributions of commercial intent were measured: discrimination between programs and commercials, recognition of a commercial source, perception of an intended audience, awareness of symbolic nature of commercials, and personal experience of discrepancies between products as advertised and actual products.

The findings reveal age differences in persuasive intent but not assistive intent. Attributions of assistive intent remain constant across the three grade levels, with about half of the children mentioning the information function of advertising. Attributions of persuasive intent, however, increase dramatically from 52.7% of first graders (6-/-7-year-olds) to 87.1% of third graders (8-/9-year-olds) to 99% of fifth graders (10-/-11-year-olds). In addition, the recognition of persuasive intent is significantly related to the antecedent conditions described above. In fact, about three fourths of the children with an understanding of persuasive intent can be identified by an assessment of these antecedent factors, especially personal experiences with discrepancies between advertised claims versus actual products and awareness of the symbolic nature of commercials.

Similar age trends have been reported in much subsequent research, though additional factors have been identified that may moderate the specific age at which a child understands persuasive intent. Family environment, for example, plays a role. Children from black families exhibit lower levels of understanding of advertising's persuasive intent (Donohue, Meyer, and Henke 1978; Meyer, Donohue, and Henke 1978). Higher levels of understanding can be facilitated by parents with higher educational levels (Robertson and Rossiter 1974; Rossiter and Robertson 1976) and by parents who take a strong consumer education role with their children (Reid 1978). Common to both types of families is a greater degree of parent-child interaction about advertising, though the interaction must have an educational component to be effective. The impact of such interaction is captured well by Reid (1978, pp. 16-17), who reports the following discussion with a five-year-old boy from a "high teaching orientation" family. The boy (identified as C7) is watching television while the observer (Ob) is present. A commercial for the Six Million Dollar Man doll appears on the television:

C7: "I got that for my birthday."

Ob: "Is it fun to play with?"

C7: "Yea! It's lots of fun."

Ob: "Boy, the *Six Million Dollar Man* sure does a lot of super things on TV—running fast as cars—jumping over buildings."

C7: "Sure does. But my *Six Million Dollar Man* don't do that."

Ob: "Why not?"

C7: "'cause! That's on TV."

Ob: "What do you mean? Your doll can't do those things you just saw in that commercial?"

C7: "Dummy! That's just stuff in a commercial."

In addition to background factors, features of the methodology used to measure children's understanding of persuasive intent have also come under scrutiny. Researchers have questioned whether measures of children's knowledge, using open-ended questions requiring abstract thinking and verbalization, result in an overly pessimistic view of what young children know about advertising intent. Employing nonverbal measures of advertising intent, Donohue, Henke, and Donohue (1980) reported high levels of understanding of commercial intent among two- to six-year-olds. In this study, children were shown a television commercial for Froot Loops cereal featuring an animated character called Toucan Sam. After viewing the ad, children were shown two pictures and asked to indicate which picture best indicated "What Toucan Sam wants you to do." The correct picture was one of a mother and child in a supermarket cereal aisle, with the child sitting in a pushcart seat and the mother standing with a box of Froot Loops in her hand, ready to put it into the cart. The incorrect picture showed a child watching television. Children in the study selected the right picture 80% of the time, with even the youngest children (2-/-3-year-olds) selecting the right picture at above-chance levels (75%).

Replications and extensions of this study have produced results more in line with traditional verbal measures. Noting that the choice between the two pictures used in the Donohue et al. study was a rather easy one, which children could have successfully completed absent any knowledge of persuasive intent, Macklin (1985) replicated the Donohue et al. procedure using a set of four pictures. Two new pictures were added to the choice set, one depicting an activity portrayed by the characters in the commercial and another showing two children sharing the advertised product. The results were vastly different in this case, with 80% of the children (3 to 5 years of age) failing to select the correct picture. Further research by Macklin (1987), using similar nonverbal measures to assess children's understanding of the informational function of advertising, corroborates these findings. In this study, none of the three-year-olds, 0% to 7.5% of the four-year-olds, and 20% to 40% of the five-year-olds provided the correct response in two different tasks. In sum, though nonverbal measures of persuasive intent may allow some children to express levels of understanding not uncovered with verbal measures, there is little reason to believe that the vast majority of children younger than seven or eight years of age have a command of advertising's persuasive intent.

Recognizing Bias and Deception in Advertising

———

By the time children reach their eighth birthday, they not only understand advertising's persuasive intent but also recognize bias and deception in advertising. The majority of children aged eight and older no longer believe that "commercials always tell the truth" (Bever et al. 1975; Robertson and Rossiter 1974; Ward 1972; Ward et al. 1977), though children from black and lower-income families are less discerning (Bearden, Teel, and Wright 1979; Meyer, Donohue, and Henke 1978). Beliefs about the truthfulness of advertising become even more negative as children move into the preadolescent years (Bever et al. 1975; Robertson and Rossiter 1974; Rossiter and Robertson 1976; Ward 1972; Ward et al. 1977). For example, Ward et al. (1977) report that the percentage of kindergartners, third graders, and sixth graders believing that advertising never or only sometimes tells the truth increases from 50% to 88% to 97%, respectively. In addition, three fifths of the kindergartners and third graders believe that advertising lies only once in a while, whereas only one third of the sixth graders believe in such a low frequency of deception.

Along with these more negative views comes a better understanding of why commercials are sometimes untruthful and how one can distinguish truthful from untruthful ads. For example, Ward et al. (1977) report that kindergartners often state no reason for "why commercials lie" (e.g., "they just lie"), whereas older children (third and sixth graders) connect lying to persuasive intent (e.g., "they want to sell products to make money, so they have to make the product look better than it is"). The ability to detect specific instances of bias and deception also increases with age. Bever et al. (1975) report that most of the seven- to 10-year-olds in their study could not discriminate truthful from misleading advertising and admitted to their difficulties in evaluating advertising: " '[Advertisers] can fake well,' they said, and 'you don't really know what's true until you've tried the product' " (p. 114). These researchers also report that 11- to 12-year-olds are more discriminating, using nuances of voice, manner, and language to detect misleading advertising: "as clues that commercials were not telling the truth, 11- and 12-year olds most commonly cited 'overstatements and the way they [the actors] talk,' and times 'when they use visual tricks or fake things,' 'when it just doesn't sound right,' and when the commercial 'goes on and on in too much detail' " (p. 119). Discriminations of this sort allow children to progress from global beliefs about misleading advertising (e.g., "all commercials lie") to more specific beliefs about when advertising is misleading and when it is not.

The ability to recognize bias and deception in ads, coupled with an understanding of advertising's persuasive intent, results in less trust and less liking of commercials (Robertson and Rossiter 1974; Rossiter and Robertson 1976). Robertson and Rossiter (1974) found, for example, that the percentage of children "liking all ads" decreased dramatically from 68.5% for first graders to 55.9% for third graders to 25.3% for fifth graders. Similar studies have replicated this general pattern, noting downward trends in liking or overall attitudes toward advertising in children from the early elementary school grades to high school (Lindquist 1978; Moore and Stephens 1975).

Family environment, peer relationships, and television exposure also contribute to the development of skeptical attitudes toward advertising. For younger children, more critical attitudes seem to be furthered by more parental control over television viewing (Soley and Reid 1984) and less television viewing in general (Atkin 1975; Rossiter and Robertson 1974). By the teenage years, skepticism toward advertising seems to be related more to the development of independent thinking and access to alternative information sources. For example, Mangleburg and Bristol (see Chapter 2, this volume) report higher levels of advertising skepticism among high school students who have alternative sources (friends) of information and come from families that foster critical (concept-oriented) thinking, despite self-reports of heavier television viewing. Less skepticism was observed among students conforming to peer group norms, consistent with a pattern of less independent thinking and overreliance on a single (peer) information source.

Using Cognitive Defenses
Against Advertising?

The evidence just reviewed points to a dramatic shift in how children see advertising as they move from the preschool years to early adolescence. The preschooler who believes that commercials are entertaining and informative turns into a skeptical adolescent who knows that commercials are meant to persuade and believes them to be untruthful in general. The knowledge and skepticism about advertising that is typical of children eight years of age or older is often viewed as a "cognitive defense" against advertising. That is, armed with knowledge about advertising's persuasive intent and skepticism about the truthfulness of advertising claims, children of this age and above are often viewed as having the abilities to respond to advertising in a mature and informed manner. Younger children (under 8 years), without these cognitive defenses, are seen as an "at-risk" population for being easily misled by advertising.

Although this scenario seems straightforward, evidence regarding the extent to which children's general attitudes and beliefs about advertising function as cognitive defenses against advertising is quite mixed. Early survey research was successful in finding moderate links between children's knowledge of advertising's persuasive intent and their desire for advertised products (Robertson and Rossiter 1974) and children's negative attitudes toward advertising and their desire for advertised products (McNeal 1964). A more pessimistic view is suggested by more recent experimental research, which finds that children's cognitive defenses have little or no effect on evaluations of and preferences for advertised products. For example, Christenson (1982) found that an educational segment on commercials, discussing the intent and credibility of advertising, was successful in increasing the awareness of advertising's persuasive intent and decreasing the perceived truthfulness of advertising in general. However, the segment had little effect on younger (first and second graders) or older (fifth and sixth graders) children's rankings of the advertised product versus its competitors or on ratings of important attributes of the advertised products. Even knowledge that commercial segments have been staged, and are therefore misleading about product performance, has been found to have little effect on preferences for advertised products for children across a wide age range from eight to 14 years (Ross et al. 1984).

Several possibilities exist to explain why children's developing knowledge about advertising does not necessarily translate into more discerning responses to advertising. Perhaps the most obvious reason is that general knowledge and beliefs about advertising cannot be expected to dampen a child's enthusiasm for an enticing snack or toy. Clearly, adults with the same or higher cognitive defenses often want and purchase advertised products, even products with advertised claims that are "just too good to be true." As Robertson and Rossiter (1974, p. 19) note: "Children's ability to recognize persuasive intent in commercials should not be taken as implying immunity to all commercials; clearly, individual commercials may be highly persuasive for children, just as for adults."

A second possibility is that children's advertising knowledge can serve as a cognitive defense only when that knowledge is accessed during commercial viewing. Given the difficulty that children experience in retrieving stored information of all kinds, through elementary school and even junior high, access to and use of their advertising knowledge may be more restricted than previously thought. Brucks, Armstrong, and Goldberg (1988) present evidence to this effect in an experimental study with nine- and 10-year-olds, an age at which children typically understand the persuasive intent of advertising and are relatively skeptical of advertising claims. In the first research session, Brucks and her colleagues created a high level of advertising knowledge in one half of the children by showing and discussing two educational films about the persuasive nature of advertising, including information about specific advertising techniques and tricks. An irrelevant film was shown to the remaining children. Three days later, in the second research session, students were shown actual commercials for children's products, completed cognitive response measures, and answered questions about the perceived deceptiveness of the commercials. Immediately prior to commercial viewing, one half of the children were given a short quiz measuring children's attitudes about advertising, which served as a cue to help children access their advertising knowledge. The remaining children were given the same quiz after viewing the films in the first session, which rendered the quiz ineffective as a cue at the time of commercial viewing.

The most important, and interesting, findings relate to the number of counterarguments children raised after viewing each commercial. Over 70% of the counterarguments occurred in the high knowledge-cue present condition, in which children had been shown educational films and had received a cue encouraging them to access this knowledge prior to commercial viewing. Students in the high knowledge-cue absent condition generated advertising counterarguments for one commercial, which used techniques very similar to those critiqued in the educational films, but failed overall to use what they had learned about advertising at the time of commercial viewing. Children in the low knowledge condition failed to generate advertising counterarguments for any of the commercials, regardless of whether a cue for advertising knowledge was present or absent. These results support the idea that access to advertising knowledge is a bottleneck preventing children from using what they know as a cognitive defense against advertising. Equally important, the findings suggest that general advertising knowledge and beliefs are not sufficient defenses. As Brucks et al. (1988, pp. 480-481) conclude: "children (at least 9 to 10-year-olds) need more than just a skeptical or critical attitude toward advertising. They also need a more detailed knowledge about the nature of advertising and how it works."

Adolescence: Knowledge of Advertising Tactics and Appeals

What do children of different ages know about specific advertising tactics and appeals? Surprisingly, we have very few answers to this question, probably because most researchers have focused on advertising knowledge and beliefs possessed by children during their elementary school years (5- to 11-year-olds). Advertising knowledge of a more specific form, involving an understanding of what tactics and appeals are used by advertisers and why they are used, emerges much later in the developmental sequence as children approach early adolescence (11 to 14 years of age) (Boush, Friestad, and Rose 1994; Paget, Kritt, and Bergemann 1984).

A study by Paget, Kritt, and Bergemann (1984) offers an illustration of the knowledge differences existing between early childhood, middle childhood, and young adulthood. Children and college students were shown commercials for food products and asked to comment on the particular persuasive strategies used in different ads. For example, for one commercial, the researchers asked participants: "Why did they use this particular scene between the two siblings in order to sell the product?" Kindergartners did not mention any persuasive intent (e.g., "So people could watch it"), whereas third and sixth graders mentioned the advertiser's motivation (e.g., "They want kids to eat it and mothers to buy it so they get more money"). College students were more sophisticated in their reasoning, exhibiting their knowledge about how advertisers use persuasive appeals, for example: "According to stereotypes, little boys love baseball and collect baseball cards and to have a product that competed with younger brother's typical pastimes would be a way of selling the product."

The development of advertising knowledge develops during early adolescence, as is well illustrated by Boush, Friestad, and Rose (1994). Sixth through eighth graders were asked a series of questions about what advertisers are trying to accomplish when they use particular tactics, such as humor, celebrity endorsers, and product comparisons. Students were asked to rate eight possible effects (e.g., "grab your attention" and "help you learn about the product") for each tactic, responding to the question, "When TV ads [insert tactic], how hard is the advertiser trying to [insert list of effects]?" Ratings for each effect were obtained on a scale from "not trying hard at all" to "trying very hard." These ratings were compared to those from an adult sample to derive an overall knowledge score. In addition, skepticism toward advertising was measured by a series of questions assessing understanding of advertising intent as well as beliefs about the truthfulness of ad claims.

The results indicate that knowledge about specific advertising techniques increases during the period from sixth to eighth grade, as expected. Interestingly, skepticism about advertising was high among all students and did not vary across grades. Boush and his colleagues (1994, p. 172) conclude:

the current results suggest that negative or mistrustful predispositions toward advertising are well established as early as grade 6. This pattern of development, where skeptical attitudes precede more sophisticated knowledge structures, suggests that adolescent schemer schemas about advertisers' persuasive attempts start with general attitudes and then are filled in with more specific beliefs.

In light of these trends, and the degree of advertising skepticism and sophistication exhibited by adolescents, it would be tempting to conclude that advertising is easily dismissed and unappreciated by this age group. Of course, this is hardly the case. Although adolescents have acquired significant knowledge about advertising, and often voice negative attitudes about advertising in general, they also are discriminating consumers of advertising. They usually have firm ideas of what commercials they like and dislike and usurp whatever appeals to them as a basis for social conversation and identity. Adolescents often appear less focused on the selling message as intended and more focused on using advertising messages and meaning to suit their own purposes.

For example, in a recent study with high school students from England, Ritson and Elliott (1998) find that advertisements are often the topic of group conversations, a means of belonging and group membership, and a conduit for transferring and conveying meanings in day-to-day life. Far from being dismissed, advertisements seem to be part of the social "currency" for teens and adolescents, along with money, possessions, status, and athletic ability. One of Ritson's and Elliott's subjects sums up this sentiment well:

> If you're sitting here and someone starts talking about adverts (advertisements) and you haven't got a clue what they're going on about, you feel dead left out . . . and you can't, you know. . . . You say, "Oh, I didn't see that" and then they just carry on talking around you. But if you've seen it, you can join in and you know what they're going on about so it makes you feel . . . like . . . more in line with the group . . . part of it more.

Discussion

What do we know about children's knowledge and understanding of advertising? Three conclusions seem warranted on the basis of the evidence reviewed here. First, children's knowledge and understanding of advertising develops throughout childhood and into early adolescence. Second, children's knowledge and understanding of advertising progresses in a series of steps, beginning with the basic ability to distinguish commercials from television programs; advancing to a central understanding that advertising has a persuasive intent accompanied by a certain degree of bias or deception; and culminating in a sophisticated view of advertising that includes detailed knowledge of selling tactics, a healthy degree of skepticism regarding advertising, and an appreciation for advertising as a conduit for social discourse and meaning. Third, these levels of understanding proceed in a clear developmental sequence, with each new level emerging in a predictable way as children mature and become more experienced consumers.

Less clear is the underlying mechanism(s) responsible for the development of children's knowledge and understanding in this domain. Though a number of individual theories have been recruited for this purpose, it is unlikely that any one theory or set of concepts will be capable of explaining the wide range of effects summarized here. Instead, it is more likely that individual theories or general approaches are capable of shedding light on only certain aspects of children's knowledge development. A complete explanation probably rests with a variety of approaches, each focusing on a different set of contributing factors such as age-related improvements in cognitive abilities and cumulative increases in advertising-related experiences. With this in mind, we turn our attention to a number of factors that contribute to the developmental trends we have just reviewed.

Cognitive Development

The predominant explanation given for developmental differences in children's understanding and knowledge of advertising focuses on aspects of cognitive development that occur during childhood. Children undergo dramatic changes in the way they perceive, organize, and think about stimuli in their environment. These changes are thought to underlie and characterize many of the changes observed in how children of different ages view advertising.

Piaget's theory of cognitive development has been the most popular reference point for this line of reasoning. Piaget proposed four main stages of cognitive development, which roughly correlate with chrono-logical age: sensorimotor (birth to 2 years), preoperational (2 to 7 years), concrete operational (7 to 11 years), and formal operational (11 through adulthood) (Ginsburg and Opper 1988). There are vast differ-ences in the cognitive abilities and resources available to children at these stages, especially at the preoperational, concrete operational, and formal operational stages of most interest in the advertising domain. The preoperational stage features children who are developing symbolic thought but are still very focused on perceptual properties of stimuli. Preoperational children tend to be "perceptually bound" to the readily observable aspects of their environment, unlike concrete operational children, who do not accept perception as reality but can think about stimuli in their environment in a more thoughtful way. Preoperational children are also characterized by "centration," the tendency to focus on a single dimension or limited amount of information. In contrast, the concrete operational child can consider several dimensions of a stimuli at a time and relate the dimensions in a thoughtful and relatively abstract way. Finally, in the formal operational stage, children progress to more adultlike thought patterns, capable of even more complex and abstract thought for concrete and hypothetical objects and situations.

These stage descriptions provide an explanation for several aspects of how children view advertising messages. Consider, for example, children's ability to distinguish advertising from television programming. The fact that younger children (preschoolers) distinguish commercials on the basis of perceptual features (e.g., length) instead of persuasive intent fits nicely with notions of perceptual boundness in preoperational children. An understanding of persuasive intent emerges later among concrete operational children, who are able to think more abstractly about advertising beyond its perceptual features and no longer take commercial messages at face value. More complex knowledge about advertising tactics and appeals surfaces at the formal operational stage among adolescents who are capable of more complex thought and more hypothetical reasoning.

Beyond Piaget's approach, concepts associated with information processing theories provide additional explanatory power for several aspects of children's advertising knowledge. Though several formulations of information processing theory exist, all share a focus on the acquisition, encoding, organization, and retrieval of information from memory. Throughout childhood, children develop more sophisticated and flexible ways to encode, organize, and retrieve information. To illustrate, Roedder (1981) characterizes children as belonging to one of three segments based on their information-processing skills: strategic processors, cued processors, and limited processors. Strategic processors (age 12 and older) use a variety of strategies for storing and retrieving information, such as verbal labeling, rehearsal, and use of retrieval cues to guide memory searches. Cued processors, generally ranging in age from seven to 11, are able to use a similar set of strategies to enhance information storage and retrieval, but only if aided by explicit prompts or cues. Cued processors exhibit "production deficiencies," referring to the fact that they have the ability to use processing strategies but do not spontaneously produce these strategies when needed. Finally, most children under the age of seven are limited processors, with processing skills that are not yet fully developed or successfully utilized in learning situations. These children are characterized as having "mediational deficiencies," referring to the fact that they often have difficulty using storage and retrieval strategies even when prompted to do so.

This framework is quite useful for explaining why younger children do not utilize cognitive defenses against advertising, even when the evidence is clear that they possess quite a bit of knowledge about advertising's persuasive intent, bias and deception, and untrustworthiness. Simply having advertising knowledge does not mean that children necessarily access this information in response to advertising messages that should be questioned. Viewers must detect cues in the commercial that would trigger retrieval of information about advertising in general or about specific advertising tactics and techniques. Although eight- to 12-year-olds have a good deal of general knowledge about advertising, their ability to retrieve and use whatever knowledge they have acquired is still developing as cued processors. Strategic processors should be more equipped to handle these situations, although truly effective cognitive defenses may not be available until more specific types of advertising knowledge about manipulative tactics have been acquired by midadolescence (see Brucks et al. 1988 for a more extended discussion).

Social Development

Less attention has been given to theories of social development as potential explanations for children's developing knowledge about advertising. This seems quite reasonable given the fact that most aspects of advertising knowledge that have been studied focus on the processing and interpretation of advertising messages, not on social aspects of advertising viewing and social interaction. Yet, there is at least one theoretical perspective, Selman's framework of social perspective-taking, that is quite informative about how children develop abilities to understand advertisers' motives and intent.

Selman (1980) proposes that children's abilities to understand another person's perspective progress through a series of five stages. At first, in the ego-centric stage (ages 3 to 6), children are unaware of any perspective other than their own. Next, in the social information role-taking stage (ages 6 to 8), children become aware that others may have different opinions or motives, but do not exhibit the ability actually to think about others from their perspective. The self-reflective stage (ages 8 to 10) follows next, with children understanding that others may have different opinions or motives and exhibiting an ability to consider another person's viewpoint. However, the ability simultaneously to consider another person's viewpoint at the same time as one's own does not surface until the fourth stage, mutual role taking (ages 10 to 12). The final stage, social and conventional system role taking (ages 12 to 15 and older), features simultaneous consideration of different viewpoints based on the context or situation in which it occurred.

This framework provides an additional explanation for why younger children do not understand advertising's persuasive intent until they reach elementary school. The ability to discern persuasive intent requires one to view advertising from the advertiser's perspective. According to Selman's stages, this does not typically occur until children are eight to 10 years of age, which is compatible with the findings reviewed here. The ability to reason about advertisers' motives for specific advertising tactics and techniques, such as celebrity endorsers and humor, requires even more detailed thinking about how an advertiser thinks about a viewer who thinks about advertising. Not only is there consideration of dual viewpoints, but also reasoning about what techniques would be effective for what types of situations. Consistent with abilities characterized by Selman's last stage, we see knowledge of advertising tactics and appeals emerging only in early adolescence and developing thereafter.

Experiential Base and Environment

Clearly, children do not develop a knowledge and understanding of advertising in a vacuum. Knowledge development can certainly be guided by parental involvement, direct experience with advertising and consumption, and interaction with friends and peers. Though general frameworks that capture the scope of these influences are unavailable, it is important to explore the extent to which experience and interaction with others might explain the development of children's knowledge in the advertising domain.

At early ages, children use television advertising as their "window to the world" of toys, candy, food products, restaurants, and such. Though their knowledge of the consumer marketplace is augmented by trips to the store with parents, or interactions with playmates, television advertising is an important source of information for young children. Part of the reason they see advertising as informational is because it truly is a source of information about the latest toys, newest cereals, and most recent premium offers at local fast food restaurants. Given the informational function it plays, and the lack of general marketplace experience that young children bring to the viewing situation, it is quite understandable why these children do not view advertising in a more critical and less trustworthy manner.

Children's worlds expand once they enter elementary school. Here children find a vast pool of peers who can serve as a sounding board for what toys are "cool," what candy is really "neat," and what brand of clothes is "cheesy." Advertising still serves as an information source, but now children have a set of their own experiences and peer experiences to serve as a basis for comparison. Through this set of experiences, they learn that commercials sometimes exaggerate, that advertisers are not always truthful, and that they need to access a variety of information sources to find out what they should buy. Discrepancies between advertising promises and actual experience is dealt with harshly, as children develop quite negative attitudes and become skeptical toward advertising.

This viewpoint explains many of the findings regarding environmental factors that influence children's understanding and beliefs about advertising. In general, the more children rely on advertising as an informational source, the more they trust and like advertising. Children who come from disadvantaged backgrounds, have less frequent or successful interactions with parents, or watch a great deal of television, have fewer contacts in their immediate environment to serve as information sources. There are also fewer opportunities for the type of discussion and sharing of experiences that gives children a more balanced view of advertising in their lives. Given few alternatives to television advertising, it is not surprising that children in these situations are less skeptical of advertising and find advertising to be more informative, truthful, and entertaining than the norm (see Van Evra 1995 for similar arguments).

Conclusion

Over 25 years of research on the topic of children's understanding and knowledge of advertising have produced an impressive picture of how children view advertising at different ages. We know when children learn to distinguish commercials from television programs, when they discern the persuasive intent of advertising, when they perceive bias and deception in advertising, when they understand the purpose for specific advertising tactics and techniques, and when they use or do not use this knowledge as a cognitive defense against advertising. We are also aware of many of the factors, such as age-related cognitive abilities and family environment, that contribute to these developmental trends.

Further advances to our knowledge can be made by focusing our future attention on several important issues. One, we need to understand better the type of knowledge development that takes place among adolescents, such as knowledge about advertising tactics and techniques. Past research has focused on younger children, usually from kindergarten to preadolescence, but many interesting developments in children's understanding of advertising appear to surface during adolescence. Second, we need a better understanding of how children's knowledge and understanding of advertising comes into play as children view, interpret, and judge commercial messages. Past research has focused on the acquisition of advertising knowledge and skepticism, without commensurate attention being paid to how this acquired knowledge is utilized as children view and respond to advertising messages. Finally, it would be interesting to examine the more positive aspects of advertising as they relate to children's everyday lives. For example, it may be that advertising actually facilitates children's understanding of persuasion and enhances their critical reasoning skills. Or, as we have seen with adolescents, advertising may serve as a conduit for positive social interaction and identity. With new issues such as these to explore, perhaps the next 25 years of research will be as productive as the last.

References

Atkin, Charles K. (1975), *Effects of Television Advertising on Children: First Year Experimental Evidence, Report No. 1,* East Lansing: Michigan State University, Department of Communication.

Bearden, William O., Jesse E. Teel, and Robert R. Wright (1979), "Family Income Effects on Measurement of Children's Attitudes Toward Television Commercials," *Journal of Consumer Research,* 6 (December), 308-311.

Bever, Thomas G., Martin L. Smith, Barbara Bengen, and Thomas G. Johnson (1975), "Young Viewers' Troubling Response to TV Ads," *Harvard Business Review,* 53 (November-December), 109-120.

Blatt, Joan, Lyle Spencer, and Scott Ward (1972), "A Cognitive Developmental Study of Children's Reactions to Television Advertising," in *Television and Social Behavior, Vol. 4, Television in Day-to-Day Life: Patterns of Use,* Eli A. Rubinstein, George A. Comstock, and J. P. Murray, eds., Washington, DC: U.S. Department of Health, Education, and Welfare, 452-467.

Blosser, Betsy J. and Donald F. Roberts (1985), "Age Differences in Children's Perceptions of Message Intent: Responses to TV News, Commercials, Educational Spots, and Public Service Announcements," *Communication Research,* 12 (October), 455-484.

Boush, David M., Marian Friestad, and Gregory M. Rose (1994), "Adolescent Skepticism Toward TV Advertising and Knowledge of Advertiser Tactics," *Journal of Consumer Research,* 21 (June), 165-175.

Brucks, Merrie, Gary M. Armstrong, and Marvin E. Goldberg (1988), "Children's Use of Cognitive Defenses Against Television Advertising: A Cognitive Response Approach," *Journal of Consumer Research,* 14 (March), 471-482.

Butter, Eliot J., Paula M. Popovich, Robert H. Stackhouse, and Roger K. Garner (1981), "Discrimination of Television Programs and Commercials by Preschool Children," *Journal of Advertising Research,* 21 (April), 53-56.

Christenson, Peter Gilbert (1982), "Children's Perceptions of TV Commercials and Products: The Effects of PSAs," *Communication Research,* 9 (October), 491-524.

Donohue, Thomas R., Lucy L. Henke, and William A. Donohue (1980), "Do Kids Know What TV Commercials Intend?" *Journal of Advertising Research,* 20 (October), 51-57.

———, Timothy P. Meyer, and Lucy L. Henke (1978), "Black and White Children: Perceptions of TV Commercials," *Journal of Marketing,* 42 (October), 34-40.

Ginsburg, H. and S. Opper (1988), *Piaget's Theory of Intellectual Development,* Englewood Cliffs, NJ: Prentice Hall.

Leonhardt, David (1997), "Hey Kid, Buy This!" *Business Week* (April 11), 62-67.

Levin, Stephen R., Thomas V. Petros, and Florence W. Petrella (1982), "Preschoolers' Awareness of Television Advertising," *Child Development,* 53, 933-937.

Lindquist, Jay D. (1978), "Children's Attitudes Toward Advertising on Television and Radio and in Children's Magazines and Comic Books," in *Advances in Consumer Research,* Vol. 6, William L. Wilkie, ed., Ann Arbor, MI: Association for Consumer Research, 407-412.

Macklin, M. Carole (1985), "Do Young Children Understand the Selling Intent of Commercials?" *Journal of Consumer Affairs,* 19 (Winter), 293-304.

——— (1987), "Preschoolers' Understanding of the Informational Function of Television Advertising," *Journal of Consumer Research,* 14 (September), 229-239.

McNeal, James U. (1964), *Children as Consumers,* Austin: Bureau of Business Research, University of Texas at Austin.

——— (1998), "Tapping the Three Kids' Markets," *American Demographics,* 20 (April), 37-41.

Meringoff, Laurene Krasny and Gerald S. Lesser (1980), "Children's Ability to Distinguish Television Commercials From Program Material," in *The Effects of Television Advertising on Children,* Richard P. Adler, Gerald S. Lesser, Laurene Krasny Meringoff, Thomas S. Robertson, John R. Rossiter, and Scott Ward, eds., Lexington, MA: Lexington Books, 29-42.

Meyer, Timothy P., Thomas R. Donohue, and Lucy L. Henke (1978), "How Black Kids See TV Commercials," *Journal of Advertising Research,* 18 (October), 51-58.

Moore, Roy L. and Lowndes F. Stephens (1975), "Some Communication and Demographic Determinants of Adolescent Consumer Learning," *Journal of Consumer Research,* 2 (September), 80-92.

Palmer, Edward L. and Cynthia N. McDowell (1979), "Program/Commercial Separators in Children's Television Programming," *Journal of Communication,* 29 (Summer), 197-201.

Paget, K. Frome, D. Kritt, and L. Bergemann (1984), "Understanding Strategic Interactions in Television Commercials: A Developmental Study," *Journal of Applied Developmental Psychology,* 5, 145-161.

Raju, P. S. and Subhash C. Lonial (1990), "Advertising to Children: Findings and Implications," *Current Issues and Research in Advertising,* 12 (2), 231-274.

Reid, Leonard N. (1978), "The Impact of Family Group Interaction on Children's Understanding of Television Advertising," *Journal of Advertising*, 8 (Summer), 13-19.

Resnik, Alan J., Bruce L. Stern, and Barbara Alberty (1979), "Integrating Results From Children's Advertising Research," *Journal of Advertising*, 8 (Summer), 3-12 and 48.

Ritson, Mark and Richard Elliott (1998), "The Social Contextualization of the Lonely Viewer: An Ethnographic Study of Advertising Interpretation," Working Paper, University of Minnesota.

Robertson, Thomas S. and John R. Rossiter (1974), "Children and Commercial Persuasion: An Attribution Theory Analysis," *Journal of Consumer Research*, 1 (June), 13-20.

Roedder, Deborah L. (1981), "Age Differences in Children's Responses to Television Advertising: An Information Processing Approach," *Journal of Consumer Research*, 8 (September), 144-153.

Ross, Rhonda P., Toni Campbell, John C. Wright, Aletha C. Huston, Mabel L. Rice, and Peter Turk (1984), "When Celebrities Talk, Children Listen: An Experimental Analysis of Children's Responses to TV Ads With Celebrity Endorsement," *Journal of Applied Developmental Psychology*, 5, 185-202.

Rossiter, John R. and Thomas S. Robertson (1976), "Canonical Analysis of Developmental, Social, and Experiential Factors in Children's Comprehension of Television Advertising," *The Journal of Genetic Psychology*, 129, 317-327.

——— and ——— (1974), "Children's TV Commercials: Testing the Defenses," *Journal of Communication*, 24 (Autumn), 137-144.

Rubin, Ronald S. (1974), "The Effects of Cognitive Development on Children's Responses to Television Advertising," *Journal of Business Research*, 2 (October), 409-419.

Selman, Robert L. (1980), *The Growth of Interpersonal Understanding*, New York: Academic Press.

Sheikh, Anees A., V. Kanti Prasad, and Tanniru R. Rao (1975), "Children's TV Commercials: A Review of Research," *Journal of Communication*, 24 (Autumn), 126-136.

Soley, Lawrence C. and Leonard N. Reid (1984), "When Parents Control Children's TV Viewing and Product Choice: Testing the Attitudinal Defenses," in *Marketing Comes of Age: Proceedings of the Annual Meeting of the Southern Marketing Association*, Boca Raton, FL: Southern Marketing Association, 10-13.

Stephens, Nancy and Mary Ann Stutts (1982), "Preschoolers' Ability to Distinguish Between Television Programming and Commercials," *Journal of Advertising*, 11 (2), 16-26.

Stutts, Mary Ann, Donald Vance, and Sarah Hudleson (1981), "Program-Commercial Separators in Children's Television: Do They Help a Child Tell the Difference Between Bugs Bunny and the Quik Rabbit?" *Journal of Advertising*, 10 (Spring), 16-25.

Van Evra, Judith P. (1995), "Advertising's Impact on Children as a Function of Viewing Purpose," *Psychology & Marketing*, 12 (August), 423-432.

Ward, Scott (1972), "Children's Reactions to Commercials," *Journal of Advertising Research*, 12 (April), 37-45.

————, Greg Reale, and David Levinson (1972), "Children's Perceptions, Explanations, and Judgments of Television Advertising: A Further Explanation," in *Television and Social Behavior, Vol. 4, Television in Day-to-Day Life: Patterns of Use*, Eli A. Rubinstein, George A. Comstock, and J. P. Murray, eds., Washington, DC: U.S. Department of Health, Education, and Welfare, 468-490.

————, Daniel B. Wackman, and Ellen Wartella (1977), *How Children Learn to Buy*, Beverly Hills, CA: Sage.

Young, Brian M. (1990), *Television Advertising and Children*, New York: Oxford University Press.

CHAPTER

2

Socialization and Adolescents' Skepticism Toward Advertising

TAMARA F. MANGLEBURG
TERRY BRISTOL

Understanding adolescents' attitudes toward advertising is important for several reasons. The spending power of teens is substantial and likely to grow in the future as members of the baby boomlet enter adolescence. Indeed, teens are estimated to have spent $63 billion of their own money and $36 billion of their family's money in 1994 (Zollo 1995). A greater understanding of teens' attitudes toward advertising may help marketers and advertisers who want to appeal to that substantial and growing market. Consumer researchers also are interested in understanding the dynamic processes related to consumer learning among teens, in part because the behaviors and attitudes learned during adolescence may have implications for consumers' behavior later in life. Finally, a greater understanding of teens' attitudes toward advertising

AUTHORS' NOTE: Reprinted from *Journal of Advertising*, Vol. XXVII, Number 3, Fall 1998. Reprinted with permission.

may help public policy officials develop effective programs and policies to help teens evaluate marketing communications.

We examine one aspect of adolescents' attitude toward advertising, skepticism toward advertising. Skepticism is defined as consumers' negatively valenced attitude toward the motives of and claims made by advertisers (Boush, Friestad, and Rose 1994). Skepticism implies that consumers recognize that advertisers have specific motives, such as persuading consumers, and therefore that advertisers' communications may be biased and varied in their truthfulness (Boush, Friestad, and Rose 1994; Brucks, Armstrong, and Goldberg 1988). Hence, skepticism is a critical approach to evaluating and coping with advertising messages and therefore seems to be an important skill for consumers to acquire.

We conducted a study to examine factors that may be related to teens' learning of skeptical attitudes toward advertising. Parental socialization tendencies, or the family communication environment, may be especially important in fostering the development and learning of such attitudes. In addition, adolescents' skepticism toward advertising may be related to their susceptibility to being influenced by peers (Boush, Friestad, and Rose 1994). The amount of teens' television exposure also may be related to the development of skeptical attitudes toward advertising, in part, because a greater degree of exposure may give teens more experience by which to judge ads. Finally, specific aspects of interaction with the three socialization agents—parents, peers, and television—may enhance teens' marketplace knowledge, which in turn may affect their skepticism toward advertising. The effects on skepticism of specific dimensions of interaction with socialization agents may, thus, be mediated by teens' marketplace knowledge. We developed and tested hypotheses about adolescent skepticism toward advertising that incorporated those ideas.

Development of Hypotheses

Socialization is the process by which "young people acquire skills, knowledge, and attitudes relevant to their functioning as consumers in the marketplace" (Ward 1974, p. 1). Skepticism toward advertising is an attitude that may be of particular importance to the consumer role because it may aid consumers in critically evaluating advertising. To the extent that one is skeptical, one is more likely to examine the claims made in ads in a critical way and not accept them at face value. Such critical evaluation, in turn, may help consumers make wiser or more informed purchase decisions. Therefore, skepticism toward advertising may be an important attitude for consumers to learn.

Socialization Agents

Family. One aspect of the socialization process that is likely to affect teens' learning of skepticism toward advertising is the family communication environment, which has been linked to general parental socialization tendencies, or parental styles (Carlson, Grossbart, and Stuenkel 1992). The family communication environment is conceptualized as having two orthogonal dimensions: socio-oriented and concept-oriented communication (see, e.g., Carlson, Grossbart, and Walsh 1990; Carlson et al. 1994; McLeod and Chaffee 1972; McLeod and O'Keefe 1972; Moore and Moschis 1981; Moschis 1985; Moschis and Mitchell 1986; Moschis and Moore 1979b). Socio-oriented communication centers on creating and maintaining harmonious relations in the family and promoting deference to authority, thereby leading parents to control and monitor children's consumption activities (see, e.g., Moschis 1985; Carlson, Grossbart, and Stuenkel 1992). Concept-oriented communication centers on encouraging children to develop their own views of the world and to consider alternative points of view, thereby fostering "development of childrens' own skills and competence as consumers" (Carlson, Grossbart, and Stuenkel 1992, p. 32).

Because concept-oriented communication stresses the development of consumer competence, we would expect it to be associated positively with adolescents' skepticism toward advertising. Indeed, mothers whose family communication patterns are based on concept orientation tend to mediate media influence on children by discussing and coviewing ads with children (Carlson, Grossbart, and Walsh 1990). Such discussions are likely to foster more critical attitudes toward advertising. In contrast, because socio-oriented communication stresses obedience and conformity to parents, we would expect it to be related negatively to adolescents' skepticism toward advertising. Such communication teaches children to yield to parental authority, and teens exposed to it may be more likely to yield to claims made in ads with little questioning or critical evaluation.

> H1:   Concept-oriented communication is related positively to adolescents' skepticism toward advertising.

> H2:   Socio-oriented communication is related negatively to adolescents' skepticism toward advertising.

Peers. Other socialization agents who are likely to be particularly relevant for teens include peer groups (see, e.g., Moschis 1978, 1985). Research suggests that frequency of communication with peers is related positively to adolescents' attitudes toward advertising (Moschis 1978). Similarly, Boush, Friestad, and Rose (1994) hypothesized that adolescents' susceptibility to peer influence is related negatively to skepticism toward advertising. Susceptibility to influence is defined as "the need to identify or enhance one's image with significant others through the acquisition and use of products and brands, the willingness to conform to the expectations of others regarding purchase decisions [normative influence], and/or the tendency to learn about products and brands by observing others and/or seeking information from others [informational influence]" (Bearden, Netemeyer, and Teel 1989, p. 474). Susceptibility to influence, then, has two dimensions, a normative dimension reflecting a willingness to comply with the wishes of others or to conform to others to enhance one's self-esteem and an informational dimension reflecting one's willingness to accept and internalize information from another.

Boush et al. (1994) found a positive relationship between conformity and trust in advertising. On the basis of these findings, Boush, Friestad, and Rose (1994) hypothesized that mass media sources such as advertising would serve as a type of normative influence, and therefore teens high in susceptibility to influence would be less skeptical toward advertising. However, those researchers combined items designed by Bearden, Netemeyer, and Teel (1989, 1990) to measure susceptibility to normative influence with items designed to measure informational influence. They found that susceptibility to influence was related negatively to disbelief in advertising, as expected, but positively to mistrust of advertiser motives, counter to expectation. Perhaps one reason for these results is the way in which susceptibility to influence was operationalized. Because susceptibility to informational influence and susceptibility to normative influence may have different effects on skepticism, we operationalized both types of susceptibility to influence. In particular, we expected susceptibility to normative peer influence to be related negatively to skepticism toward advertising, consistent with Boush, Friestad, and Rose (1994). However, we expected susceptibility to informational peer influence to be associated positively with skepticism toward advertising. Peers may provide information that is critical of advertising and/or provide information that may help teens acquire a skeptical outlook. Consistent with this view, the frequency of communication with peers has been found to be associated positively with adolescents' ability to filter puffery in ads (Moschis 1978).

H3:   Adolescents' susceptibility to normative peer influence is related negatively to their skepticism toward advertising.

H4:   Adolescents' susceptibility to informational peer influence is related positively to their skepticism toward advertising.

Television. Exposure to the mass media may be another important socializing influence on teens (see, e.g., Moschis 1978, 1984; Moschis and Churchill 1978). To the extent that teens watch a lot of television, their experience with ads is enhanced. That greater experience with television ads may help teens to develop knowledge of the techniques and tactics used and, as a result, may enhance their skepticism toward advertising. The more ads one sees, the more likely one may be to recognize differences among ads in truthfulness, for example, and hence to become more skeptical toward ads. Consistent with this reasoning, Moschis (1984) found amount of television viewing to be associated positively with teens' discontent with the consumption process, in which skepticism may play a part.

H5:   The extent to which adolescents watch television is related positively to their skepticism toward advertising.

Socialization Agents and Marketplace Knowledge

In addition to helping teens develop skeptical attitudes toward advertising, interaction with socialization agents may help them acquire other skills and behaviors, such as marketplace knowledge, which in turn may be related to skepticism. Marketplace knowledge is defined as teens' knowledge of consumer-related factors, such as stores, shopping, and prices. One function of the socialization process is to help teens acquire marketplace knowledge so that they will be able to adapt adequately in their roles as consumers (McNeal 1987; Moschis and Churchill 1978; Ward 1974).

Parents. Teens may acquire marketplace knowledge from many sources or socialization agents, such as parents, peers, and the mass media (see, e.g., Churchill and Moschis 1979; Moschis and Churchill 1978; Moschis and Moore 1979a; Ward 1974). It may be that specific aspects or types of interaction with and exposure to socialization agents are related more closely to creating marketplace knowledge in teens, whereas others (i.e., socio-oriented communication, susceptibility to normative peer influence) are not. In other words, certain types of interaction with socialization agents may enhance teens' learning of marketplace knowledge. In the family communication environment, concept-oriented communication, in particular, is likely to be related positively to teens' learning of marketplace knowledge. Such communication fosters development of children's consumer competence and problem-solving abilities (Carlson, Grossbart, and Stuenkel 1992). Hence, we would expect concept-oriented communication to enhance teens' marketplace knowledge.

H6: Concept-oriented communication is related positively to teens' marketplace knowledge.

Peers. Peers may also contribute to teens' acquisition of marketplace knowledge. Indeed, studies have found that peers are important reference sources for teens in selecting products (see, e.g., Gilkison 1973; Mascarenhas and Higby 1993; Saunders, Samli, and Tozier 1973). In particular, teens may be susceptible to being influenced by friends because friends supply needed information in ambiguous consumption situations. The tendency to seek information from friends and to be influenced by knowledgeable friends is likely to be related positively to teens' acquisition of marketplace knowledge. Presumably the information that friends provide is internalized by the teen, thereby enhancing teens' marketplace knowledge.

H7:   Teens' susceptibility to informational influence from friends is related positively to their marketplace knowledge.

Television. Exposure to the mass media may enhance teens' knowledge of the marketplace. Goldberg (1990) found that children who were exposed to American television had greater awareness of toys than children who were not exposed to it. By watching television, teens may gain information about products, brands, stores, and shopping, as well as information about how products are used and fit with certain lifestyles (see, e.g., Moschis 1978). Such learning may follow from ads, which have an explicit goal of providing consumer-related information, and from programming, which provides implicit information about how products are used in "everyday" life (i.e., what products are used and how by sitcom celebrities, or "social motivations for watching television," Moschis 1978).

H8:   The extent to which teens watch television will be related positively to their marketplace knowledge.

Marketplace Knowledge

Teens' level of marketplace knowledge is likely to be related positively to skepticism toward advertising. With greater knowledge, teens may be more familiar with alternative brands and stores, for example, and therefore better able to differentiate between truthful and misleading claims. Generally, the increased knowledge resulting from greater experience in the marketplace may enable teens to understand that ads provide a point of view that is biased toward the marketer's position and hence may result in a more skeptical attitude toward such persuasion attempts. Boush, Friestad, and Rose (1994) found that age was related positively to skepticism toward advertising. Older teens may have had more experience in the marketplace and more opportunity for negative experiences than younger teens and consequently may have more knowledge of the marketplace, which in turn may make them more skeptical (Boush, Friestad, and Rose 1994).

> H9:   Teens' marketplace knowledge is related positively to their skepticism toward advertising.

Mediation

The effects of specific dimensions of interaction with and exposure to socialization agents on skepticism toward advertising are likely to be mediated by teens' marketplace knowledge. In particular, the effects of concept-oriented communication, susceptibility to informational influence from friends, and teens' extent of television viewing on skepticism are likely to be mediated by teens' marketplace knowledge. These three variables, or aspects of interaction with the three socialization agents (parents, peers, and television) are expected to be related positively to marketplace knowledge, which in turn is expected to be associated positively with adolescents' skepticism toward advertising. Moschis and Moore (1979b) found that the effect of concept-oriented communication on adolescents' ability to filter puffery in ads was indirect through its effect on exposure to public affairs.

> H10a: The effects of concept-oriented communication on teens' skepticism toward advertising are mediated by their marketplace knowledge.
>
> H10b: The effects of teens' susceptibility to informational influence from friends on their skepticism toward advertising are mediated by their marketplace knowledge.
>
> H10c: The effects of teens' extent of television viewing on their skepticism toward advertising are mediated by their marketplace knowledge.

Method

To test the socialization model of skepticism toward advertising, we collected survey data from a sample of 353 students in classes at a public high school in a city in the Southeast. Respondents were informed that the purpose of the research was to learn what teenagers think about various consumer-related issues and that their responses would remain anonymous. They were asked not to discuss their responses with classmates because we wanted to learn what they themselves thought about the issues. A $2 contribution was made to the school for every completed student questionnaire to encourage the school's participation in the project. However, the respondents were unaware of the incentive.

Because of missing data, usable responses were obtained from 296 of the students. Analyses indicated that data were missing on a random basis; therefore, students who did not provide complete data were dropped from the analysis. The average age of respondents was 16 years, and 57% were female. The sample was predominantly lower middle class. Seventy-six percent were white, 17% were black, not of Hispanic origin, and 7% were members of other ethnic groups.

Measures

The self-report items used to measure constructs are listed in the Appendix. All constructs were measured by multiple items, with the exception of teens' television viewing, which was measured by responses to the item, "I watch a lot of television," recorded on a 7-point Likert-type scale (mean = 4.17, SD = 1.90). Whenever possible, we used items from previously validated scales to measure other constructs. Items designed to measure concept-oriented and socio-oriented communication were drawn from Moschis, Moore, and Smith (1984). To measure susceptibility to normative and informational influence from friends, we used items from scales developed and validated by Bearden, Netemeyer, and Teel (1989). As in the study by Boush, Friestad, and Rose (1994), these items were modified slightly to focus on susceptibility to influence from friends, in particular. The items measuring skepticism toward advertising were based on Gaski and Etzel's (1986) measure of sentiment toward advertising and, for the most part, pertained to television advertising. The items used to measure teens' marketplace knowledge tapped teens' subjective perceptions of their level of knowledge about consumer-related phenomena (i.e., stores, prices, and general knowledge) and were developed specifically for our study.

We assessed unidimensionality and reliability of the measures by maximum-likelihood confirmatory factor analyses with the covariance matrix as input. Given poor fit of the initial solution of any scale, items associated with large standardized residuals (i.e., those > $|2.58|$) were dropped and the model reestimated (Jöreskog and Sörbom 1989). Large residuals often indicate model misspecification and potential multidimensionality (Steenkamp and van Trijp 1991). Acceptable models were obtained for each scale (nonsignificant chi-square statistic, low standardized residuals, low root mean square residuals, significant loadings, and adequate composite reliability, i.e., > .60 per Bagozzi and Yi 1988). Composite reliability ranged from .64 to .84 (see the Appendix). Descriptive statistics and simple correlations are reported in Table 2.1.

Results

We used regression models to test the hypothesized effects. The relationships hypothesized were specific in direction, so all t-test probability levels reflect one-tailed tests. Because marketplace knowledge was hypothesized to mediate the effects of the socialization agents on teens' skepticism toward advertising, we estimated three separate models suggested by Baron and Kenny (1986) to detect such mediation (see Table 2.2). Specifically, we used ordinary least-squares regression to estimate:

$$SK = f(CO, SO, SNPI, SIPI, TV) \qquad (2.1)$$
$$MK = f(CO, SO, SNPI, SIPI, TV) \qquad (2.2)$$
$$SK = f(MK, CO, SO, SNPI, SIPI, TV), \qquad (2.3)$$

where:

TABLE 2.1 Descriptive Statistics and Simple Correlations[a]

	SK	CO	SO	SNPI	SIPI	TV	MK
CO	.25						
SO	.13	.27					
SNPI	−.01	−.04	.22				
SIPI	.16	.16	.20	.55			
TV	.21	.06	.19	.10	.09		
MK	.51	.32	.14	.02	.14	.13	
Mean	4.80	1.68	1.17	3.12	4.07	4.17	4.59
S.D.	1.06	.82	.80	1.46	1.19	1.90	1.07

a. SK is skepticism toward advertising, CO is concept-oriented communication, SO is socio-oriented communication, SNPI is susceptibility to normative peer influence, SIPI is susceptibility to informational peer influence, TV is amount of television watched, and MK is marketplace knowledge.

SK   =   skepticism toward advertising
CO   =   concept-oriented communication
SO   =   socio-oriented communication
SNPI =   susceptibility to normative peer influence
SIPI =   susceptibility to informational peer influence
TV   =   amount of television watched, and
MK   =   marketplace knowledge.

We tested H1 through H5 by using model 2.1. The results show concept-oriented communication, teens' susceptibility to informational peer influence, and the amount of television teens watch to be related positively to teens' skepticism toward advertising ($p < .05$). Teens' susceptibility to normative peer influence is related negatively to skepticism, as predicted ($p < .05$). However, a socio-oriented family environment is unrelated to skepticism ($p > .10$). Hence, H1, H3, H4, and H5 are supported, but H2 is not.

We used model 2.2 to test H6 through H8. The results show both a concept-oriented family communication environment and the amount of TV a teen watches to be related positively to teens' marketplace knowledge ($p < .05$). Susceptibility to informational peer influence also is related to marketplace knowledge ($p < .06$). Hence, H6, H7, and H8 are supported.

TABLE 2.2 Regression Results

Independent variables	Beta	Std. beta	t-value	p-value
Model 1 (criterion = skepticism)[a]				
Concept-oriented communication	.26	.20	3.41	.000
Socio-oriented communication	.04	.03	.45	.675
Normative peer influence	−.09	−.12	−1.73	.042
Informational peer influence	.16	.17	2.57	.005
Amount of TV watched	.10	.19	3.32	.001
Constant	3.52		14.01	.000
Model 2 (criterion = marketplace knowledge)[b]				
Concept-oriented communication	.37	.29	4.89	.000
Socio-oriented communication	.04	.03	.56	.714
Normative peer influence	−.03	−.05	−.67	.251
Informational peer influence	.10	.11	1.57	.058
Amount of TV watched	.06	.11	1.88	.030
Constant	3.38		13.35	.000
Model 3 (criterion = skepticism)[c]				
Marketplace knowledge	.45	.45	8.59	.000
Concept-oriented communication	.09	.07	1.30	.097
Socio-oriented communication	.02	.01	.22	.598
Normative peer influence	−.07	−.10	−1.60	.055
Informational peer influence	.11	.13	2.07	.019
Amount of TV watched	.08	.14	2.75	.003
Constant	2.01		7.03	.000

a. Overall model: $F(5,290) = 8.01, p < .001, R^2 = .121.$
b. Overall model: $F(5,290) = 8.28, p < .001, R^2 = .125.$
c. Overall model: $F(6,289) = 20.65, p < .001, R^2 = .300.$

Baron and Kenny (1986) specified four conditions among the independent variables, mediator, and dependent variable that are necessary to establish mediation. First, the independent variables must each significantly affect the mediator. The results from model 2.2 establish such effects. Specifically, a concept-oriented family communication environment, susceptibility to informational peer influence, and the amount of TV watched are related significantly to marketplace knowledge. Second, the independent variables must each significantly affect the dependent variable. The results from model 2.1 indicate that concept-oriented communication, informational peer influence, and amount of TV watched are related significantly to skepticism toward advertising. Third, the mediator must significantly affect the dependent variable as hypothesized in H9. The results from model 2.3 support H9; teens' marketplace knowledge is related positively to skepticism toward advertising ($p < .05$). Fourth, and finally, Baron and Kenny (1986) suggested that each of the effects of the independent variables on the dependent variable must be reduced given the presence of the mediator in the model. In other words, the effect coefficients for each of the independent variables must be less in model 2.3 than those estimated in model 2.1. The results from model 2.3 indicate that the effect of concept-oriented family communication, as indicated by the standardized regression coefficient, diminished considerably (65%) given the presence of the mediator in the model. The effects of susceptibility to informational peer influence and the amount of TV watched did not decrease as much when the mediator was present, as estimated in model 2.3 (reduction of about 23% and 26%, respectively). We used an approximate t-test suggested by Baron and Kenny (1986) to test the significance of the mediated effects. The indirect effects of concept-oriented communication ($t(288) = 4.23, p < .001$), informational peer influence ($t(288) = 1.54, p < .10$), and amount of TV watched ($t(288) = 1.83, p < .05$) on skepticism toward advertising via marketplace knowledge are all significant. Hence, H10a through H10c are supported with the effects of concept-oriented family communication on skepticism toward advertising mediated more by marketplace knowledge than were the other two variables.

Discussion

In general, the results provide strong support for the socialization model of adolescent skepticism toward advertising, with the included variables explaining more than 30% of the variance in skepticism. Specific dimensions of interaction with the three socialization agents—parents, peers, and the mass media—are found to be related to skepticism (H1, H3-H5). Moreover, teens' marketplace knowledge is related positively to skepticism (H9), and appears to mediate the effects of certain aspects of interaction with socialization agents on skepticism (H10).

The pattern of results suggests that skepticism toward advertising is an attitude learned through interaction with parents, peers, and television. Moreover, socialization-agent-based effects appear to be due in large part to the nature of teens' interaction with each of those agents. In particular, concept-oriented family communication, susceptibility to informational peer influence, and the extent of television viewing enhance skepticism, largely because of their positive effects on teens' marketplace knowledge. Indeed, marketplace knowledge, which is itself an outcome of the socialization process (H6-H8), appears to be a particularly important factor in promoting the development of adolescents' skepticism toward advertising. Greater knowledge appears to give teens a basis by which to evaluate the motives of and claims made by advertisers and provides an informational foundation for skepticism.

Family. Concept-oriented family communication is related positively to skepticism, as expected. By stressing the development of children's problem-solving skills, parents who use concept-oriented communication help children to learn skeptical attitudes toward advertising, thereby enhancing children's consumer competence. Given that relationship, examining antecedents related to concept-oriented communication would be interesting. For example, does family communication differ on the basis of family type? If so, public policy officials should direct consumer education efforts toward families less likely to use concept-oriented communication.

Counter to expectation, socio-oriented communication has no significant effect on skepticism. Because such communication focuses on creating deference to authority, we hypothesized that teens exposed to it would be more likely than others to accept ad claims as well. However, teens may not view the sponsors of ads as authority figures. Alternatively, parents who practice socio-oriented communication may insulate teens from factors related to creating skeptical attitudes, and, hence such communication may have little effect on teens' skepticism.

Peers. Our results indicate that peers are also an important socializing influence in helping teens acquire skeptical attitudes toward advertising. In particular, the tendency for teens to yield to peer influence, or teens' susceptibility to peer influence, is related to skepticism. Boush, Friestad, and Rose (1994) suggested that advertising serves as a normative influence, and therefore children who are susceptible to peer influence would be likely to yield to advertising as well. However, they found conflicting effects of susceptibility to influence on skepticism. One reason for their conflicting results may be that no distinction was made between susceptibility to normative versus informational peer influence. One of the important contributions of our study is that we provide evidence for the unique effects of each of those types of influence on skepticism.

In particular, we found susceptibility to normative peer influence to be related negatively to skepticism toward advertising, as expected. To the extent that one is likely to conform to peers to enhance self-esteem and/or receive rewards and avoid punishment (e.g., wanting friends to think you're "cool" and to avoid their making fun of you), one may also be more likely to accept the portrayals of "coolness" or "what's in" depicted in ads, and therefore less likely to be critical of ad claims. Susceptibility to normative influence, then, would reduce tendencies toward skepticism.

Alternatively, we found susceptibility to informational peer influence to be related positively to adolescents' skepticism toward advertising, as expected. Teens may be susceptible to being influenced by friends who have relevant knowledge about advertising, which is likely to enhance teens' skepticism. The information that friends provide to teens may aid teens in developing a critical orientation toward ads. Our results, then, shed light on the conflicting findings of Boush, Friestad, and Rose (1994). In particular, the distinction between susceptibility to normative and susceptibility to informational peer influence is important because they have opposite effects on skepticism.

Television. Though exposure to television is often cast in a negative light (Grossbart and Crosby 1984; Goldberg 1990), our results indicate that the extent of television viewing can have positive effects on teens' consumer socialization. In particular, we found the extent of teens' television viewing to be related positively to adolescents' skepticism toward advertising, as expected. One might suspect that teens who watch more television would be more at risk, that is, more likely to use ads as a significant source of information about the marketplace than to use other sources. However, the greater skepticism toward ads that results from increased exposure to television may serve as a counterweight to such presumed effects. Further, we might assume that teens who watch less TV gain much of their information about products from non-mass-media sources, and hence are not under any greater risk of accepting subjective claims. That assumption needs to be substantiated.

Regardless, exposure to television seems to give teens experience by which to judge ads, thereby enhancing their skepticism. Though public policy officials traditionally have viewed television as having detrimental effects on children, our results suggest that television can be a positive force as well. Perhaps public policy officials can use the medium even more effectively; that is, these effects we found with traditional programming might be even stronger if specific consumer education programming were included. Television might be an important medium for public policy officials to use in the future for consumer education efforts.

The positive relationship between the amount of TV watched and skepticism may also have implications for marketers. Specifically, marketers may have to be careful in presenting implied and/or subjective claims to heavier viewers of television, because such viewers are likely to have wary attitudes and a discerning eye toward such claims.

Marketplace Knowledge. Marketplace knowledge plays a particularly crucial role in adolescent skepticism toward advertising. We found marketplace knowledge, itself an outcome of the socialization process, to be related positively to skepticism. Greater knowledge of the marketplace appears to give teens a basis by which to evaluate ads. With greater knowledge, teens are more likely to recognize techniques that advertisers use to effect persuasion. Also, with greater knowledge of stores, shopping, and the like, teens are better able to tell when ads are truthful and when they are misleading. Our results suggest that public policy officials who want to help teens develop skeptical attitudes should focus on enhancing teens' marketplace knowledge.

Our results also suggest that interaction with socialization agents affects skepticism primarily because of its effects on teens' marketplace knowledge (i.e., marketplace knowledge mediates the effects of specific dimensions of interaction with socialization agents on skepticism, as expected). In other words, not all types of interaction are equally effective in fostering skepticism. Dimensions of interaction with socialization agents that involve disseminating information to teens and thereby enhancing teens' marketplace knowledge (i.e., concept-oriented communication, susceptibility to informational peer influence, and extent of television viewing) appear to be particularly relevant in fostering skepticism.

Limitations and Directions for Future Research

Our study had certain limitations, and our conclusions and the results on which they are based should be tempered by the research choices we made. We examined only parents, peers, and television as socialization agents. It would be interesting to explore how interaction with other socialization agents, such as schools and retailers, might be related to adolescents' skepticism toward advertising. Further, we examined only certain types of interaction with the three socialization agents. Other dimensions of interaction not included in our study (e.g., frequency of communication with parents, peers, etc.; modeling effects; reinforcement) also may be important in explaining adolescents' skepticism toward advertising. For example, because parental styles may be an antecedent of family communication patterns (Carlson, Grossbart, and Stuenkel 1992), parental styles may provide a particularly fruitful explanation for adolescents' skepticism toward advertising. Finally, we examined only television viewing for mass media effects, but exposure to other media such as magazines also may be related to skepticism. We used only a single item to tap the extent of television viewing. Our study should be replicated with alternative, better measures of television viewing. The effects on skepticism from viewing programs versus viewing ads also may be important. Our measure of skepticism tended to focus on television advertising; hence, future research should be broadened to include other forms of advertising explicitly.

Our study centered on general marketplace knowledge and skeptical attitudes toward advertising. Wright (1986) suggested that consumers develop intuitive schemas of the scheming tactics that advertisers may use, or "schemer schemas." Future research should go beyond marketplace knowledge to examine teens' schemer schemas (specific knowledge about persuasion tactics) and the implications of such schemas for skepticism. In addition, given the importance of teens' marketplace knowledge to our understanding of their skepticism toward advertising, researchers should examine other factors, not included in our study, that may affect teens' knowledge of the marketplace.

Our findings indicate that specific aspects of the socialization process are related systematically to adolescents' skepticism toward advertising. Such skepticism is key to prevailing public policies about deceptive advertising (Ford, Smith, and Swasy 1990). Our research demonstrates that socialization is a useful theoretical framework for understanding adolescents' skepticism toward advertising.

Appendix 2.1
Measures of Constructs

Concept-oriented Family Communication[1] *(composite reliability = .74)*

My (step)mother asks me to help in buying things for the family.

My (step)mother asks me what I think about the things I buy for myself.

My (step)mother says I should decide about things I should or should not buy.

My (step)mother says that buying thing I like is important even if others do not like them.

My (step)mother lets me decide how to spend my own money.

My (step)mother asks me for advice about buying things.

Socio-oriented Family Communication[1] *(composite reliability = .80)*

My (step)mother tells me what types of things I can buy.

My (step)mother wants to know what I do with my money.

My (step) mother complains when I buy something that she does not like.

My (step)mother says that I should not ask questions about things that teenagers do not usually buy.

My (step)mother tells me that I can't buy certain things.

My (step)mother says that she knows what is best for me and that I should not question her.

Susceptibility to Normative Peer Influence[2] *(composite reliability = .84)*

When buying products, I usually buy the ones that I think my friends will approve of.

I like to know what products and brands make a good impression on my friends.

It is important that my friends like the products and brands I buy.

Susceptibility to Informational Peer Influence[2] *(composite reliability = .74)*
  If I don't have a lot of experience with a product, I often ask my friends
    about it.
  I often ask my friends to help me choose the best product.
  I often get information about a product from friends before I buy.
  To make sure that I buy the right product or brand, I often look at what
    my friends are buying and using.

Marketplace Knowledge[2] *(composite reliability = .65)*
  I am a knowledgeable consumer.
  I know a lot about different types of stores.
  I am usually well-informed about what is a reasonable price to pay for
    something.

Skepticism toward Advertising[2] *(composite reliability = .64)*
  Advertisers often exaggerate claims made about their products.
  Television ads tell only the good things about products.
  Most television advertising is very annoying.
  Television advertising does not tell much useful information about
    products.

1. Items were measured on five-point scales ranging from "never" to "very often."
2. Items were measured on seven-point scales ranging from "strongly disagree" to "strongly agree."

References

Bagozzi, Richard P. and Youjae Yi (1988), "On the Evaluation of Structural Equation Models," *Journal of the Academy of Marketing Science*, 16 (Spring), 74-94.

Baron, Reuben M. and David A. Kenny (1986), "The Moderator-Mediator Variable Distinction in Social Psychology Research: Conceptual, Strategic, and Statistical Considerations," *Journal of Personality and Social Psychology*, 51 (6), 1173-1182.

Bearden, William O., Richard G. Netemeyer, and Jesse E. Teel (1989), "Measurement of Consumer Susceptibility to Interpersonal Influence," *Journal of Consumer Research*, 15 (March), 472-480.

———, ———, and ——— (1990), "Further Validation of the Consumer Susceptibility to Interpersonal Influence Scale," in *Advances in Consumer Research*, Vol. 17, Marvin E. Goldberg et al., eds., Provo, UT: Association for Consumer Research, 770-776.

Boush, David M., Marian Friestad, and Gregory M. Rose (1994), "Adolescent Skepticism Toward TV Advertising and Knowledge of Advertiser Tactics," *Journal of Consumer Research*, 21 (June), 165-175.

———, Chung-Hyun Kim, Lynn R. Kahle, and Rajeev Batra (1994), "Cynicism and Conformity as Correlates of Trust in Product Information Sources," *Journal of Current Issues and Research in Advertising*, 15 (Fall), 1-9.

Brucks, Merrie, Gary M. Armstrong, and Marvin E. Goldberg (1988), "Children's Use of Cognitive Defenses Against Television Advertising: A Cognitive Response Approach," *Journal of Consumer Research,* 14 (March), 471-482.

Carlson, Les, Sanford Grossbart, and J. Kathleen Stuenkel (1992), "The Role of Parental Socialization Types on Differential Family Communication Patterns Regarding Consumption," *Journal of Consumer Psychology,* 1 (1), 31-52.

———, ———, and Ann Walsh (1990), "Mothers' Communication Orientation and Consumer Socialization Tendencies," *Journal of Advertising,* 19 (3), 27-38.

———, Ann Walsh, Russell N. Laczniak, and Sanford Grossbart (1994), "Family Communication Patterns and Marketplace Motivations, Attitudes, and Behaviors of Children and Mothers," *Journal of Consumer Affairs,* 28 (1), 25-53.

Churchill, Gilbert A., Jr. and George P. Moschis (1979), "Television and Interpersonal Influences on Adolescent Consumer Learning," *Journal of Consumer Research,* 6 (June), 23-35.

Ford, Gary T., Darlene B. Smith, and John L Swasy (1990), "Consumer Skepticism of Advertising Claims: Testing Hypotheses from Economics of Information," *Journal of Consumer Research,* 16 (March), 433-441.

Gaski, John F. and Michael J. Etzel (1986), "The Index of Consumer Sentiment Toward Marketing," *Journal of Marketing,* 50 (July), 71-81.

Gilkison, Paul (1973), "Teen-agers' Perceptions of Buying Frames of Reference: A Decade in Retrospect," *Journal of Retailing,* 49 (2), 25-37.

Goldberg, Marvin E. (1990), "A Quasi-Experiment Assessing the Effectiveness of TV Advertising Directed to Children," *Journal of Marketing Research,* 27 (November), 445-454.

Grossbart, Sanford L. and Lawrence A. Crosby (1984), "Understanding the Bases of Parental Concern and Reaction to Children's Food Advertising," *Journal of Marketing,* 48 (Summer), 79-92.

Jöreskog, Karl and Dag Sörbom (1989), *LISREL VII: Analysis of Linear Structural Relationships by the Methods of Maximum Likelihood,* Mooresville, IN: Scientific Software, Inc.

Mascarenhas, Oswald A. J. and Mary A. Higby (1993), "Peer, Parent, and Media Influences in Teen Apparel Shopping," *Journal of the Academy of Marketing Science,* 21 (Winter), 53-58.

McLeod, Jack M. and Steven R. Chaffee (1972), "The Construction of Social Reality," *The Social Influence Process,* J. T. Tedeschi, ed., Chicago: Aldine-Atherton, 50-99.

——— and Garrett J. O'Keefe, Jr. (1972), "The Socialization Perspective and Communication Behavior," in *Current Perspectives in Mass Communication Research,* F. G. Kline and P. J. Tichenor, eds., Beverly Hills, CA: Sage, 121-168.

McNeal, James U. (1987), *Children as Consumers: Insights and Implications,* Lexington, MA: Lexington Books.

Moore, Roy L. and George P. Moschis (1981), "The Role of Family Communication in Consumer Learning," *Journal of Communication,* 31 (Autumn), 42-51.

Moschis, George P. (1978), "Teenagers' Responses to Retailing Stimuli," *Journal of Retailing,* 54 (4), 80-93.

——— (1984), "A Longitudinal Analysis of Consumer Socialization," in *Winter AMA Educator's Conference Proceedings,* Paul F. Anderson and Michael J. Ryan, eds., Chicago: American Marketing Association, 189-192.

——— (1985), "The Role of Family Communication in Consumer Socialization of Children and Adolescents," *Journal of Consumer Research,* 11 (March), 898-913.

——— and Gilbert A. Churchill, Jr. (1978), "Consumer Socialization: A Theoretical and Empirical Analysis," *Journal of Marketing Research,* 15 (November), 599-609.

——— and ——— (1979), "An Analysis of The Adolescent Consumer," *Journal of Marketing,* 43 (Summer), 40-48.

——— and Linda G. Mitchell (1986), "Television Advertising and Interpersonal Influences on Teenagers' Participation in Family Consumer Decisions," in *Advances in Consumer Research, Vol. 13,* Richard J. Lutz, ed., Provo, UT: Association for Consumer Research, 181-186.

——— and Roy L. Moore (1979a), "Decision Making Among the Young: A Socialization Perspective," *Journal of Consumer Research,* 6 (September), 101-112.

——— and ——— (1979b), "Family Communication and Consumer Socialization," in *Advances in Consumer Research, Vol. 6,* William Wilkie, ed., Ann Arbor, MI: Association for Consumer Research, 359-363.

———, ———, and Ruth B. Smith (1984), "The Impact of Family Communication on Adolescent Consumer Socialization," in *Advances in Consumer Research, Vol. 11,* Thomas C. Kinnear, ed., Provo, UT: Association for Consumer Research, 314-319.

Saunders, Josephine A., A. Coskun Samli, and Enid F. Tozier (1973), "Congruence and Conflict in Buying Decisions of Mothers and Daughters," *Journal of Retailing,* 49 (3), 3-18.

Steenkamp, Jan-Benedict E. M. and Hans C. M. van Trijp (1991), "The Use of LISREL in Validating Marketing Constructs," *International Journal of Research in Marketing,* 8 (November), 283-299.

Ward, Scott (1974), "Consumer Socialization," *Journal of Consumer Research,* 1 (September), 1-16.

Wright, Peter (1986), "Schemer Schema: Consumers' Intuitive Theories About Marketers' Influence Tactics," in *Advances in Consumer Research, Vol. 13,* Richard J. Lutz, ed., Provo, UT: Association for Consumer Research, 1-3.

Zollo, Peter (1995), "Talking to Teens," *American Demographics,* 17 (November), 22-28.

CHAPTER

3

Evaluating the Impact of Affiliation Change on Children's TV Viewership and Perceptions of Network Branding

ROBERT ABELMAN
DAVID ATKIN

Today, children aged four to 12 influence more than $165 billion in spending in the United States (McGee 1997) and six- to 12-year-olds directly purchase $9 billion worth of merchandise each year (Zier 1994). Television provides the bulk of that advertising, as the average American child watches more than thirty thousand commercials a year, or roughly 82 advertisements a day (Robinson and Bianchi 1997). Children thus now represent the fastest growing segment of the ad market since 1980. This growth has, in conjunction with a rapidly changing media environment, created a highly competitive children's television marketplace that includes the Fox Children's Network, the Warner Bros. (WB) television network's programming block called "Kids' WB" and ABC's "Disney Afternoon" (Tobenkin 1994).

Increased competition has created a television landscape in which new series' failures have doubled since the mid-1980s (Adams, Eastman, and Levine 1993). The tendency of young viewers to watch programs on the same channels (channel loyalty), especially between adjacent programs (inheritance effects), and repeat viewing across different episodes of the same program (duplication of viewing) has also eroded (Abelman 1995), much to the chagrin of advertisers (see, e.g., "Children's TV Ad Spending" 1994).

In response, the major networks have waged various campaigns to maintain their young audiences and attract advertisers, tethering each to a different conception of children's motives and viewing patterns (Adams 1993; Lin 1995). Recent efforts artificially to cultivate inheritance include cameo "visitations" of children's characters from one program to its adjacent program (see Gay 1996) and the infusion of 3-D gimmickry across a block of family-oriented prime-time fare (Bowles 1997).

Most significantly, believing that children display an affinity for and distinguish between television networks, network executives have upgraded efforts to promote identifiable logos ("ABC to Show Logo" 1993; Mandese 1993). Networks have also redoubled their efforts in corporate "branding" (Jensen 1996)—the establishment of a network image to which all programming and program stars are tied (e.g., "FOXKIDS TV"). In the words of Larry Light, president of branding consultancy Arcature Corp., "Branding is exactly what helped Fox become successful. They didn't sell call letters, they sold the name and played down individual stations" (Levin 1995, p. 22).

A growing number of network executives believe that young viewers are largely attracted to local stations and distinguish between channels within the marketplace to guide their televiewing (see "Affiliation Switches Impact Network News" 1991). Based on the assumption that brands enjoy top-of-mind awareness when they've been recently advertised (e.g., Wansink 1997), the commercial networks have redoubled their campaigns to strengthen station affinity by highlighting affiliated station identification and inspiring viewers' station loyalty (Abelman, Atkin, and Rand 1997; Gantz and Eastman 1983; Schofield and Driscoll 1991). Promotional efforts notwithstanding, the networks continue to see lower ratings and diminished inheritance effects across programs, as they reconsider programming strategies for the $1 billion a year in advertising aimed at children.

The Uses and Gratifications Perspective

As the networks scramble to stem audience erosion, researchers grounded in uses and gratifications theory are continuing their exploration of what it is that governs viewer choice, viewing patterns, and audience interpretations of program content. Uses and gratifications was aptly summarized by Katz, Blumler and Gurevitch (1974, p. 20) as an approach to media use that examines:

> (1) the social and psychological origins of (2) needs, which generate (3) expectations of (4) the mass media or other sources, which lead to (5) differential patterns of media exposure (or engagement in other activities), resulting in (6) need gratifications.

Katz et al. (1974) go on to note that the perspective is founded on three basic tenets: (a) viewers are goal directed in their behavior; (b) they are active media users; and (c) they are aware of their needs and select media to gratify these needs. Theorists in this tradition thus hypothesize a self-motivated audience actively seeking gratifications (Blumler 1979). Children, in particular, make distinct choices across media channels and programs (Greenberg 1974).

Lin (1993) confirmed that child viewers remain a distinctive segment of the viewing audience, displaying characteristic viewing activities—but similar gratification objectives—compared to adult viewers. Important elements of the psychological context in which exposure to and affinity for television programming occurs are outlined in a great many studies (see, e.g., Rosengren, Wenner, and Palmgreen 1985; Rubin and McHugh 1987; Rubin, Perse, and Powell 1985). Most recently, they have identified two primary types of television viewing: ritualized (habitual use of television for diversionary reasons) and instrumental (goal-oriented use of television to gratify various needs or motives; see Abelman 1987, 1988; Babrow 1987; Houlberg 1984; Rubin et al. 1986).

Although uses and gratifications is a well-accepted theory, the concept of a self-motivated audience actively seeking gratifications is not without its detractors (Bauer 1964; Bogart 1965; Elliot 1974). In criticizing the "audience activeness" notion, Biocca (1987) questioned the validity of "active" versus "passive" audience conceptions, calling instead for a wider consideration of medium and sociocultural media-use orientation factors. A similar weakness noted in this tradition is that, rather than measuring program choice empirically, the majority of studies examining media context or environment factors treat this concept as part of the institutional structure, or outputs (Lin 1993). In the wake of expanded viewing choices, the significance of program options in the overall media consumption process has dramatically increased (e.g., Atkin, Greenberg, and Baldwin 1991).

That most uses and gratifications studies predict media exposure with gratifications sought has also been criticized, as the correlation between these two constructs is often weak (Rosengren et al. 1985) or insignificant (e.g., Babrow 1987). Another criticism is that these general concepts remain of little value to the television industry—that is, they provide no information as to *what* young ritualized and instrumental viewers watch in order to gratify their needs (Abelman et al. 1997). Thus, they offer no insight into the salience of network branding, relevancy of promoting station identification, or effectiveness of programming strategies in maintaining an audience.

A dimension of uses and gratifications theory that is particularly relevant for off-air viewing, functional equivalence, implies that different content within the same medium may be functionally equivalent for child viewers (e.g., Levy and Windahl 1984). Thus children with divergent viewing motivations may seek out a particular feature—a network, station, or program—if it is perceived as capable of fulfilling a particular function or satisfying a particular need. Yet as researchers (Krugman 1985; Lin 1994) suggest, symbiotic investigations that build communication theory and also have direct pragmatic appeal for the professional community are rare, particularly in the children's televiewing domain.

Affiliation Changes

As the networks enter an unprecedented era of competition, we see an increased need for information that can help predict children's responses to affiliation shifts and, thus, provide guidance for programming, promotional strategies, and advertising. Abelman et al. (1997, p. 363) maintain there can be no better scenario through which to evaluate viewing preferences and perceptions of network branding than when local television stations change network affiliation:

> When affiliation changes occur within a given market, viewing behaviors are challenged because: (a) channel numbers remain the same but network identity shifts across channels; (b) local and syndicated entertainment programming typically remains intact on a given station but network programming shifts occur across stations; (c) local newscasts often shift times to accommodate new network programming; and (d) local program personalities often remain situated, but network news and entertainment program personalities must be sought elsewhere. In general, chaos reigns and viewing motivations and behaviors are potentially laid bare as viewers attempt to make sense of the new-found television landscape.

According to David Tobenkin (1994, p. 52) of *Broadcasting & Cable,* "a shuffling of channels and time periods could dislocate kids from their shows and impede across-the-board clearances and promotions for the networks." Although there is a paucity of research on the topic, investigations on affiliation swaps suggest that the results—in terms of audience impact and composition—are difficult to predict (Coe 1995; McClellan 1995).

Academic inquiries in this area have been criticized for focusing overly on the individual (Biocca 1987), and producing little in the way of industry-relevant findings. Samples are often comprised of college-age students and attempt to generalize audience viewing behavior based on viewership of specific genres (e.g., soap operas). Industry studies, on the other hand, are more "how to" oriented (Krugman 1985) and have relied exclusively on audience ratings as a measure of viewing behavior. Studies in both traditions generally fail to distinguish between local and network programming and are focused upon single markets. Greater insight into viewing behavior would have been generated by examining both local and network programming across a wider cross section of markets. In addition, none of these investigations examined the impact of affiliation shift on children's televiewing habits and practices.

As researchers (Abelman et al. 1997) note, a unique opportunity to examine multiple case study markets arose when, from September 1994 to January 1995, an unparalleled 68 stations in 37 markets across the country changed affiliations. Inspired by an agreement between Fox Television and New World Communications in May 1994, 21 stations moved from a traditional network to Fox, and 27 moved from independence to an affiliate. According to Steven Rattner, managing director of Lazard Freres & Co., "the deal between New World and Fox constituted one of the seminal events in broadcasting history" (Abelman et al. 1997, p. 363). It also created the opportunity to examine children's responses to affiliation shifts and the light these changes cast on viewing patterns and preferences in multiple markets.

Toward that end, the present study reaffirms Rubin's (1983, p. 39) call to "further the line of heuristic development which recognizes that viewing motivations are not isolated, static traits, but rather, comprise a set of interactive needs and expectations." That a complex pattern of interrelationships exists between these variables is firmly established in the literature and offers the guiding hypothesis that children's viewing motivations, preferences, and attitudes will be interrelated.

In the context of children's viewing, Webster and Wakshlag's (1983) program choice model incorporates program options and viewer needs along with program preference, viewer availability, viewer awareness, and viewing groups. It posits that these are all distinguishable and antecedent variables for program choice behavior that, in turn, determines subsequent exposure behavior (see Greenberg 1974). Activities such as purchasing behavior motivated by media exposure (Lin 1994) are indicators for the dimension of behavioral involvement with the viewing process.

Drawing from that work, we expect that viewing motivations would causally influence viewing exposure, television affinity, network affinity, and station affinity. These assumptions are largely in agreement with the logic of Levy and Windahl's (1984) model, in which viewing exposure is the dependent variable for gratifications obtained. However, subsequent work (Lin 1993) brings into question the direction of these interactions, particularly amid significant affiliation changes within multiple markets and among children. Thus, we pose the following research questions:

RQ1: What are the salient patterns of interactions among television viewing motivations for children?

RQ2: What patterns of television use during affiliation shifts help define what children watch on television?

RQ3: What patterns of television use help predict children's responses to affiliation shifts and, thus, provide guidance for programming, promotional strategies, and advertising?

Method

This study is based on a stratified sample of nine markets, representing the widest variety of affiliation shifts, as selected from the 37 markets experiencing affiliation shifts mentioned earlier. From mid- to late-January 1995, telephone surveys were administered by 20 professional interviewers to a multimarket sample using random digits. Of 700 criterion respondents contacted, 532 completed the survey (50-78 per market), representing an overall response rate of 76%. Respondents ranged in age from seven to 16 (M = 12.32, SD = 3.82) and were primarily male (57.7%).

Our instrument contained measures of children's TV viewing motives, awareness of local station and individual program network affiliation, and awareness of national advertising brand symbols. It also gauged awareness of local station affiliation shifts and of television viewing patterns—including television affinity, network affinity, local station affinity, and viewing levels and genre preferences.

Television Viewing Motivations

Consistent with past work (see Abelman 1987; Rubin 1983), respondents indicated their levels of agreement with each of 30 statements of motives for watching television, which were subdivided into 10 motivations. Response options ranged from "strongly disagree" (1) to "strongly agree" (5) with that reason, and were repeated for each statement. Specific items, along with their means and standard deviations, can be found in Table 3.1.

TABLE 3.1 Television Viewing Motivations

	Mean	SD
Relaxation		
"It relaxes me"	3.24	1.02
"It allows me to calm down"	3.08	0.98
"It's a pleasure"	2.87	1.12
Companionship		
"So I won't have to be alone"	2.72	0.76
"When there's no one else to talk to"	2.37	0.93
"Because it makes me feel less lonely"	2.33	1.02
Habit		
"Because it's there"	3.21	1.08
"Because I just like to watch"	3.22	1.04
"Because it's a habit, just something I do all the time"	2.32	1.13
Pass Time		
"I have nothing better to do"	2.96	0.97
"It passes the time away when I'm bored"	2.83	0.76
"It gives me something to do to occupy my time"	2.31	0.87
Entertainment		
"It entertains me"	3.91	0.96
"It's enjoyable"	3.33	1.08
"It amuses me"	3.12	1.01

We determined patterns of viewing motivations by intercorrelating the items and conducting a principal factor analysis with oblique rotation, which was selected because viewing motives were interrelated. Eigenvalues of at least 1.0 and a minimum of three primary loadings of .40 or greater (and no secondary loadings above .30 on any other factors) served as the retention criteria. The factor solution, summarized in Table 3.2, identified five factors and explained 68.4% of the total variance.

In particular, Factor 1 (Pass Time/Habit) had an eigenvalue of 6.89 and explained 49.5% of the common variance. Three habit items and two pass time items loaded highly on this factor. Factor 2 (Entertainment) had an eigenvalue of 3.21 and explained 24.0% of the common variance. The three entertainment items loaded highly on this factor. Factor 3 (Information) had an eigenvalue of 2.28 and explained 12.3%

TABLE 3.1 Continued

	Mean	SD
Social Interaction		
"It's something to do with my friends"	2.20	1.21
"So I can talk with other people about what's going on"	2.15	1.17
"So I can be with family/friends who are watching"	1.43	1.22
Information		
"It helps me learn things about myself and others"	3.02	0.87
"So I can learn how to do things which I haven't done before"	2.31	1.05
"So I can learn about what could happen to me"	2.20	1.11
Arousal		
"It's thrilling"	2.32	1.12
"It's exciting"	2.24	1.14
"It peps me up"	1.32	1.07
Escape		
"So I can forget about school or other things"	2.85	1.12
"So I can get away from the rest of the family or others"	1.88	1.30
"So I can get away from what I'm doing"	2.03	1.16
Moral Support		
"It proves the lessons my parents and other adults teach me"	1.12	0.76
"It lets me believe that how I treat others is correct"	1.21	0.83
"It helps me figure out the right way to treat others"	1.07	0.69

of the common variance. Three information and one social interaction item loaded highly on this factor. Factor 4 (Companionship) had an eigenvalue of 1.44 and explained 9.7% of the common variance. Our three companionship items loaded on this factor. Factor 5 (Escape) had an eigenvalue of 1.22 and explained 7.2% of the common variance. The three escape items loaded highly on this factor.

Awareness Measures

We next included a series of Awareness indices, involving a ratio of generated correct responses to total possible correct responses. Classifications included: "low awareness" (0%-33% correct), "moderate

TABLE 3.2 Oblique Rotated Factor Matrix
of Viewing Motivations

Viewing Motivation Items	Time/ Habit	Entertainment	Information	Companionship	Escape
		Viewing Motivation Factors			
Habit (1)	[.82]	−.26	−.12	.12	−.14
Pass Time (1)	[.76]	−.03	.09	−.04	.08
Pass Time (2)	[.74]	−.18	.09	−.07	.08
Habit (2)	[.68]	−.18	−.11	.18	−.06
Habit (3)	[.62]	−.13	−.03	.14	−.03
Entertainment (2)	−.21	[.87]	−.12	.11	.12
Entertainment (1)	−.24	[.81]	−.17	.09	.18
Entertainment (3)	−.10	[.71]	−.10	.07	.12
Social Interaction (1)	.05	[.60]	.02	.24	−.12
Information (1)	.01	−.04	[.72]	.09	−.23
Information (3)	.02	−.02	[.70]	.02	.02
Information (2)	.04	.02	[.64]	.02	−.16
Social Interaction (2)	.21	.12	[.51]	.25	−.11
Companionship (1)	.04	.08	.09	[.83]	−.03
Companionship (2)	−.08	.07	.07	[.80]	−.04
Companionship (3)	−.06	.03	.12	[.71]	−.06
Escape (2)	.15	−.18	−.03	.04	[.68]
Escape (3)	.12	−.12	.05	.06	[.65]
Escape (1)	.14	−.12	−.02	.06	[.58]
Pass Time (3)	.38	.04	.11	−.05	−.06
Relaxation (1)	.22	−.09	.12	.12	−.04
Relaxation (2)	.18	−.07	−.01	.12	.12
Relaxation (3)	.09	.05	.15	.08	.21
Social Interaction (3)	.09	.18	.09	.21	−.21
Arousal (1)	−.14	.22	.22	.11	.12
Arousal (2)	−.09	.18	.34	.08	.22
Arousal (3)	.01	.21	.18	.11	.23
Moral Support (1)	−.24	.09	−.05	.14	−.12
Moral Support (2)	−.18	.04	.01	.12	.03
Moral Support (3)	−.16	.08	.07	.19	−.01

awareness" (34%-66% correct), and "high awareness" (67%-100% correct). In all cases, a point was awarded for each correct response and no point was awarded for each wrong response or nonresponse:

Program Affiliation Awareness. Respondents were read the previous week's daytime and prime-time network television lineup, one day at a time (with offerings presented in random order), and asked to identify the programs "they typically watch on a weekly basis." After the program preferences were identified, respondents were asked to identify the network on which each program currently appeared.

Local Station Awareness: Call Letters. Respondents were asked to identify each of their local broadcast television stations by their station call letters.

Local Station Awareness: Channel Number. Respondents were asked to identify each of their local stations by their broadcast channel number.

Network Affiliation Awareness. Respondents were then provided with the correct channel numbers and call letters for each of the stations in their market, and asked to identify each station by its network affiliation prior to the recent shifts.

Affiliation Change Awareness. Respondents were asked to identify, by either channel or call letters, each station that changed network affiliation in the past few months.

Affiliation Change Identification. Respondents were then provided with the channel, call letters, and previous network affiliation of each station in their market that underwent a recent affiliation shift, and asked to identify the new network affiliation of each station.

Product Brand Awareness. Respondents were asked to identify, by name (see Fischer et al. 1991), the product associated with 10 brand advertising symbols including Ronald McDonald (McDonald's), Tony the Tiger (Frosted Flakes), Toucan Sam (Froot Loops), Dough Boy

(Pillsbury), Chester Cheetah (Chee-tos), Snap, Crackle, & Pop (Rice Krispies), Bunny with Drum (Energizer), Swoosh (Nike), Joe Camel (Camel), and Cat in the Hat (Dr. Seuss).

Television Viewing Patterns

Genre Preferences. Children's genre preferences were derived from the diary entry information submitted three weeks after the telephone survey, where respondents (or parents) indicated the names of the daytime and prime-time programs they had watched during that period. Three independent coders assigned the programs to one of 14 genre types, using commonly accepted categories (see Lin 1995). Intercoder agreement exceeded 95%. The number of program mentions by respondents was summed to formulate 14 separate genre preference measures.

Viewing Levels. At the same time, viewing levels were derived from diary entry information submitted by mail. For each of six 3-hour time periods, respondents indicated how much television they had viewed and the names of the programs they had watched. An index of viewing levels was constructed by summing responses for the six time periods, with a potential range of 0 to 18 hours per day, for a week. The average amount of viewing was 2.96 hours per day (SD = 1.12). In comparison with A. C. Nielsen's (1995) measures of average child audience viewing activity, respondents viewing: (1) under one hour per day were identified as "low consumers" (6% of the sample); (2) between one and three hours per day were identified as "moderate consumers" (38% of the sample); and (3) over three hours per day were identified as "high consumers" (56% of the sample).

Television Affinity. Five affinity measures, representing respondents' perceptions of the importance of TV in their lives, formed a summated TV affinity index (see Rubin 1983). Items included: "Watching TV is one of the most important things I do each day," "I would rather watch TV than do anything else," "I could easily do without television for several days," "I would feel lost without television to watch," and "If the TV wasn't working, I would not miss it." Responses were then coded so that a "5" indicated a high level and "1" a low level of television affinity. The affinity index (M = 3.82, SD = 1.22) had a .89 Cronbach alpha reliability coefficient.

Network Affinity. Five affinity measures, representing respondents' perceptions of the importance of broadcast networks in their lives, formed a summated network affinity index (see Abelman 1987). Items included: "I feel comfortable watching any program that appears on a favorite network," "I use the network on which a program appears to help determine the quality of the program," "When I turn on the TV, I turn to a particular network to find programs I might be interested in watching," "I tend to choose one network over another when choosing television programs to watch," and "I am more likely to watch a program that appears on a channel connected with a television network than a program that appears on a channel without any connection to a television network." Responses were coded so that a "5" indicated a high level and "1" a low level of network affinity. The affinity index (M = 2.56, SD = .85) had a .87 Cronbach alpha reliability coefficient.

Station Affinity. Five affinity measures, representing respondents' perceptions of the importance of local broadcast stations in their lives, formed a summated station affinity index. Items included: "I use the channel number or call letters on which a program appears to help determine the quality of the program," "I feel comfortable watching any program that appears on a favorite channel," "I tend to watch programs that appear on the same channel," "When choosing a program to watch, what channel it is on is more important than which network is presenting the program," and "Local hosts of kids programs and local talk show personalities are very important to me." Responses were coded so that a "5" indicated a high level and "1" a low level of television affinity. The affinity index (M = 2.62, SD = .82) had a .84 Cronbach alpha reliability coefficient.

Statistical Analysis

Pearson product-moment correlations were computed to examine the interrelationships among children's viewing motives. Canonical correlation was selected to examine the multivariate associations between viewing motives and viewing patterns, owing to its ability to accommodate metric as well as nonmetric (e.g., ratings) data for either the dependent or independent variables (Hair et al. 1992); it was also selected in studies with which our findings will be compared (e.g., Abelman 1988; Rubin 1984). To reduce possible misinterpretations that might result from multicollinearity, structure coefficients were computed by summing the product of canonical loadings and standardized scores of the variables for each set. Multiple regression techniques were then used to assess further the proposition that children's viewing motivations can effectively predict viewing patterns by determining whether or not motivation factors can aid in the explanation of viewing levels and attitudes. The significance level for all tests was set at .05.

Results

Viewing Motivation Interrelationships

Across our measures, we find support for the notion that children's viewing motivations will be interrelated. The use of oblique rotation procedures in the factor analysis recognized the potential interrelatedness of certain viewing motives. By way of outlining the salient patterns of interaction tapped by RQ1, Table 3.3 displays the product-moment correlations among viewing motives. As the correlations suggest, the conception of distinctive types of television use among children is supported by the fact that only information and pass time/habit viewing motivation factors are unrelated; all other viewing motivation factors are moderately to strongly interrelated.

In particular, the strongest of these viewing motivation correlates are between pass time/habit and both companionship and escapism. Escapist viewing is also associated with using television to acquire information, for companionship, and to be entertained. Habitual viewing and information-driven viewing is also associated with using television as a vehicle for entertainment. For the entertainment viewer, companionship and information are additional viewing motivations. Companionship viewers are also watching television to be informed.

TABLE 3.3 Viewing Motivation Correlation Matrix

	Pass Time/Habit	*Information*	*Entertainment*	*Companionship*
Pass Time/Habit	—			
Information	.08	—		
Entertainment	.34	.36	—	
Companionship	.58	.38	.29	—
Escape	.46	.34	.34	.38

$r = .15, p < .05$; $r = .18, p < .01$; $r = .22, p < .001$.

Viewing Motivation, Viewer Awareness, and Viewing Patterns

RQ2 asked whether patterns of television use become evident during affiliation shifts that help define what young viewers watch when they watch television. Comparisons were made among and between the set of viewing motives (as computed from factor scores) and patterns and the set of awareness measures. Interpretation of the data focused on the canonical variate scores as redefined by the structure coefficients. The canonical correlation analysis (see Table 3.4) indicates that three roots are significant at the .001 level.[1]

Some 45.7% of the variance in common between the canonical variates was explained by the first canonical root (Rc = .66). Set 1 was dominated by pass time/habitual, escape, and entertainment motivations, and included positive associations between viewing levels and television affinity, both of which were associated negatively with network affinity and station affinity. Set 2 included negative associations between local station awareness, network affiliation awareness, affiliation change awareness and identification, program affiliation awareness, and product brand awareness. This root points to the existence of a *medium-oriented viewer*. Comparisons across the two sets indicate that these young habitual, escapist consumers are neither aware of nor have strong affinity for network affiliation or station identification, although they have a strong affinity for television itself. Relatively oblivious to affiliation changes within their markets, these avid viewers of television are also relatively indiscriminant consumers, except where individual programs are concerned. These children do not have strong

(text continued on p. 66)

TABLE 3.4 Canonical Correlates

	Root 1		Root 2		Root 3	
	Canonical Variate	Structure Coefficient	Canonical Variate	Structure Coefficient	Canonical Variate	Structure Coefficient
Set 1: Viewing Motivations and Patterns						
Entertainment	.79	.89*	.45	.73*	.15	.18
Pass Time/Habit	.87	.92*	-.14	-.24*	-.48	-.54*
Information	-.23	-.19	.68	.78*	.56	.58*
Escape	.83	.84*	.12	.14	-.09	.16
Companionship	.09	.03	.02	.16	.65	.86*
Viewing Level	.82	.94*	.19	.31*	.12	.19
Television Affinity	.73	.88*	.17	.29*	.09	.14
Network Affinity	-.56	-.75*	.74	.93*	-.24	-.32*
Station Affinity	-.28	-.31*	-.33	-.67*	.45	.66*
Live-Action Comedy	.26	.32*	.19	.32*	.09	.14
Animated Comedy	.23	.34*	.59	.57*	.14	.21*
Live-Action Action/Drama	.19	.29*	.07	.12	-.08	-.07
Animated Action/Drama	.17	.21*	.17	.22*	-.12	.06
Live-Action Educational	-.12	-.19	.52	.54*	.26	.37*
Animated Educational	-.16	-.23*	.36	.46*	.18	.20*
Network News Viewing	-.03	-.19	.12	.17	-.13	-.15
Local News Viewing	.17	-.13	-.01	-.09	.17	.20*

TABLE 3.4 Continued

	Root 1		Root 2		Root 3	
	Canonical Variate	Structure Coefficient	Canonical Variate	Structure Coefficient	Canonical Variate	Structure Coefficient
Local Talk Show Viewing	.12	-.15	-.17	-.34*	.18	.21*
Syn. Talk Show Viewing	.14	.18	-.32	-.26*	.14	.20*
Sports Viewing	.09	.16	.08	.18	.25	.31*
Soap Opera Viewing	.05	.18	.09	.13	.07	.11
Game Show Viewing	.32	.54*	.23	.17	.43	.62*
Redundancy Coefficients	[.06]	[.16]	[.08]	[.12]	[.04]	[.06]
Set 2: Awareness Levels						
Local Station—Channel	-.46	-.64*	.62	.82*	.86	.92*
Local Station—Call	-.38	-.56*	.03	.12	.29	.22*
Network Affiliation	-.60	-.77*	.79	.88*	-.72	-.80*
Affiliation Change	-.49	-.75*	.51	.82*	-.43	.62*
Affiliation Identification	-.52	-.76*	.39	.77*	-.16	.16
Program Affiliation	-.75	-.88*	.56	.83*	-.59	.77*
Product Brand Symbol	-.34	-.42*	.65	.85*	.17	.19
Redundancy Coefficients	[.04]	[.12]	[.04]	[.16]	[.04]	[.06]

Root 1: Rc = .66, eigenvalue = .46, $\chi^2(238)$ = 432.18, $p < .001$; Root 2: Rc = .54, eigenvalue = .28, $\chi^2(175)$ = 257.32, $p < .001$; Root 3: Rc = .43, eigenvalue = .19, $\chi^2(119)$ = 154.25, $p < .001$; * $p < .001$.

genre preferences nor are they necessarily aware of which network is providing their entertainment menu.

Our second canonical root (Rc = .54) explained a more modest 27.6% of the variance in common between the canonical variates. Set 1 was dominated by the information and entertainment motives, and included positive associations among network affinity and a wide variety of network-originated entertainment and educational programming, as well as a negative association between network affinity and station affinity and various forms of locally originated programming, including local news, syndicated talk shows, and game shows. Set 2 included strong positive associations among program affiliation awareness, network affiliation awareness, local station channel awareness, and affiliation change awareness and identification. This root would seem to identify the *network-oriented viewer*. Comparisons across the two sets indicate that these entertainment- and information-seeking viewers have a strong affinity for TV and its networks. They possess a greater awareness of a station's network affiliation than its local identification (i.e., call letters) and are highly aware of brand advertising symbols. These viewers are also well aware of the network affiliation of the programs they watch and station affiliation changes that occurred within their markets.

Finally, the third canonical root (Rc = .43) explained 18.8% of the variance in common between the canonical variates. Set 1 was dominated by the information and companionships motives, and included a negative correlation with pass time/habit. It also included positive associations between station affinity and the viewing of syndicated game shows, syndicated and local talk shows, and sports programming. Set 2 included positive associations with both assessments of local station awareness, both of which were negatively associated with network affiliation awareness and program affiliation awareness. This root would seem to identify a *station-oriented viewer*. Comparisons across the two sets indicate that these young nonhabitual, information seekers also use television for companionship. They have a strong affinity with their local television station and are attracted to locally originated programming. Interestingly, the stations' network affiliation is not salient to these viewers, and they are relatively unaware of network affiliation shifts occurring in their market.

TABLE 3.5 Multiple Regression: Viewing Motivations as Predictors of Viewing Levels, Television Affinity, Network Affinity, and Station Affinity

Viewing Motivations	Viewing Levels		Television Affinity		Network Affinity		Station Affinity	
	b	*F*	*b*	*F*	*b*	*F*	*b*	*F*
Entertainment	.22***	18.24	.32***	41.22	.26***	18.34	.01	0.01
Time/Habit	.27***	41.32	.21***	15.41	−.19**	15.21	.05	0.03
Information	−.24***	31.66	.06	1.14	.24***	31.54	.14*	5.12
Escape	.26***	34.26	.21***	26.34	.25***	18.13	.05	0.12
Companion	−.18**	13.50	−.05	0.24	.05	0.1	.28***	35.66

F = 35.67	F = 33.56	F = 29.71	F = 30.98
df = 5/530	df = 5/530	df = 5/530	df = 5/530
R = .58***	R = .54***	R = .47***	R = .49***
R^2 = .29	R^2 = .27	R^2 = .20	R^2 = .24

* $p < .05$.
** $p < .01$.
*** $p < .001$.

Given the significant associations among viewing motivations and patterns, and viewer awareness, RQ3 explores how the structures of viewing motivations can aid in the explanation of children's TV viewing levels and affinity. This final question further considers the consequences of television use by examining motivational contributors to four important television viewing patterns. To address this question, four multiple regression analyses were performed and are summarized in Table 3.5.

These models—which explain between 20% and 29% of the variance observed—generally confirm our assumption that viewing motivations would causally influence viewing exposure, television affinity, network affinity, and station affinity. The four viewing behaviors and attitudes can be significantly explained by the viewing motivation factors. First, viewing levels increase with the salience of pass time/habit, escape, and entertainment motivations, and decrease with the salience of the information and companionship motivations. Second, television affinity also increases with the salience of pass time/habit, escape, and entertainment motivations. Third, network affinity increases with the salience of the entertainment and information motivations, and decreases with the salience of pass time/habit and escape motivations. Finally, station affinity increases with the salience of companionship as a viewing motivation. Taken together, these models provide support for the guiding hypothesis that children's viewing motivations, preferences, and attitudes will be interrelated.

Discussion

————

Rust, Kamakura, and Alpert (1992) suggested that researchers need to "disentangle the influences of audience psychological and behavioral dimensions" (p. 17) relevant to media selection and advertising effectiveness in order to be pragmatic. The present study served this purpose by profiling young television consumers in light of uses and gratifications theory. By identifying the variety of viewer motives that reflect the utility, selectivity, and intentionality of children's viewing, this study provided strong support for the hypothesis that viewing motivations and viewing patterns will be interrelated. This proposition was investigated during one of the great network upheavals in broadcasting history, via a nationwide sample of young television consumers. Utilizing a framework that includes diverse aspects of viewer preference and viewer perception, we were able to identify three distinctive categories of child audience segmentation—medium-, network-, and station-oriented viewers—which presents challenges as well as opportunities for advertisers seeking to reach children.

At a general level, the direct theoretical implications of these findings suggest that young viewers—during a time of affiliation change—may attend differently to network or station images in pursuing various viewing gratifications. Of particular interest to advertisers, we found that the need for entertainment is strongly predictive of television affinity, along with escapism. The fact that none of these motivations is inversely related to television exposure suggests that there are, as yet, few media or external leisure pursuits that can satisfy these needs for children as well as television in general and network television in particular. Since the literature provides little indication about the sufficiency level for continued audience loyalty, the child audience segments identified here should help programmers and advertisers distinguish between those for whom the program context in which an ad is placed is paramount and those for whom a given station or network brand is paramount and content is secondary. In general, the distinctive viewer archetypes identified here reinforce past work with adults (Abelman et al. 1997), confirming the need for advertisers to consider carefully the context in which their message appears and the diverse nature of the child audience.

Working from the assumption that viewer needs lead to differential patterns of media exposure, this investigation confirms the existence of ritualized/habitual viewers (see Rubin 1984; Sprafkin et al. 1992). Yet our analysis also suggests that these young viewers are relatively indiscriminant consumers with regard to program sources, network branding activities notwithstanding. Ritualized viewers display little network and station affinity, are neither aware of nor particularly interested in network affiliation or station identification, and are relatively oblivious to affiliation changes within the market. Thus, these viewers seem highly medium-oriented in their television usage; that is, they tend to watch television itself, focusing less on genre, networks, or stations. A post hoc, systematic review of viewer diary information also suggests that these children tend to fit the profile of active channel surfers and advertising "zappers" identified in previous research (see Cronin and Menelly 1992; Heeter and Greenberg 1985; Lin 1994).

Insofar as that active viewing undermines ad viewership, this segment of child viewers is likely a source of great frustration for advertisers. Where past work reveals that children are generally able to recognize key features of advertising (e.g., EPM Communications 1997; Macklin 1987), medium-oriented viewers seem relatively unresponsive to efforts to foster channel loyalty and tie programming to network branding (i.e., "Kids' WB," Fox Children's Network). Although this segment creates associations with product branding, they may prove oblivious to duplication of viewing strategies. Despite their receptivity to efforts to bolster inheritance effects—such as NBC's "Must See TV" campaign—medium-oriented viewers have little station or network loyalty and, thus, are more likely responding to a body of potentially interesting programming (and the accompanying advertising) than the fact that it is tied to NBC. Similarly when, in early 1997, CBS raided ABC's programming lineup (see "CBS Has Concluded 'Family' Really Matters" 1997) and stole the eighth year of the family-oriented comedy *Family Matters,* these children would most likely follow the program regardless of where on the dial it resided.

The segment of instrumental viewers identified here is also consistent with past work involving adults, although we've expanded this goal-oriented viewer profile beyond traditional TV use needs, linking it to a strong affinity for television networks, a higher level of awareness of a station's network affiliation than its local identification, an awareness of the network affiliation of the programs one views, a high level of awareness of affiliation changes within one's market, and a significant awareness of product brand symbols. Thus, instrumental viewers have been found to be highly network-oriented in their television usage—that is, they tend to watch networks and programs associated with network identification.

Of particular import to advertisers, these viewers are likely to be highly responsive to efforts to foster network and product branding, but such campaigns are redundant reinforcements, as that group has the least need for such information. In a similar vein, counter programming and other network efforts to cultivate inheritance effects may merely reinforce existing viewing habits among these children; that is, they're unlikely to be receptive to efforts to inspire station loyalty and station identification. Even so, affiliation shifts are a crucial time to cultivate station allegiance among these instrumental child viewers, as they are most likely to be following network programming to new dial locations. These efforts might prove particularly fruitful for the ad hoc (Fox, WB, and UPN) affiliates, as the introduction of a new outlet encourages a restructuring in the way these young consumers view established outlets (see Krugman 1985; Krugman and Rust 1987, 1993).

Our analysis also identified young viewers who use television for companionship purposes. Such viewing motivations are related to an attraction to locally originated and syndicated children's programming, a strong affinity with local television stations, and little interest in network affiliation or affiliation changes. Although these children tend to watch stations when they watch TV, affiliation shifts nevertheless afford an opportunity to link station identification attributes more closely with branding of new network personalities. When designing these campaigns, programmers should keep in mind that station affinity is predicted only by companionship and, to a lesser extent, information. Thus, successful stations may well be the ones that cultivate an image as child-friendly by providing blocks of syndicated, thematic programming that can stand out in a rapidly changing channel environment.

The regression finding that viewing motivations causally influence TV viewing exposure is consistent with Levy and Windahl's (1984) model, in which viewing exposure is the dependent variable for gratifications obtained. At a general level, careful consideration of the types of gratifications fulfilled by a given program can help advertisers select appropriate vehicles for their products. For instance, if advertisers can establish that a given program fulfills escape gratifications (e.g., travelogues), they have another basis upon which to match topically relevant messages (e.g., amusement park promotions).

Even so, the amount of variance accounted for by our motivational measures—ranging from 20% to 29%—can perhaps be bolstered by the inclusion of other variables not considered here. Later work could provide a more extensive accounting of other viewing influences, including demographics, child age, ability to make viewing decisions, and related sociocultural factors, such as family lifestyle and mediation (Atkin et al. 1991) or personal values of viewers (McCarty and Shrum 1993).

On balance, study findings should help broadcasters and advertisers to promote themselves more effectively in a rapidly changing media environment. We were able to confirm and extend interrelationships among viewing motives to children, even as the TV industry was undergoing unprecedented tumult. This, in conjunction with the typology of medium, network, and station-oriented viewers uncovered here, should allow broadcasters to segment their viewing audience more carefully when crafting messages for various children's TV promotions. Thus, much in the same way that demographics have yielded diminished returns—relative to psychographics—in studies of product adoption (e.g., Krugman 1985), our own results give advertisers some important audience characteristics to consider when planning their media buys in today's turbulent, multichannel environment.

As recent scandals with image-building suggest, particularly in the realm of tobacco promotion, children represent an important market whose brand loyalty can be cultivated from an early age (e.g., Henke 1995). This dynamic is especially important for programmers themselves, as the pace of deregulation and media acquisitions intensifies and the rate of affiliation turnover increases. As Wansink (1997, p. 15) notes, with astute management, even mature brands (e.g., NBC, CBS) can shine for new generations of users; he concludes: "The best way to jump-start a mature brand is by understanding its uniqueness and equity, and making the most of them."

As network-affiliate relations become more volatile, local affiliates must continue to build a stable constituency of "station-loyal" viewers if they're to weather future affiliation changes. By the same token, networks will need to establish strong national brand-images so that children can follow favorite programs to a new dial location (or market, in the case of the 16% of American families that move every year).

Investment in strong station or network IDs can also pay dividends in the short term, as a steady audience flow during late afternoon ("children's ghetto") daytime hours may enhance a station's nighttime ratings. Given the specter of increased competition from multichannel providers, broadcasters would be wise to increase copromotion—between the networks and their affiliates—to strengthen their station/network identity. This, in turn, should act as a hedge against further audience deterioration. It will be important, in later work, to assess how these changing allegiances influence child loyalty for prominent brands as well as networks and individual stations.

Note

1. The significance of canonical roots is assessed through the Bartlett's chi-square test.

References

"ABC to Show Logo During Programs," (1993), *Kansas City Star (February 7)*, H 13.

A. C. Nielsen Company (1995), *Year End Report*, New York: Author.

Abelman, Robert (1995), *Reclaiming the Wasteland: TV & Gifted Children,* Cresskill, NJ: Hampton Press.

—— (1988), "Motivations for Viewing the '700 Club,' " *Journalism Quarterly,* 64, 112-118.

—— (1987), "Religious Television Uses and Gratifications," *Journal of Broadcasting & Electronic Media,* 31 (3), 293-307.

Abelman, Robert, David Atkin, and Michael Rand (1997), "What Viewers Watch When They Watch TV: Affiliation Change as a Case Study," *Journal of Broadcasting & Electronic Media,* 41, 360-379.

Adams, William J. (1993), "TV Program Scheduling Strategies and Their Relationship to New Program Renewal Rates and Rating Changes," *Journal of Broadcasting & Electronic Media,* 37, 465-474.

——, Susan T. Eastman, and Robert F. Levine (1993), "Prime-Time Network Television Programming," in *Broadcast/Cable Programming: Strategies and Practices,* 4th ed., Susan T. Eastman, ed., Belmont, CA: Wadsworth, 115-159.

"Affiliation Switches Impact Network News" (1991), *Broadcasting* (January 7), 97.

Atkin, David, Bradley Greenberg, and Thomas S. Baldwin (1991), "The Home Ecology of Children's Viewing: Parental Mediation in the New Video Environment," *Journal of Communication,* 41, 40-53.

Babrow, Austin S. (1987), "Student Motives for Watching Soap Operas," *Journal of Broadcasting & Electronic Media,* 31 (3), 309-321.

Bauer, Robert A. (1964), "The Obstinate Audience: The Influence Process From the Point of View of Social Communication," *American Psychologist,* 19, 314-328.

Biocca, Frank (1987), "Opposing Conceptions of the Audience: The Active and Passive Hemispheres of Mass Communication Theory," in *Communication Yearbook, 11,* J. Anderson, ed., Beverly Hills, CA: Sage, 51-80.

Blumler, J. G. (1979), "The Role of Theory in Uses and Gratifications Studies," *Communication Research,* 6, 9-36.

Bogart, L. (1965), "The Mass Media and the Blue Collar Worker," *The Blue Collar World,* A. Bennett & W. Gombert, eds., Englewood Cliffs, NJ: Prentice Hall, 66-83.

Bowles, J. (1997), "Viewers Beware, Objects in Glasses Are Only TV 3D," Associated Press (reprinted in *The Plain Dealer,* May 5, p. 9D).

"CBS Has Concluded 'Family' Really Matters" (1997), *Los Angeles Times* (Reprinted in *The Plain Dealer,* February 4, p. 11E).

"Children's TV Ad Spending in a Slump" (1994), *Broadcasting & Cable* (July 25), 67.

Coe, Steve (1995), "WB Network Makes Weak National Debut," *Broadcasting & Cable* (January 16), 3, 10.

Cronin, John J. and Nancy E. Menelly (1992), "Discrimination vs. Avoidance: 'Zipping' of Television Commercials," *Journal of Advertising,* 21, 1-8.

Elliot, P. (1974), "Uses and Gratifications Research: A Critique and a Sociological Alternative," in *The Uses of Mass Communications: Current Perspectives on Gratification Research,* Jay G. Blumler and Elihu Katz, eds., Beverly Hills, CA: Sage, 249-269.

EPM Communications (1997), *The Market for Children's Entertainment and Media,* New York: Author.

Fischer, Paul M., Meyer P. Schwartz, John W. Richards, Jr., Adam O. Goldstein, and Tina H. Rojas (1991), "Brand Logo Recognition by Children, Aged 3 to 6 Years," *Journal of the American Medical Association,* 266 (22), 3145-3148.

Gantz, Walter and Susan T. Eastman (1983), "Viewer Uses of Promotional Media to Find Out About Television Programs," *Journal of Broadcasting,* 27 (3), 269-277.

Gay, V. (1996), "Diet Coke Promotion Could Cap Frenzy Over NBC 'Friends,' " *Newsday* (reprinted in *The Plain Dealer,* January 26, p. 5E).

Greenberg, B. S. (1974), "Gratifications of Television Viewing and Their Correlates for British Children," in *The Uses of Mass Communications: Current Perspectives on Gratification Research,* Jay G. Blumler and Elihu Katz, eds., Beverly Hills, CA: Sage, 71-82.

Hair, Joseph F., Ronald E. Anderson, Ronald L. Tatham, and William C. Black (1992), *Multivariate Data Analysis,* New York: Macmillan.

Heeter, Carrie and Bradley S. Greenberg (1985), "Profiling the Zappers," *Journal of Advertising Research,* 25 (2), 15-19.

Henke, Lucy L. (1995), "Young Children's Perceptions of Cigarette Brand Advertising Symbols: Awareness, Affect, and Target Market Identification," *Journal of Advertising,* 24 (Summer), 13-28.

Houlberg, Rick (1984), "Local Television News Audiences and the Para-Social Interaction," *Journal of Broadcasting,* 28, 423-429.

Jensen, Elizabeth (1996), "Fox TV Network Takes Another Stab at Offering News," *Wall Street Journal* (March 28), B1, B4.

Katz, Elihu, Jay G. Blumler, and Michael Gurevitch (1974), "Utilization of Mass Communication by the Individual," in *The Uses of Mass Communications: Current Perspectives on Gratification Research,* Jay G. Blumler and Elihu Katz, eds., Beverly Hills, CA: Sage, 19-32.

Krugman, Dean (1985), "Evaluating the Audiences of the New Media," *Journal of Advertising,* 14 (Summer), 21-27.

—— and Roland T. Rust (1987), "The Impact of Cable TV Penetration on Network Viewing," *Journal of Advertising Research,* 27 (October/November), 9-13.

—— and —— (1993), "The Impact of Cable and VCR Penetration on Network Viewing: Assessing the Decade," *Journal of Advertising Research,* 33 (January/February), 67-74.

Levin, G. (1995), "Making a Name for Yourself," *Variety* (December 11), 3, 22, 28.

Levy, Mark R. and Sven Windahl (1984), "Audience Activity and Gratifications: A Conceptual Clarification and Exploration," *Communication Research,* 11, 51-78.

Lin, Carolyn (1995), "Network Prime-Time Programming Strategies in the 1980s," *Journal of Broadcasting & Electronic Media,* 39, 482-495.

—— (1994), "Audience Fragmentation in a Competitive Video Marketplace," *Journal of Advertising Research,* 34 (6), 1-17.

—— (1993), "Modeling the Gratification-Seeking Process of Television Viewing," *Human Communication Research,* 20 (2), 224-244.

Macklin, M. Carole (1987), "Preschoolers' Understanding of the Information Function of Television Advertising," *Journal of Consumer Research,* 14 (2), 229-239.

Mandese, J. (1993), "NBC and Kellogg Co-Star," *Advertising Age* (July 18), 1.

McClellan, Steve (1995), "The Mixed Bag of Affiliate Switches," *Broadcasting & Cable* (April 24), 15.

McCarty, John A. and L. J. Shrum (1993). "The Role of Personal Values and Demographics in Predicting Television Viewing Behavior: Implications for Theory and Application," *Journal of Advertising,* 22 (4), 77-101.

McGee, Tom (1997), "Getting Inside Kids' Heads," *American Demographics* (January), 53-55, 59.

Robinson, John P. and S. Bianchi (1997), "The Children's Hour," *American Demographics* (December), 20, 22-24.

Rosengren, Karl E., Lawrence A. Wenner, and Phillip Palmgreen, eds., (1985), *Media Gratification Research: Current Perspectives,* Beverly Hills, CA: Sage.

Rubin, Alan M. (1983), "Television Uses and Gratifications: The Interactions of Viewing Patterns and Motivations," *Journal of Broadcasting,* 27, 37-51.

——— (1984), "Ritualized and Instrumental Television Viewing," *Journal of Communication,* 34 (3), 67-77.

———, Elizabeth M. Perse, and Richard A. Powell (1985), "Loneliness, Parasocial Interaction, and Local Television News Viewing," *Human Communication Research,* 12, 155-180.

Rubin, Rebecca B. and M. P. McHugh (1987), "Development of Parasocial Interaction Relationships," *Journal of Broadcasting & Electronic Media,* 31, 279-292.

———, Alan M. Rubin, Elizabeth M. Perse, Cameron Armstrong, Michael McHugh, and Nora Faix (1986), "Media Use and Meaning of Music Video," *Journalism Quarterly,* 63, 353-359.

Rust, Roland, Wagner A. Kamakura, and Mark I. Alpert (1992), "Viewer Preference Segmentation and Viewing Choice Models for Network Television," *Journal of Advertising,* 21, 1-18.

Schofield, Lemuel B. and Paul D. Driscoll (1991), "Effects of Television Network Affiliation Changes: A Miami Case Study," *Journal of Broadcasting & Electronic Media,* 35, 367-374.

Sprafkin, Joyce, Kenneth D. Gadow, and Robert Abelman (1992), *Television and the Exceptional Child,* Hillsdale, NJ: Lawrence Erlbaum.

Tobenkin, David (1994), "Warner Bros. Wants to Capture Kids," *Broadcasting & Cable* (July), 16.

Webster, James and Jacob J. Wakshlag (1983), "A Theory of TV Program Choice," *Communication Research,* 16, 59-67.

Wansink, B. (1997), "Making Old Brands New," *American Demographics* (December), 53-56.

Zier, Julie K. (1994), "Can You Say 'Merchandising'?" *Broadcasting & Cable* (July 25), 66.

4

Youth, Advertising,
and Symbolic Meaning

CINDY DELL CLARK

The gap between academic theory and practical application persists as a recognized concern, both in marketing circles (Root 1998) and by government officials (Schmidt 1998). Fundamentally different approaches typify, for example, the scholarly study of children and advertising, as contrasted with research done by advertisers and other practitioners. Research on children and advertising touches an issue of considerable practical and social importance, yet academic studies of this subject are seldom salient in the eyes of practitioners nor broadly applied outside the academy. Scholarly consumer research on children generally has had an experimental focus, with an emphasis on logical processes, memory, and cognition. Ethnographic or interpretive consumer research rarely makes an impact on academic studies of youngest consumers, despite the recent influence of Belk's (1991) Consumer Behavior Odyssey as a catalyst for interpretive research among adult consumers.

In contrast to the generally experimental research on children done by scholars, applied research usually has broader goals, endeavoring to explore the role of imagination, affect, social context, and culturally derived practices as issues that intermingle with (and often drive) children's language, cognition, and memory. In the practical world of applied research, young consumers are generally considered within their everyday context of culture and meaning in order to account for their behavior in holistic, inclusive terms.

Children, of course, are the true subject matter to be reckoned with in understanding youth's interactions with advertising. Inquiry into controlled variables drawn from scholarly theories of childhood cognition and memory begs other, crucial issues. The worlds of American children abound in nonlogical, expressive entities, such as vitamins shaped like cavemen, bandages decorated with TV superheroes, purple dinosaurs who are neither powerful nor prehistoric (Mitchell 1998), mutant tortoise characters who live in subterranean hideouts, boxes to leave teeth for the Tooth Fairy (Clark 1995), and diminutive bears whose form is reflected in graham cookies. Construing children's consumer behavior as a straightforward matter of learning theory (e.g., Roedder 1981; Ward, Wackman, and Wartella 1977) or an artifact explained by cognitive development (e.g., Macklin 1983, 1985; McNeal 1987) is insufficient if commonplace consumer experience is to be fully accounted for and understood.

In recent classroom research on educational processes, academic investigators have broadened beyond strictly cognitive studies, such as through Vygotsky's (1978) social-cognitive orientation (Wertsch 1985). An impressive array of scholars in developmental research (outside of marketing) have been arguing for a framework broader than strict cognition, aiming toward a more socioculturally informed study of development (Bruner 1990; Cole 1996; Dunn 1988; Nelson 1996; Rogoff 1990; Shore 1996; Shweder 1991; Valsiner 1997). A vanguard of young scholar-experimentalists have also called for more culturally contextualized research on children (e.g., Lillard 1998; Taylor 1997). Emerging examples of culturally informed research are now widely cited (e.g., Corsaro and Miller 1992; Goodnow, Miller, and Kessel 1995). Given the changing field of developmental studies, academic advertising research has an opportunity to exercise broader options than the strict cognitive experiment—and thereby a better opportunity to link academic work with practitioner's approaches.

In this chapter, I will frame children's advertising beyond the confines of the narrow cognitive model. I offer ideas of how children respond to advertising, derived from extensive applied research experience. The ideas here are influenced by my full-time consulting research practice and my past experience as an "insider" at a large advertising agency with major children's accounts. As an author with academic teaching credentials and peer-approved publications, I respectfully reach out to scholarly researchers who study children and advertising. I believe that as the world grows smaller and more multicultural, the time has come to think bigger, which is to say more inclusively, about research with children.

This chapter is not intended to pose a grand theory with ambitions to universal laws. Some readers might wish for more "data" to substantiate the concepts proposed. Such a requirement, in effect, would have censored this chapter, which is inductively derived from extensive, but proprietary, research. The concepts sketched out in this chapter have received pragmatic validation in the marketplace, thus enjoying the form of validation endorsed by that venerable psychologist, William James. These are conceptual insights that have been useful to successful companies that operate in the for-profit world of children and advertising. The proprietary status of findings used to derive this scheme requires me to explain and illustrate my ideas in hypothetical terms. I nevertheless offer the chapter as a well-intentioned, initial stepping-stone across the theory-practice gap.

The Brand

From Barbie to McDonald's to Cheetos, products that succeed with children over time are rich reservoirs of meaning: that is, the product itself and its advertising symbols are meaningful and valued. The value of the brand derives in large part from its symbolic value for the child. In other words, the product plays a symbolic role for the child, just as adult products serve symbolic purposes in the lives of adults (Levy 1959).

Children, from a very young age, are adept at imputing symbolic meanings. Even as babies, for example, tots use a possession such as a stuffed bear or blanket as a "transitional object" that comforts them in the absence of their mother (Winnicott 1971). The metaphorical comprehension involved in symbolism, experimental research shows, is an early emergent mental process (Goswami 1992; Marks, Hammeal, and Bornstein 1987; Winner 1988). Symbols encompass meaning at both the affective and the cognitive levels for children, as demonstrated by pretend play—a domain studied as a cognitive structure (e.g., Rubin, Fein, and Vandenberg 1983) and yet also studied and utilized for feeling-based therapy (e.g., Clark and Miller 1997; O'Connor 1991). Through the representative symbolism of play, children indirectly "practice" social and cultural behaviors (through toys and/or with companions) (Bretherton 1984; Haight and Miller 1993; Roopnarine, Johnson, and Hooper 1994). The domain of symbols, in children's lives, traverses many sociocultural meanings as well as personal meanings, both affective and cognitive. The allure of reductionism (to view a symbol as merely cognitive, or merely personally emotive, etc.) diminishes the inherently manifold, dense meaning of symbols.

In practice, children are prone to symbolic transformation of everything from food (alphabet soup as a spelling toy, pancake syrup as an art material, etc.) to bed sheets (for which the pictured characters may serve as nighttime "companions") to toys meant for symbolic play (even nonrepresentative toys, such as blocks). A brand's meaning to children is revealed by understanding how it is used, symbolically, in their lives. Children make choices about how to use objects to signify, such as when rejecting a particular item of clothing or plaything along perceived gender lines ("Pink is for girls") or along perceived maturity lines ("Purple dinosaurs are for babies"). Some items connote security, such as a particular bedtime story or toy (Albert et al. 1979). Other items encode empowerment (a two-wheel bicycle), rebellion (baggy jeans), social connection (pizza shared with friends), mastery (a sports trophy), or manifold other meanings. A branded product takes on symbolic meaning from the actions and observations of everyday use, even though the manufacturer did not intentionally set out to communicate such product symbolism. For example, medications can symbolize safety and trust, although pharmaceutical companies did not intend this kind of meaning (Clark 1996, 1998; Van der Geest 1996).

It is important to emphasize that as a symbol, a brand's meaning is subject to the rules of expressive symbolism, semiotics, and metaphor (e.g., Belk, Bahn, and Mayer 1982; Fernandez 1986; Forceville 1994; Goswami 1992; Lakoff and Johnson 1980; McCracken 1988; Mick 1986; Turner 1967; Wiseman and Groves 1997). Meanings can operate at many levels, often encompassing paradoxical meanings that seem (at face value) to be mutually contradictory (Leach 1976). For example, a brand of in-line skates (according to children) provides a sense of "safe" yet "adventurous" enjoyment, an experience that incorporates an apparent contradiction: A child feels a sense of free-flowing smoothness and comfort, yet that very comfort makes it safe to attempt adventure-seeking stunts on the skates. The paradoxical qualities of the skates (safe, yet also adventure-seeking) infuse them with oppositional meanings.

Another example of a product embodying oppositional meanings is a premium brand of baseball cards. For young collectors, baseball cards are a chance to exercise computational logic and precision; indeed, the back of each card displays the relevant statistics summarizing each player's performance. Yet the front of the card shows not calculated facts, but a photo of the player in action, recalling the awe-striking aura of excellent achievement. Thus, while baseball cards are in some ways rational tokens of processed information, they are simultaneously quasi-sacred instruments of awe and transcendence (in the case of basketball cards, this can involve a near-magical sense that a particular player, namely Michael Jordan, "flies" amidst competing players).

Brand Advertising

Communicating brand meaning through advertising, it follows, calls for a powerful medium capable of encoding multivocal (even oppositional) meaning. This explains why so much of successful children's advertising uses expressive symbolism (characters, icons, and narratives) to bring meaning through metaphor. Poetic or symbolic devices hold potential for adept multivocal communication. As already stated, children understand expressive symbolism, metaphor, and narrative from an early age and are able to relate these elements to a brand's deep symbolic meaning. (They may not be aware that they are making symbolic connections, on a meta-level; but the ability to articulate what is communicated is a separate capacity from internalized communication.)

The response of children to brand advertising is largely based in its symbolic content, its metaphorical meaning. The successful advertising program creates a metaphor for the product's symbolic meaning. A poetic equation exists between, first, the product's felt meaning (in a child's expressive world of day-to-day life) and second, the dramatized meanings encoded in the commercial. That is, the advertising carries meanings that correspond to the product's expressive meaning in everyday use. Often, successful children's advertising uses a symbol, such as a character that literally personifies the brand's symbolic meaning, through appearance and behavior (see Figure 4.1). Such advertising demonstrates the effectiveness of both narrative and metaphor as means to convey higher order constructs through nonverbal means (Zaltman and Higie 1993) among youth.

As a hypothetical example, consider Trix cereal and its long-standing character, the Trix Rabbit. The Trix rabbit, no doubt loosely connected to the widespread folkloric symbol, the trickster, is adept at formshifting, much as other trickster characters (or a magician's rabbit; cf. Abrams and Sutton-Smith 1977; Radin 1997). Like many successful advertising icons, the Trix Rabbit derives from the culture's semiotic reservoir (full of well-known rabbits as well as diverse animal tricksters), thereby having recognizable meaning that a child can discern through a base of prior experience (Sullenberger 1974).

In each commercial, the Rabbit shifts form as a means of disguise, with a goal to get the Trix away from the children in the story. Inevitably, the Rabbit is unable to fool the children (who, for once, outsmart an adult figure). The Rabbit is reminded that, "Silly Rabbit. Trix are for kids"; that is, Trix constitutes the exclusive preserve of the young.

The desirability of Trix is communicated metaphorically by the Rabbit's struggle to get the cereal. In fact, Trix cereal seems to have a transformative impact on the Rabbit, as his mood and concentration are mesmerized by the Trix. The Rabbit is a multivocal symbol: adult-sized, but in some ways (such as in pursuing pleasure above all else) not entirely adult. To add another level of irony, note that rabbits are culturally associated with the "nursery" years of childhood (Clark

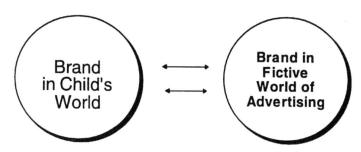

Figure 4.1.

1995), such that the adult Rabbit may literally embody both childlike ("Silly" rabbit) and nonchild values ("Trix are not for you"), set in opposition.

The stimulating fruit flavors, colors, and shapes of Trix have a symbolic impact in a child's real-life world apart from advertising: to whit, adding fun and mood enhancement. This is an experience denied adults (who are associated with "dull" cereals and "serious" lives by children). Trix cereal, through its advertising story line and spokesrabbit, is emblematic of preserving childlike abandon and fun, even from the intrusions of staid adult values. In other words, the meaning of the brand (in the symbolic world of the child) corresponds metaphorically to the Trix Rabbit story (in the fictive, dramatized world; see Table 4.1).

Turning to a second hypothetical example, another time-proven character worth considering is the Kool-Aid Pitcher. Here, the metaphorical tie between the brand and its advertising symbol seems obvious, at least on some level. The Pitcher is drawn as smiling, and the refreshing impact of the drink within is evident by the gleaming condensation on the Pitcher. The metaphor here seems to be simple: a pleasurable, refreshing beverage.

But recall that the Pitcher, over years of advertising, displayed one recurring habit or trait. The Pitcher liked to emerge on the scene by entering forcefully through the wall: the Pitcher is dramatized as a wall-destroyer or barrier-breaker. What could this have to do with a drink for school-aged children?

Among school-aged children, favorite drinks are those that part ways with normative, staid behavior. This quality of the drink, an informant child once explained to me, helps to "get you away from the

TABLE 4.1

Brand in Child's World	Brand in Fictive Advertising World
Colorful and stimulating	Rabbit wants stimulating experience (of Trix)
A fun-associated, kid-associated eating experience	Kids win ("kids rule")

normal world," much as the feeling of a "party" or "adventure" provides a break from routine. Off-beat wackiness is called for by school-age children in a drink (as evidenced by the success of blue-colored drinks, or unconventional packages such as oddly shaped squeezable plastic bottles). In light of the desired off-beat wackiness of a drink, the Pitcher's practice of breaking through walls provides a metaphor that is apt, indeed (Table 4.2).

Children's Response to Advertising

In some ways, the interpretations just shared correspond to a theory of (adult-directed) celebrity endorsers proposed by Grant McCracken (1989). According to McCracken, celebrities embody symbolic meaning developed over the course of their fame (through their acting appearances or other persona-building activities) that is then transferred, through the process of advertising, to the brand. By this model, the Trix Rabbit and Kool-Aid Pitcher are instruments of meaning transfer, relocating the quality of the character to the product itself. The meaning transfer notion fits well with some cases of children's products (vitamins or adhesive bandages depicting superheroes, for example) that operate as cases where the "power" of the character is indeed transferred to the product (producing vitamins or bandages that impart "super" resilience or strength).

But note that the meaning transfer model assumes a fairly passive viewing experience on the part of the consumer. The concept I am proposing assumes an interactive process in which the child actively

TABLE 4.2

Brand in Child's World	Brand in Fictive Advertising World
Refreshing and pleasurable	Smiling Pitcher, moist with "cool" condensation
Counter-normative escape from routine and restrictions	Pitcher breaks barriers, enters where pleases

participates in the act of communication. I endorse a model of "interactive meaning exchange" rather than unidirectional meaning transfer. Thus, a mutual feedback or dynamic exchange takes place between child and advertising. Children bring to this exchange their experiences and expectations regarding the product itself, as well as their experiences and expectations relevant to viewing the narrative genre, characters, and other symbolic elements of the commercial.

An interactive quality pervades both the imputing of symbolic value to the brand within the child's world, as well as the way meaning is constituted while watching advertising. In children's experience, drinks, cereal, or vitamins are ingested, or Band-Aids put on, and these actions are interpreted by the child, resulting in an active construction of meaning, based on everyday practices. The experience of viewing brand advertising (in the distraction-filled setting of home, remote control at hand, perhaps while simultaneously doing other activities) is fraught with "clutter" well known to marketing practitioners. Amid this busy context, the child's attention and involvement cannot be assumed to be a one-way process. The viewing process has a dialogic or interactive quality, just as the viewing of television programming has been so well documented to involve an active child viewer (Alwitt et al. 1980; Anderson and Lorch 1983; Anderson, Lorch, Field, and Sanders 1981; Anderson, Lorch, Smith, et al. 1981; Levin and Anderson 1976). Both the making of brand meaning and the making of advertising meaning are active processes in which the child has agency and impact.

In this sense, the agency attributed to the consumer by the reader-response model of advertising (Scott 1994) is relevant to how children derive symbolic meaning from products and commercials. Interpretations that are different from assumptions of the adult marketer need not impute "error" to the viewer (Fish 1980). The meaning is constructed as the child interacts with the advertising, not static or predetermined. Advertising communicates in a manner open to personal as well as shared cultural meanings. This includes systematically varying meanings, such as the differing significance that girls and boys impute to narrative (Nicolopoulou, Scales, and Weintraub 1994) or varied meanings for older versus younger children. Adult interpretations are not the standard or "correct" meaning, and indeed may be irrelevant to how children interpret the advertising.

A meaning-based view of children's advertising, then, borrows the assumption of reader-response theory that research should examine communication as an active process with many feasible outcomes. This contrasts with an approach that assumes children "miscomprehend" if they do not interpret advertising in the single "correct" manner assumed by the adult researcher (Waksler 1991).

Just as reader-response theory is grounded in the practices of the reader, the notion of advertising response argued here is grounded in the practices of the viewer, as an active imputer of meaning in the worlds of: (1) product use and (2) advertising symbolism. The process of meaning-making is taken to be dynamic rather than fixed. For example, children coming of age in a social era of technical innovation (exposed to videotape, multiple cable channels, remote control, and interactive computer activities) will have practices that reflect this historical, social context. The child needs to be grasped in total, encompassing notions of thought, feeling, developmental transformation, family life, and sociocultural framework. The full context should be explored and understood, rather than "controlled for" and thereby essentially ignored (Jacob 1997).

Symbolic Meaning and Youth Smoking

No minor matter, consumption is one of the most culturally significant aspects of contemporary American society. A telling case in point is youth smoking, which has dire health implications (Escobedo and Peddicord 1997; Greenlund et al. 1997; Urberg, Degirmencioglu, and Pilgrim 1997). Given the widely known health risks of smoking, no amount of computational logic can explain the youthful decision to smoke. Smoking is largely driven by expressive and social meanings (U.S. Department of Health and Human Services 1994). Knowledge of the role of advertising in sustaining positive meanings about smoking could hold advantage in countering youth smoking. (Research that only tapped cognition, though, would construe the problem too narrowly.)

In a past study examining advertising levels and market share (among teens and adults), Pollay and collaborators (1996) found the following levels of market share attained by cigarette brands among teens during 1979 to 1993. Table 4.3 gives these market share data, along with the corresponding "share of voice" or proportion of advertising spending, for the same brand.

If a further analytical step is applied to the data from Pollay and collaborators, calculating the index of market share relative to advertising share of voice, some brands can be shown to be disproportionately successful at building market share with young smokers. In part, heavy promotional emphasis may be a factor in the disproportionately strong performance of high-index brands. In addition, the share/voice ratio demonstrates that meaningful content (and not just amount of advertising per se) has differential impact on youth market share—as is well known by advertising practitioners (Burnett 1958). The leader in marketing efficiency, among these brands, is Marlboro (an imagery-based brand with ads using expressive symbolism) and the trailing brand is Merit (a brand with relatively less expressive imagery in its ads).

Index: Market Share Versus Share of Voice

Advertising content that features a cowboy amid rustic wilderness, then, outperforms in sales to youth the other brands (to a degree that would be difficult to explain through promotional spending alone). The model proposed in this chapter—by which advertising forms a metaphor for the product's multivocal meaning—provides an intriguing approach to account for Marlboro's market share success.

Cigarettes are first smoked during the years of transition out of childhood, when a desire for individual efficacy and independence can

TABLE 4.3   Levels of Market Share Attained by Cigarette Brands
Among Teens, 1979 to 1993

Brand	Market Share (Teen) (%)	Share of Advertising Voice (%)	Index Market Share vs. Share of Voice
Marlboro	59.5	12.7	469
Newport	11.1	4.7	236
Camel	8.7	4.9	178
Kool	4.3	4.8	90
Salem	3.8	5.4	70
Winston	2.5	6.9	36
Virginia Slims	2.2	4.8	46
Benson & Hedges	2.1	5.3	40
Merit	0.9	6.3	14

sometimes outpace the ability to face and accept true adult demands (DeVaron 1972). Smoking is in part a behavior of "rebelliousness" (Brook et al. 1997; Robinson et al. 1997) as teens break away from childhood dependency. Yet the emerging responsibilities of the post-childhood years can be demanding. Smoking, an oral and sedating experience (Lynch and Bonnie 1994; Orleans and Slade 1993), may bring regressive comfort so as to lessen the felt vulnerability of maturity.

Thus, the meaning of smoking may embody a paradox: a "mature" parting of ways with childhood, yet with reassuring consolation for the vicissitudes of maturity. The act of smoking might well signify, dissonant though this may seem, both maturity and regression. If so, a question follows: Is the oppositional meaning of cigarettes metaphorically communicated in Marlboro advertising?

About thirty years ago, Lohof (1969, p. 448) speculated about the meaning of Marlboro advertising (which has since translated the format of its former television commercials into print and billboard ads):

> The Marlboro image is not evocative of simple escape. To be sure the Marlboro Man stands apart from civilization. Like civilization . . . Marlboro country makes demands upon its inhabitants. But responsibilities there are simple . . . The Marlboro image represents escape, not from the responsibilities of civilization, but from its frustrations . . . Innocence

TABLE 4.4

Brand in Teen's World	Brand in Fictive Advertising World
A means to individual independence, perceived maturity	Rugged individualism amid "open trail"
A sedating, comforting sensation	Innocence apart from demands of civilization

and individual efficacy are the touchstones of the metaphor employed on behalf of Marlboro cigarettes.

The motif of the cowboy, of course, has been associated with the frontier, and with the rugged individuals who survived on the open land (Dary 1989). The individual "hitting the trail" (or facing the open range) carries meaning that likely resonates with adolescents on the personal frontier of young adulthood. Marlboro cigarettes, depicted in advertising as rugged-but-innocent, are a trope for the symbolic purpose of cigarettes, to confer maturity and independence without vulnerability or anxiety. The advertising succeeds dramatically, through metaphorical aptness (Table 4.4).

Discussion

It should be emphasized that recognizing advertising viewership as an interactive, symbolic process does not exempt advertisers from responsibility. Advertisers need to understand their interactive relationship with young viewers, so as to reduce undesirable residual outcomes (including harmful addiction). Many advertisers already exercise this kind of responsibility, though (as the case of Marlboro illustrates) not all.

If marketers, regulators, and growing consumers are to be served by academic research, the full range of human response (not just logical processes of cognition and memory) needs to be explored. Children relate to commercials (and, for that matter, to products) in a manner that is as much poetic as cognitive, as much sociocultural as informational, as much dissonant as logical. Expressive meanings adhere in products and in the narrative and metaphor structures of advertising. We can fully understand the human encounter with advertising only by acknowledging its complexity and multifaceted context. If we miss the richly meaningful role of symbolism in advertising, we miss a powerful influence in children's lives. In a society where children are a "market" as well as a group to nurture, omitting from inquiry nonlogical processes (such as emotion and imagination) seems itself a case of flawed logic, in the face of today's crucial issues.

References

Abrams, David and Brian Sutton-Smith (1977), "The Development of the Trickster in Children's Narrative," *Journal of American Folklore, 90*, 29-47.

Albert, Stuart, Terry Amgott, Mildred Krakow, and Howard Marcus (1979), "Children's Bedtime Rituals as a Prototype Rite of Safe Passage," *Journal of Psychological Anthropology, 2* (January), 85-105.

Alwitt, Linda, Daniel Anderson, Elizabeth Lorch, and Stephen Levin (1980), "Preschool Children's Visual Attention to Attributes of Television," *Human Communication Research, 7* (Fall), 52-67.

Anderson, Daniel and Elizabeth Lorch (1983), "Looking at Television: Action or Reaction?" in *Children's Understanding of Television,* San Diego: Academic Press.

——, ——, Diane Field, and Jeanne Sanders (1981), "The Effects of TV Program Comprehensibility on Preschool Children's Visual Attention to Television," *Child Development, 52*, 151-157.

——, ——, Robin Smith, Rex Bradford, and Stephen Levin (1981), "Effects of Peer Presence on Preschool Children's Television-Viewing Behavior," *Developmental Psychology, 17*, 446-453.

Belk, Russell (1991), *Highways and Byways: Naturalistic Research From the Consumer Behavior Odyssey,* Provo, UT: Association for Consumer Research.

——, Kenneth Bahn, and Robert Mayer (1982), "Developmental Recognition of Consumption Symbolism," *Journal of Consumer Research, 9* (June), 4-17.

Bretherton, Inge (1984), *Symbolic Play: The Development of Social Understanding,* Orlando FL: Academic Press.

Brook, J., M. Whiteman, L. Czeisler, J. Shapiro, and P. Cohen (1997), "Cigarette Smoking in Young Adults: Childhood and Adolescent Personality, Familial and Peer Antecedents," *Journal of Genetic Psychology, 158*, 172-188.

Bruner, Jerome (1990), *Acts of Meaning,* Cambridge, MA: Harvard University Press.

Burnett, Leo (1958), "The Marlboro Story: How One of America's Most Popular Filter Cigarettes Got That Way," *The New Yorker, 34*, 41-43.

Clark, Cindy Dell (1995), *Flights of Fancy, Leaps of Faith: Children's Myths in Contemporary Society,* Chicago: University of Chicago Press.

———— (1996), "Imaginal Coping and Childhood Illness: How Children Relate to Treatments for Chronic Illness," Presentation to International Society for the Study of Behavioral Development (ERIC Catalogue No. ED 401 666).

———— (1998), "Childhood Imagination in the Face of Chronic Illness," in *Believed-in Imaginings: The Narrative Construction of Reality,* Ted Sarbin and Joe DeRivera, eds., Washington, DC: American Psychological Association.

———— and Peggy J. Miller (1997), "Play," in *Encyclopedia of Mental Health,* Howard Freeman, ed., San Diego, CA: Academic Press, 189-194.

Cole, Michael (1996), *Cultural Psychology: A Once and Future Discipline,* Cambridge, MA: Belknap Press.

Corsaro, William and Peggy Miller (1992), *Interpretive Approaches to Children's Socialization,* San Francisco: Jossey-Bass.

Dary, D. (1989), *Cowboy Culture: A Saga of Five Centuries,* Lawrence: University Press of Kansas.

DeVaron, T. (1972), "Growing Up," in *Twelve to Sixteen: Early Adolescence,* Jerome Kagan and Robert Coles, eds., New York: Norton.

Dunn, Judy (1988), *The Beginnings of Social Understanding,* Cambridge, MA: Harvard University Press.

Escobedo, L. and J. Peddicord (1997), "Long-term Trends in Cigarette Smoking Among Young U.S. Adults," *Addictive Behaviors,* 22, 427-430.

Fernandez, James (1986), *Persuasions and Performances: The Play of Tropes in Culture,* Bloomington: Indiana University Press.

Fish, Stanley (1980), *Is There a Text in This Class?* Cambridge, MA: Harvard University Press.

Forceville, Charles (1994), "Pictorial Metaphors in Advertisements," *Metaphor and Symbolic Activity,* 9, 1-29.

Goodnow, Jacqueline, Peggy Miller, and Frank Kessel (1995), *Cultural Practices as Contexts for Development,* San Francisco: Jossey-Bass.

Goswami, Usha (1992), *Analogical Reasoning in Children,* Hove, UK: Lawrence Erlbaum.

Greenlund, K., C. Johnson, L. Webber, and G. Berenson (1997), "Cigarette Smoking Attitudes and First Use Among Third- Through Sixth-grade Students: The Bogalusa Heart Study," *American Journal of Public Health,* 87, 1345-1348.

Haight, Wendy and Peggy J. Miller (1993), *Pretending at Home: Early Development in a Sociocultural Context,* Albany: State University of New York Press.

Jacob, Evelyn (1997), "Context and Cognition: Implications for Educational Innovators and Anthropologists," *Anthropology and Education Quarterly,* 28 (March), 3-21.

Lakoff, George and Mark Johnson (1980), *Metaphors We Live By,* Chicago: University of Chicago Press.

Leach, Edmund (1976), *Culture and Communication: The Logic by Which Symbols Are Connected,* New York: Cambridge University Press.

Levin, Stephen and Daniel Anderson (1976), "The Development of Attention," *Journal of Communication,* 26 (Spring), 126-135.

Levy, Sidney (1959), "Symbols for Sale," *Harvard Business Review,* 37 (July-August), 117-124.

Lillard, Angeline (1998), "Ethnopsychologies: Cultural Variations in Theories of Mind," *Psychological Bulletin,* 123, 3-32.

Lohof, Bruce (1969), "The Higher Meaning of Marlboro Cigarettes," *Journal of Popular Culture,* 3, 441-450.

Lynch, Barbara and Richard Bonnie (1994), *Growing Up Tobacco Free: Preventing Nicotine Addiction in Children and Youths,* Washington, DC: National Academy Press.

Macklin, M. Carole (1983), "Do Children Understand TV Ads?" *Journal of Advertising Research,* 23 (February-March), 63-70.

—— (1985), "Do Young Children Understand the Selling Intent of Commercials?" *Journal of Consumer Affairs,* 19 (Winter), 293-304.

Marks, Lawrence, Robin Hammeal, and Marc Bornstein (1987), *Perceiving Similarity and Comprehending Metaphor,* Chicago: Monographs of the Society for Research in Child Development.

McCracken, Grant (1988), *Culture and Consumption: New Approaches to the Symbolic Character of Consumer Goods and Activities,* Bloomington: Indiana University Press.

—— (1989), "Who Is the Celebrity Endorser?" *Journal of Consumer Research,* 19 (September), 196-213.

McNeal, James (1987), *Children as Consumers: Insights and Implications,* Lexington, MA: Lexington Books.

Mick, David Glen (1986), "Consumer Research and Semiotics: Exploring the Morphology of Signs, Symbols, and Significance," *Journal of Consumer Research,* 13 (September), 196-213.

Mitchell, W. J. T. (1998), "Dinos R Us," *University of Chicago Magazine,* 90 (February), 16-22.

Nelson, Katherine (1996), *Language in Cognitive Development,* New York: Cambridge University Press.

Nicolopoulou, Ageliki, Barbara Scales, and Jeff Weintraub (1994), "Gender Differences and Symbolic Imagination in the Stories of Four-Year Olds," in *The Need for Story: Cultural Diversity in Classroom and Community,* Anne Haas Dyson and Celia Genishi, eds., Urbana IL: National Council of Teachers of English.

O'Connor, Kevin (1991), *The Play Therapy Primer: An Integration of Theories and Techniques,* New York: John Wiley.

Orleans, C. Tracy and John Slade (1993), *Nicotine Addiction: Principles and Management,* New York: Oxford University Press.

Pollay, R., S. Siddarth, M. Siegel, A. Haddix, R. Merritt, G. Giovino, and M. Eriksen (1996), "The Last Straw? Cigarette Advertising and Realized Market Shares Among Youths and Adults, 1979-1993," *Journal of Marketing,* 60, 1-16.

Radin, Paul (1997), *The Trickster: A Study in American Indian Mythology.* New York: Schocken Books.

Robinson, Leslie, Robert Klesges, Susan Zbikowski, and Renita Glaser (1997), "Predictors of Risk for Different Stages of Adolescent Smoking in a Bi-racial Sample," *Journal of Consulting and Clinical Psychology,* 65, 653-662.

Roedder, Deborah (1981), "Age Differences in Children's Responses to Television Advertising: An Information-Processing Approach," *Journal of Consumer Research,* 8 (September), 144-153.

Rogoff, Barbara (1990), *Apprenticeship in Thinking: Cognitive Development in a Social Context,* New York: Oxford University Press.

Root, H. Paul (1998), "From the President: Closing the Gap Between Knowledge and Practice," *Marketing Science Institute Review,* Spring, 3.

Roopnarine, Jaipaul, James Johnson, and Frank Hooper (1994), *Children's Play in Diverse Cultures,* Albany: State University of New York Press.

Rubin, K., Greta Fein, and B. Vandenberg (1983), "Play," in *Handbook of Child Psychology: Socialization, Personality and Social Development,* New York: John Wiley, 693-774.

Schmidt, Peter (1998), "Governors Want Fundamental Changes in Colleges, Question Place of Tenure," *The Chronicle of Higher Education,* 44 (June 19), A38.

Scott, Linda (1994), "The Bridge From Text to Mind: Adapting Reader-Response Theory to Consumer Research," *Journal of Consumer Research,* 21 (December), 461-480.

Shore, Bradd (1996), *Culture in Mind: Cognition, Culture and the Problem of Meaning,* New York: Oxford University Press.

Shweder, Richard (1991), *Thinking Through Cultures: Expeditions in Cultural Psychology,* Cambridge, MA: Harvard University Press.

Sullenberger, Tom (1974), "Ajax Meets the Jolly Green Giant: Some Observations on the Use of Folklore and Myth in American Mass Marketing," *Journal of American Folklore,* 87, 53-65.

Taylor, Majorie (1997), "The Role of Creative Control and Culture in Children's Fantasy/Reality Judgements," *Child Development,* 68 (December), 1015-1017.

Turner, Victor (1967), *The Forest of Symbols,* Ithaca, NY: Cornell University Press.

U.S. Department of Health and Human Services (1994), *Preventing Tobacco Use Among Young People: A Report of the Surgeon General,* Washington, DC: U.S. Department of Health and Human Services.

Urberg, K., S. Degirmencioglu, and C. Pilgrim (1997), "Close Friend and Group Influence on Adolescent Cigarette Smoking and Alcohol Use," *Developmental Psychology,* 33, 834-844.

Valsiner, Jaan (1997), *Culture and the Development of Children's Action: A Theory of Human Development,* New York: John Wiley.

Van der Geest, Sjaak (1996), "Grasping the Children's Point of View? An Anthropological Reflection," in *Children, Medicine and Cultures,* Patricia Bush, Deanna Trakas, Emilio Sanz, Rolf Wirsing, Tuula Vaskilampi, and Alan Prout, eds., Binghamton, NY: Pharmaceutical Products Press.

Vygotsky, Lev Semyonich (1978), *Mind in Society: The Development of Higher Psychological Processes,* Cambridge, MA: Harvard University Press.

Waksler, Frances (1991), *Studying the Social Worlds of Children, Sociological Readings,* London: Falmer Press.

Ward, Scott, Daniel Wackman, and Ellen Wartella (1977), *How Children Learn To Buy,* Beverly Hills, CA: Sage.

Wertsch, James (1985), *Vygotsky and the Social Formation of Mind,* Cambridge, MA: Harvard University Press.

Winner, Ellen (1988), *The Point of Words: Children's Understanding of Metaphor and Irony,* Cambridge, MA: Harvard University Press.

Winnicott, Donald (1971), *Playing and Reality,* London: Tavistock.

Wiseman, Boris and Judy Groves (1997), *Introducing Levi-Strauss,* New York: Totem Books.

Zaltman, Gerald and Robin Higie (1993), "Seeing the Voice of the Customer: The Zaltman Metaphor Elicitation Technique," Marketing Science Institute Working Paper 93-114, Cambridge, MA: Marketing Science Institute.

PART

II

Societal Impact and Concerns

CHAPTER

5

"We'll Be Back In a Moment"

A Content Analysis of Advertisements in
Children's Television in the 1950s

ALISON ALEXANDER
LOUISE M. BENJAMIN
KEISHA L. HOERRNER
DARRELL ROE

The 1950s were a seminal decade in the development of marketing to children. McNeal (1987, 1992) and Schneider (1987) describe the era as one in which the number of children increased dramatically as the baby boomers were born, and general economic stability brought consumer goods within the reach of most families. Parents who had been through the deprivations of the Depression and World War II vowed that their children would experience affluence. Consequently, children became a market. Halberstam (1993) describes the 1950s as a decade of general goodwill and expanding prosperity in which few Americans

AUTHORS' NOTE: Reprinted from *Journal of Advertising*, Vol. XXVII, Number 3, Fall 1998. Reprinted with permission.

97

doubted the essential goodness of their society, but also as a time of growing challenge to the old order, much of it produced by critical changes in technology, including television.

The children's television advertising environment generally is studied from the 1970s onward. So little academic research was reported in the 1950s that Pecora (1995) refers to the decade as the prehistory of research on children's television advertising. Early academic literature considered children as developing markets and focused on their recall of television advertising (Brumbaugh 1954), buying habits (Guest 1955), and influence on parental purchases (Munn 1958).

We rectify the oversight by examining what happened during the 1950s, when television advertising to children began, and describing the television ads designed to appear in children's programs of that decade. Our research shows that advertisements of the 1950s differ substantially from those of the decades that followed, and many of the differences reflect both the growth of the child audience and advertisers' recognition of that audience as an emerging market. Because the evolutionary changes in television, TV audiences, and children as a market began in the 1950s, we review them briefly as background for our discussion of the evolution of children's television advertisements to 1960.

Factors in Television, TV Advertising, and the Evolution of Children's Programming in the 1950s

—

Growth of Television

The 1950s were a time of great change in television. In 1950, 9% of American homes had television sets; by decade's end, sets were present in 87% of homes (Sterling and Kittross 1990). Most stations broadcast monochrome signals to the black-and-white television sets. Studio cameras were monochrome, bulky, equipped with turret lenses instead of zoom lenses for changes in camera shot perspective, and primitive in technology. Studio switchers lacked sophisticated special effects, and usually the director could select only from a sequence of simple in-studio shots. Most programs at the decade's beginning were live. Any copies were recorded by a kinescope projector, a device in which a motion picture camera photographed images on a television picture tube. Videotape was introduced in 1956 but was not widely used until the 1960s (Sterling and Kittross 1990). Consequently, copies of programs and commercials from the 1950s are difficult to obtain (Schneider 1987).

The broadcast day increased during the 1950s. The first daypart filled by networks and stations was 6:00 to 11:00 p.m., and the total evening hours offered remained fairly constant during the decade. During the 1950s daytime and weekend programs increased tremendously. From 1949 to 1960 total daytime broadcast hours more than quadrupled, and weekend hours increased tenfold. Much of the increase occurred from 1949 through 1955. Overall, the network time devoted to children's programming declined dramatically in the evening hours, but rose almost as dramatically during daytime and weekends (Lichty and Topping 1975).

Because most households in the 1950s had only one television set, programs appealing to adults as well as children were seen as a way of attracting the entire family. At the decade's beginning such shows often had one sponsor that underwrote the entire program, or dual (shared) sponsorship with noncompeting advertisers rotating sponsorship. That system was imported from radio. As production costs increased in the early to mid-1960s the 30- to 60-second spot announcements familiar today replaced sole or dual sponsorship. During the 1950s most children's programs, and many adult shows, were controlled by the sponsor and its advertising agency, which often packaged the program, commercials and all. Early children's shows were designed to sell TV sets by enhancing television's appeal to the entire family (Sterling and Kittross 1990; Lichty and Topping 1975). Hence, much advertising that supported family/children's programming was for adult-oriented products. By decade's end children's programs had shifted to less valuable morning, early afternoon, or Saturday morning hours from more valuable evening hours (Palmer and Dorr 1980).

Growth of Television Advertising

Television expanded the field of advertising. At first the agencies' television departments were small and understaffed, but that situation

moved into the market. Kellogg's created cartoon characters for its cereals, including Tony the Tiger (Frosted Flakes) and Snap! Crackle! and Pop! (Rice Krispies), and advertised to children and adults alike. General Mills also designed cartoon characters for its cereals. One of the longest running commercial gags began in the 1950s with the Trix Rabbit's attempts to taste Trix cereal (Hall 1984, p. 105-111). Over the next 15 to 20 years, television for children became an industry unto itself. Most of the standards, including marketing and advertising techniques, took form during those years (Schneider 1987).

By the early 1960s, broadcasters and regulators alike had recognized TV's growing impact on children. In its 1960 program policy statement, the FCC listed "Programs for Children" as one of the 14 major elements necessary for broadcasters to meet their public interest obligations (FCC 1960). In his famous "vast wasteland" speech, Minow (1961) chastised broadcasters for their poor offerings for child audiences, especially because broadcasters themselves had recognized children as a special audience in their television code and had adopted guidelines regulating toy advertising on TV (Palmer and Dorr 1980). Clearly, the decade of the 1950s had brought a transformation in children's programming and advertising.

Research Focus and Justification

The authors cited above relied on anecdotal evidence to describe the evolution of advertising in children's programming. None provided a rigorous academic review of material from the 1950s, largely because this "live" decade's programming is difficult to find. Fortunately, the Peabody Collection at the University of Georgia has copies of programs from that decade, including children's programs. The collection is a fortuitous outgrowth of the prestigious George Foster Peabody Awards housed and administered by the College of Journalism and Mass Communication at the University of Georgia. Commercials used in our study came from the collection's 1950s programming specifically designated by the industry as targeting a child audience.

Systematically characterizing and analyzing children's television advertisements from the 1950s gives unique insight to rarely seen or studied ads and how children's ads in general evolved over the course of that formative decade. Our research asks what has endured since then, what was borrowed from other media, what was created specifically for television, and what was discarded in the evolution of the contemporary children's television advertising environment. Because extensive research into children's television advertising began in the 1970s and because 1970s research provides many variables, we adopted those variables to facilitate comparisons to ads in the 1950s.

Advertising Studies from the 1970s to the 1990s

In a series of studies, Barcus (1977, 1978) and Winick et al. (1973) described a 1970s environment in which total commercial time averaged from 12 to nine minutes per hour (diminishing over the decade), product types advertised to children were limited primarily to four types (toys, cereals, candies and snacks, and fast foods), and promotional appeals were primarily to fun and happiness (Atkin and Heald 1977; Doolittle and Pepper 1975). Information was presented about the product but not always in a manner understandable to children (Barcus 1980). The handful of studies from the 1980s examined Saturday morning network children's television with basically the same results (Condry, Bence, and Scheibe 1988; Stern and Harmon 1984).

Kunkel (1992) describes the environment of 1990 in cable, affiliate and independent stations, finding diversity across those channels. Broadcast networks provided the greatest amount of advertising, and cable significantly less. Cable had the widest range of products advertised. The most prevalent promotional theme remained "fun," appearing in more than 25% of the ads, with taste and product performance each appearing in about 18% of the ads. Roughly half of all ads in 1990 included at least one disclosure/disclaimer. More than half of the ads were live action, a departure from the animated ads that made up the majority in the 1970s. Premiums appeared in 10% of all ads, consistent with research findings of the 1970s.

By adapting the research cited to the advertisements of the 1950s, we developed categories to expedite comparisons and aid analysis. The categories included total commercial time, product type, promotional appeals, age and gender of participants, production variables, and controversial techniques (see Table 5.1).

Methods

We conducted content analysis to gain basic information on the content of the commercials in children's programs of the 1950s. That method was chosen because it is deemed best at giving "a scientific, quantitative, and generalizable description of communications content" (Kassarjian 1977, p. 10). Our sample came from the Peabody Archives. We coded 75 commercials from 24 shows, which represent the bulk of all children's shows for that decade in which advertisements appeared (n = 30). Six children's shows were not coded because their condition on kinescope was too fragile for viewing.

All commercial messages were coded with the exception of the brief sponsor announcement ("This show is brought to you by . . .") found at the beginning and end of most shows. Categories were modeled on those employed by Barcus (1977) and Kunkel (1992) to facilitate comparisons. For commercials, coding included length, target audience (adult, child, mixed), participants (gender and age of all participants, primary participants, and spokespersons), presence or absence of selling techniques (including disclaimers, premium offers, host selling, and asking parents to buy the product), product type, promotional content/ appeals, and production variables.

Each of the 75 commercials was assigned to one of the major product type categories derived from previous research (Kunkel 1992; Barcus 1977) plus an "other" category. The categories, with their principal constituents from the sample, were toys (Space-O-Phone or a Winky Dink kit for drawing along with the program), cereals (Pep, Shredded Wheat, Raisin Bran), snacks (candy bars and soda), fast food (none), and other (e.g., 12 ads for dairy food such as milk, ice cream,

TABLE 5.1 Advertising in Children's Television of the 1950s, 1970s, and 1990s

	1950s All	1950s Children	1970s[a]	1990s[b]
Commercial Time				
Length	1:07	1:11	30 sec	NA
% commercial time	9	NA	15.9	16.8
Product Type				
Toys	6.7	8.3	18.1	17.0
Cereals	20.0	23.3	24.8	31.2
Candy/snacks	17.3	21.7	28.8	32.4
Fast Food	00.0	00.0	10.4[c]	8.7
Other	56.0	46.7	14.3	11.4
Promotional Appeals				
Fun	56.0	66.7	42.8[d]	26.6[e]
Taste	53.3	58.3	59.7	18.8
New/innovative	38.7	30.0	17.4	2.6
Product information	100.0	100.0	24.7[f]	NA
Production Techniques				
Animation				
Live	68.0	70.0	58.0	55.9
Animated	1.3	1.7	16.0	17.0
Mixed	30.7	28.3	26.0	27.1
Activity Level (Pace)				
Low	52.0	55.0	10.0	NA
Moderate	28.0	26.7	39.0	NA
High	17.3	18.3	51.0[g]	NA
Jingles	18.7	23.3	41.1[h]	NA
Participants				
Spokespersons[i]				
Adult Male	76.0	71.8	66.0	NA
Adult Female	16.0	12.8	6.0	NA
Children	8.0	15.4	9.0	NA
Selling Techniques				
Disclaimers	9.3	8.3	41.0	51.1
Host Selling	54.7	61.7	0.0	NA
Ask parents	12.0	15.0	1.3[j]	NA
Premiums/Prizes	14.7	18.3	19.0	13.5

a. Barcus (1977) unless otherwise noted.
b. Kunkel (1992).
c. "Eating places."
d. Winick et al. (1973).
e. Unlike data from 1950s and 1970s, only one appeal could be coded per ad.
f. "Some product description."
g. Doolittle and Pepper (1975). High = fast (26%) and very fast (25%).
h. Winick et al. (1973).
i. Percentages are of ads that had spokespersons.
j. Winick et al. (1973).

and cheese; seven for appliances, six for dog food, and four for automobiles).

Promotional content/appeals were coded for informational content (price, features of the product, product attributes, performance) and for appeals (fun/happiness, taste/flavor/smell, new/innovative, and others that proved to be less prevalent, including adventure, affiliation, energy, and conformity). Informational content emphasizes the product's features or capabilities, such as how a new toy works. Appeals link psychological motive to the product. Fun simply associates positive affect with product use; taste/flavor/smell includes such sensory descriptors as crunchy, delicious, rich; new/innovative stresses the unique attributes of the product. The use of humor in the ads was also coded. All ads were coded as revealing one or more promotional appeals.

Because production techniques of the 1950s could vary so radically from current norms, production variables also were examined. Each commercial was coded for visual format (animated, live action, or mixed), character activity (low, moderate, or high), and the presence or absence of certain visual and auditory special effects, including closeups, graphics, product display, sound effects, and others.

Four coders were trained to analyze commercials. Percentage of agreement was used to calculate intercoder reliability, which initially ranged from .75 to 1.0 (Holsti 1969). Coding discrepancies were resolved through discussion before analysis continued. Frequencies were run on all variables to determine the overall profile of the advertising studied. Cross-tabulations with chi-square tests for significance were used to assess variability due to target audience (child, adult, mixed) or time (first versus second half of the decade).

Results

Neither program length nor commercial length was completely standardized during the 1950s. Programs began on the hour, half-hour, and sometimes quarter-hour, though commercials, public service announcements, station promotions, or other "fill" materials were used to round out timing for shows running less than the allotted time. As the

decade progressed, a tendency toward today's more standardized timing developed, especially in prime time, but today's program lengths
were by no means the norm even in 1959. Programs ranged from a
low of 14.19 minutes (*Lucky Pup,* 1950) to a high of 59.35 minutes
(*Disneyland,* 1954). The mean length for programs over the decade was
37.4 minutes. Commercial length varied widely, from a low of 11
seconds to a high of three minutes 24 seconds, with a mean of one
minute nine seconds and a mode of 60 seconds (n = 12). Total commercial time in programs averaged 9%, comparable to the maximum of 12
minutes per hour weekday/nine minutes per hour weekends, or 20%
and 15%, respectively, allowed today under the Children's Television
Act of 1990.

By 1959, advertised product type had not evolved into the big four
of contemporary children's advertising: toys, cereals, candy/snacks, and
fast foods. Indeed, those traditional categories of today comprised only
44% of the advertising on children's programs in the 1950s, with other
advertisements for products such as appliances (e.g., the GE rotisserie
oven), dog food (Ken-L-Ration), and food (not fast food but staples such
as dairy products and peanut butter) comprising 56% of total advertising (see Table 5.1).

With such a large "other" category, the advertising target in the
advertisements within children's programs is an important issue. Analysis revealed that 54.7% (n = 41) of the ads were targeted to children,
25.3% (n = 19) were targeted to both parents and children (e.g., "kids,
it's delicious and mothers, it's good for them, too"), and only 15 (20%)
were targeted solely to adults. However, a significant relationship was
found between product type and target ($\chi^2 = 10.8$, $p < .01$), showing
that less than 50% of children's ads fit into the "other" category, but
more than 90% of adult ads were "other." Subsequent analyses with
target audience as a variable combined the children and the parents/
children categories. Throughout the analysis, we contrast data from all
the ads appearing in children's programs of the 1950s (all) and data
from the subset of 60 ads that had children as the target audience (kids).

Promotional appeals were imported from radio and exported to the
future. A reasonable consistency is found in appeals across the years.
The major appeal within the kids' ads in children's programs was still
the appeal to "fun" (n = 40, 61.5%). It was followed closely by appeals
to taste (n = 35, 58.3%) and new/innovative (n = 18, 30.0%). Humor

was used in 41.7% of ads (n = 25). In all cases (i.e., n = 75, 100%), some information about the product was included in the ad (e.g., "crunchy," "improved television system," and "this dog food contains horse meat"). Hence, the information-free, image-only ad did not develop in the 1950s children's television market. Chi-square analyses revealed significant differences in promotional appeals by target such that the persuasive appeals of fun and the use of humor were greater in ads to children and parents (fun: $\chi^2 = 13.9, p < .001$; humor $\chi^2 = 4.18$, $p < .05$); appeals to newness were greater in adult ads ($\chi^2 = 9.5, p < .005$), and appeals to taste were not significantly different. See Table 5.1 for the percentage of all ads in those categories.

Production values varied dramatically from contemporary norms. Of the kid commercials coded, 42 (70.0%) were live action, 17 (28.3%) combined live action and animation, and only one (1.7%) was totally animated. The physical activity of primary characters was low in 33 cases (55.0%), "moderate" in 16 (26.7%), and "high" in 11 (18.3%), reflecting the much slower pace of 1950s advertising. The most common visual and audio production techniques in kids' ads were closeups (n = 50, 83.3%), showing the product in use (n = 36, 60.0%), dissolves (n = 28, 46.7%), and using words on the screen (n = 22, 36.7%). Special effects were rare because of the primitive state of television technology in the 1950s.

The 1950s were indisputably the decade of the adult white male spokesperson. Of the 60 kids' ads coded, 28 (46.7%) had as their on-camera spokesperson a white man and 16 (26.7%) had a man as their off-camera narrator. Children appeared in 49.3% of the 1950s commercials (n = 29). They were a primary participant in only 10 commercials examined (16.7%), and in only six ads (10%) were they spokesperson for the product. Women fared worse than children; 23 ads (38.3%) had female adult participants; in only five ads (8.3%) was a woman the spokesperson for the product. Across the decade, however, the percentage of ads with adults as primary participants decreased, whereas ads with no host or children as primary participants increased ($\chi^2 = 13.3$, $p < .001$).

Selling techniques that later came to be viewed as controversial were endemic to the 1950s. The most prominent was host selling. Because production control often was in the hands of agencies that embedded the commercials within the program delivered to networks or stations, little effort was made to distinguish program content from advertising. Host selling occurred in 37 (61.7%) of the shows coded. Only nine ads (15%) urged children to ask their parents to buy the product. Disclaimers were few (n = 5, 8.3%) and included "Only available in the U.S.," "Colors sold separately," and "Only available in red/blue." In contrast, disclaimers became prevalent in the 1970s and 1980s as consumer advocates questioned what ads often omitted.

Another strategy that came under attack in the 1970s—use of premiums or prizes—was apparent in the 1950s. Eleven (18.3%) premium offers were found and the requirements ranged from sending in boxtops to entering contests to win advertised items. Interestingly, comparisons of variables in all ads across the first and second halves of the decade yielded very few differences in any area but selling techniques. A substantial decline in two selling techniques was noted across the decade. Host selling appeared in 71% of the early ads but only 27% of the ones from the last half of the decade (χ^2 = 13.99, p < .001). Similarly, the use of premiums/prizes decreased as 90.7% (n= 10) of the 11 total appeared in the first half of the decade (χ^2 = 4.76, p < .05). Both techniques were borrowed from radio.

In addition to reporting data from our study of the 1950s, Table 5.1 presents comparisons with similar studies conducted in the 1970s and 1990s. Today commercials have been standardized to the 30-second length and make up a larger percentage of commercial time. Ads for toys have increased, as have ads for candy/snacks. Other product advertising in children's programming has diminished markedly. Fun, taste, and newness remain prominent advertising appeals across the decades. A major reduction in the use of explicit product information is noted from the 1950s to the 1970s. Though the live-action form remains the most prevalent across the decades, animation jumped considerably from the 1950s to the 1970s. Not surprisingly, the activity level of the characters increased dramatically, as did the use of jingles. At least until the 1970s, men remained the dominant spokespersons. Selling techniques, many of which became controversial in the 1970s, were very different across the decades. The numbers of disclaimers increased fivefold; host selling was eliminated, in part by FCC rules forbidding it; urging children to ask parents to buy products was reduced significantly; and the incidence of premiums/prizes remained relatively stable across five decades.

Discussion

Our general findings show a stark contrast between children's advertising in the 1950s and contemporary advertising. Five compositional differences are evident. First, commercial length in the 1950s was far from the 30-seconds common today, with a trend toward 30- and 60-second spots as the decade progressed. Second, many ads were live ad-libs by a host selling the product. Host selling, banned in the 1970s, actually declined across the decade of the 1950s. Third, many ads were woven into the program's material, another form of host selling included in the ultimate ban. Fourth, products advertised were targeted to both adults and children and were diverse in comparison with today's ads that emphasize toys, cereals, candy/snacks, and fast food. Emphasis on those product types evolved in later decades. Five, total commercial time in programs averaged much less than commercial time allowed by law in programs today. The difference arose as program costs increased and advertising agencies abandoned program production, forcing remaining program producers to seek numerous sponsors for the shows. Both targeting and commercial time increased as marketers recognized the growing power of the child market and expanded niche marketing to that age group.

The ads from the 1950s that we examined also had three principal similarities with contemporary ads. First, promotional content was remarkably similar to that used today. Standard appeals, such as "fun," developed in television's earliest days. Second, in spite of the prevalence of host selling, other controversial selling techniques were not any more evident than they are in current advertisements. Third, the majority of commercials were live action then as now. Animation is still an expensive option, though its use has increased since the 1950s.

Some of our findings are understandable given the milieu of 1950s advertising and program production practices. First, full sponsorship of programming was the norm. Second, programming was limited in availability. Third, because of television's novelty, even programs aimed primarily at the child audience were watched by everyone, a fact that advertisers knew. Hence, it is not surprising that more diverse product types were available during the decade and that emphasis on the "big four" was not evident until later decades when segmentation of the viewing audience began to create the Saturday morning cartoon lineup. As multiple television sets became more common in American homes in the late 1960s, fragmentation of the audience continued.

Our findings also dispel some myths. One might assume early advertising was crude because the production techniques were new. That was not the case; film was well established and early television was done live (in film style) or on film. Nonetheless, the translation to the small screen of advertising did require much learning. Further, advertising was not substantially different in appeals, as a reasonable consistency in appeals is seen across the decades. Fun, newness, and taste were all used in the 1950s as they have been subsequently. The same appeals had been used in radio advertising. The information-free, image-only ad found today developed in later decades. Finally, much of the controversy that embroiled the 1970s had its roots in practices used from the beginning. Ironically, by the time rules had been established to prevent host selling, the practice had become much less common than it had been in the 1950s. Production control was often in the hands of agencies in the 1950s. They set commercials within programs and some made little effort to distinguish program content from advertising. That endemic practice becomes apparent when we place all 75 commercials analyzed in our study into three general categories: (1) integral, or ones that were an extension of the shows themselves, (2) segues, or ones that linked the shows' segments together, and (3) spots, or ones that were clearly external to the shows. In addition, separating commercials according to target audience (e.g., adult or child) illustrates the practice more forcefully.

Integral commercials were an elemental part of the show's lineup and provided entertainment indistinguishable from preceding and subsequent segments. That type of ad was the second most prevalent, 29.3% of all ads observed (n = 22), and featured live performances by characters who had already established themselves with the audience and then continued in their respective roles in the commercial segments. Such ads had no clear beginning or end. Of the 22 integral ads, only three were aimed at adults. When adults-only ads are factored out, 31.7% of children's ads were integral.

Indeed, in those children's ads, the sponsor's product was advocated with no observable attempt to disguise the way the product was sold (e.g., the skit, dialogue, etc.). In each case the already quick program tempo was kept moving by performers (e.g., a barker, a weight lifter, clowns, and/or hosts) in a fast-paced talent show style that highlighted their abilities as well as the product's attributes.

Segue commercials were also performed live by program characters and sometimes included preproduced clips. Though clearly separate from program performances of the characters, segue ads often functioned as transitions between show segments. They were separated from the rest of the show verbally (e.g., "It's time now to talk about Ken-L-Ration," *Zoo Parade*), by change of set, and/or by fading to and from black between the ad and the program. Among all ads, segue commercials were the third most common type (28%; n = 21), but among ads aimed at children, 31.7% were segue. As in the integral commercials, established characters (e.g., the Mouseketeers in *The Mickey Mouse Club*) or a participant-host (e.g., *Zoo Parade*) delivered the sponsor's message. Occasionally, the host(s) appeared only between show segments (e.g., *The Quaker Oats/Gabby Hayes Show*).

The 19 children's segue ads did, however, make a definite break from program action. For example, in *Space Patrol,* the host, dressed as a "Space Patroller," introduced and concluded the program and sold sponsor products on an ultramodern set resembling a rocket control room. The *Mickey Mouse Club's* live ads featured background flats and set pieces similar to play areas for the Mouseketeers. Most striking, however, were the *Rin Tin Tin* ads, which featured characters in full show dress in sets identical to or closely resembling those seen in the actual show, including occasional outside establishing shots of the Western fort where most of the show's action took place.

Among all ads, spot commercials were the most common type (42.7%; n = 32), but among children's ads, 36.7% (n = 22) were spots. Of the commercials aimed at adults (n = 15), 67% were spot advertisements. Hence, we see a clear distinction between ads aimed at adults and those aimed at children. Spot ads were generally well produced because cinematic production, directorial, and editing techniques of the time were employed. Two film styles prevailed: the Hollywood movie classic and the scientific documentary.

Ads produced in the Hollywood style featured families in daily living routines, who used the product and experienced happiness and togetherness because of the product's use. Even animated spots emphasized the family and/or the pleasure ensuing from product use.

The scientific documentary style ads typically featured only one or two people, with advertised products as diverse as automobiles and cereals. The emphasis was informational rather than emotional. For example, One-a-Day vitamins highlighted product attributes in a style closely resembling health education films shown in schools. A serious announcer voiceover narrated a script that was more clinical than emotional in tone.

Whether integral, segue, or spot approaches were used to target children in the 60 children's ads, product details in live ads were often presented in loud, enthusiastic narration or pedantic repetition of salient product attributes. High quality action shots were often diluted with over-explanation or off-screen narration, which merely provided redundant cues for viewers, such as "Here's a boy eating cereal!" (Pep) or "Take a look . . . Pretty nifty. Huh?" (Ralston cereal). Both examples are evidence of radio's influence on television advertising in its incipient stage. No clear-cut chronological progression is evident during the 1950s, but by the mid to late 1960s the audio portion in television ads had become less conspicuous, and video and audio more often shared importance.

In sum, commercials of the 1950s in programs aimed at the child market show marked distinctions from commercials of later decades. Some of the differences reflect the television technology and technical standards of the 1950s, whereas others illustrate growth in advertisers' and television executives' understanding of the medium as a way to reach specialized children's audiences. Many techniques obviously developed later and will be examined in planned further study of the evolution of children's television advertising.

References

Atkin, Charles and Gary Heald (1977), "The Content of Children's Toy and Food Commercials," *Journal of Communication*, 27 (1), 104-114.

Barcus, F. Earle (1977), *Children's Television: An Analysis of Programming and Advertising*, New York: Praeger.

——— (1978), *Commercial Children's Television on Weekends and Weekday Afternoons*, Boston: Boston University, School of Public Communications.

——— (1980), "The Nature of Television Advertising to Children," In *Children and the Faces of Television: Teaching, Violence, Selling*, E. Palmer and Aimee Dorr, eds., New York: Academic Press, 273-285.

Brumbaugh, Florence (1954), "What Effect Does TV Advertising Have on Children? *Education Digest*, 19(8), 32-33.

Condry, John, Patricia Bence, and Cynthia Scheibe (1988), "Nonprogram Content of Children's Television," *Journal of Broadcasting & Electronic Media*, 32 (3), 255-270.

Doolittle, John and Robert Pepper (1975), "Children's TV Ad Content: 1974," *Journal of Broadcasting*, 19 (2), 131-142.

Federal Communications Commission (1960), *Report and Statement of Policy re: Commission en banc Programming Inquiry*, 44 FCC 2303.

Fox, Stephan (1984), *The Mirror Makers*, New York: Vintage Books.

Guest, Lester (1955), "The Genesis of Brand Awareness," *Journal of Applied Psychology*, 39 (3), 405-408.

Halberstam, David (1993), *The Fifties*, New York: Villard Books.

Hall, James (1984), *Mighty Minutes: An Illustrated History of Television's Best Commercials*, New York: Harmony Books.

Holsti, Ole (1969), *Content Analysis for the Social Sciences and Humanities*, Reading, MA: Addison Wesley.

Kassarjian, Harold H. (1977), "Content Analysis in Consumer Research," *Journal of Consumer Research*, 4 (June), 8-18.

Kunkel, Dale (1992), "Children's Television Advertising in the Multichannel Environment," *Journal of Communication*, 42(3), 134-152.

Lichty, Lawrence and Malachi Topping (1975), *American Broadcasting*, New York: Hastings House.

McNeal, James U. (1992). *Kids as Customers*, New York: Lexington Books.

Minow, Newton (1961), "The 'Vast Wasteland': Address by Newton N. Minow to the National Association of Broadcasters, Washington, D.C.," in *1984 Documents of American Broadcasting*, 4th ed., Frank Kahn, ed., Englewood Cliffs, NJ: Prentice Hall.

Munn, Mark (1958), "The Effect of Parental Buying Habits on Children Exposed to Children's Television Programs," *Journal of Broadcasting*, 2 (2), 253-258.

Palmer, Edward and Aimee Dorr (1980), *Children and the Faces of Television: Teaching, Violence, Selling*, New York: Academic Press.

Pecora, Norma (1995),"Children and Television Advertising from a Social Science Perspective," *Critical Studies in Mass Communication*, 12 (3), 354-364.

Schneider, C.Y. (1987), *Children's Television: The Art, the Business, and How It Works*, Chicago: NTC Business Books.

Sterling, Christopher and John Kittross (1990), *Stay Tuned: A Concise History of American Broadcasting*, Belmont, CA: Wadsworth.

Stern, Bruce and Robert Harmon (1984), "The Incidence and Characteristics of Disclaimers in Children's Television Advertising," *Journal of Advertising*, 13(2), 12-16.

Turow, Joseph (1981), *Entertainment, Education, and the Hard Sell: Three Decades of Network Children's Television,* New York: Praeger.

Winick, Charles, Lorne Williamson, Stuart Chuzmir, and Mariann Winick (1973), *Children's Television Commercials: A Content Analysis,* New York: Praeger.

Woolery, George W. (1985), *Children's Television: The First Thirty-Five Years, 1946-1981: Part II: Live, Film, and Tape Series,* Metuchen, NJ: Scarecrow.

CHAPTER

6

Mothers' Preferences for Regulating Children's Television

ANN D. WALSH
RUSSELL N. LACZNIAK
LES CARLSON

Though it diminished somewhat during the deregulatory climate of the 1980s, a debate about television programming and advertising directed at children is mounting once again (Armstrong and Brucks 1988; Huston, Watkins, and Kunkel 1989; Kunkel 1997; Minow and LaMay 1995; Raju and Lonial 1990; Seiter 1995). The reasons are the increasing options for children (via cable television or ads on child-focused videotapes; Kunkel and Gantz 1992), greater public scrutiny of the practices of television station managers (largely in response to the airing of toy-based programs and ads encouraging children to call 900-numbers; Muehling, Carlson, and Laczniak 1992; Laczniak, Muehling, and Carlson 1995), responses to the passage of the Children's

---

AUTHORS' NOTE: Reprinted from *Journal of Advertising*, Vol. XXVII, Number 3, Fall 1998. Reprinted with permission.

117

Television Act in 1990 (Minow and LaMay 1995), and reactions to the release of findings from numerous studies investigating the effects of television advertising and programming, especially violence, on children (e.g., Kunkel 1997; Jensen 1995). At issue is how society should address the potential ill effects of advertising directed at children and, in a more general sense, the effects of television programming on children.

Some observers contend that government is responsible for protecting children from the potentially harmful effects of television (Huston, Watkins, and Kunkel 1989). For example, Kunkel (1997) suggests that an independent organization, similar to the one for video games, should be created to regulate television programming directed at children. Those advocates argue that parents have little control over what children view on television and can do little to mediate advertising's effects once their children are exposed to programs and ads. Others argue that parents are responsible for monitoring their children's television viewing and mediating the impact of advertising (see Becker's comments in Grimm 1989; Farhi 1995). They maintain that parents ultimately are responsible for protecting their children from the harmful effects of television (cf. Armstrong and Brucks 1988). Still, others have urged broadcasters and marketers to assume responsibility for what they offer children (Ward 1972), contending that those groups have an "implicit bargain" with parents to help develop more skilled consumers. Kunkel (1997) claims that the TV industry has yet to deliver on its promises to give parents guidance and information on children's TV.

In spite of the mounting debate and various perspectives, parents' perceptions of and preferences for the regulation of children's television are not well understood by researchers. In fact, popular press discussions about who should be responsible for children's advertising and programming are often based on opinions noticeably devoid of parental perceptions (e.g., Farhi 1995; Gunther 1995). We therefore studied the issue from the parents' point of view. Specifically, we examined mothers' perceptions and preferences about who should assume responsibility for the regulation of children's television. Further, we segmented mothers by their parental styles and examined each groups' views of various policy options. Our findings provide some insights for persons who are in a position to affect policies.

Background

Children and Television Viewing

Television is assumed to have a major impact on the lives of many people. Given children's extensive viewing, TV is potentially a more powerful socialization agent than peers and teachers (Huston, Watkins, and Kunkel 1989). TV advertising may have a particularly potent effect on young children who lack the cognitive defenses to cope with such marketplace activities (Brucks, Armstrong, and Goldberg 1988). Researchers note that exposure to TV ads strongly influences children's attitudes toward advertised products (cf. Goldberg 1990). Further, certain television programs (toy-based programs in particular) are likely to influence children's social behavior (Carlson, Laczniak, and Muehling 1994) and creative play (Greenfield et al. 1990). The debate about who is responsible continues to grow. Should parents, the television industry, the government, or independent organizations mediate the effects of television on children? Ward (1972) outlines a rationale for marketers taking responsibility for offering quality children's television. Armstrong and Brucks (1988) suggest the need for a unified effort by advertisers, government, and consumer groups to set clear and unambiguous standards for children's television. However, they recognize that such an effort would require alteration of the mindset of U.S. businesses and consumers.

Potential Solutions

Among the alternatives for addressing the problems of television and children, Armstrong and Brucks (1988) suggest (1) preparing children to cope with advertising, (2) increasing public regulation of commercials and programs directed at children, (3) encouraging parental involvement, (4) promoting advertiser and media effort, and (5) developing a self-regulation system. They argue that defenses against potential harm from television advertising must be developed in children. To defend themselves, children need training about the differences between programs and commercials. With such training, children presumably would be able to make more informed purchase decisions. However,

Armstrong and Brucks (1988) note that few school systems have the resources to undertake well-organized educational programs about advertising. They also point out that such programs may not be effective because children need "point-of-viewing" critiques of television advertising and programming. Parents are perhaps in the best situation to provide such training.

Parents can "educate" their children about television advertising in at least two meaningful ways. First, they can become *active participants* in children's viewing. For example, when parents and children watch television together, parents can encourage children to evaluate programs and advertised products, and can promote quality viewing and consumption choices. The potential for parental involvement may be limited, however, because children often watch television without their parents (Roberts 1983). Second, Armstrong and Brucks (1988) suggest that parents can mediate the effects of television and advertising by *developing rules to guide their children's viewing of television and processing of television commercials.* Such rules might limit the impact of television programs and commercials on children even when parents are not present. The extent to which parents view either of those two alternatives to be useful has yet to be examined.

According to Huston, Watkins, and Kunkel (1989), some people insist that *government intervention* is needed to offset the potential negative effects of television on children. Government could enforce a ban on commercials directed at children and carefully monitor programming during heavy viewing times, but such extreme mechanisms would have limited effectiveness (Armstrong and Brucks 1988). Alternatively, governmental agencies could set industry standards for children's television and create a more favorable (and less questionable) environment for children's viewing. Supporters of governmental involvement believe that approach to be the best alternative to consider for children's television. However, what parents think about it has yet to be reported in the literature. The TV industry has kept its promise to the President that it would support the V-chip and age-based ratings, but parents and educators are still worried (Kunkel 1997). Kunkel warns that by joint effort the government and the industry offers little substantial improvement in helping parents mediate children's viewing because age-based ratings do not give parents enough information to make intelligent decisions about what their children should see. He argues that program producers should not be allowed to determine what is suitable television for different age groups, and advocates development of an independent organization such as the Recreational Software Advisory Council that gives ratings for the video-game industry. An organization represented by more than just the television industry would be less likely to have ulterior motives.

Parental Socialization

Research on parental concern about food advertising directed at children (Crosby and Grossbart 1984) and toy-based programming (Carlson, Laczniak, and Muehling 1994) indicates that perceptions of regulatory options may vary among parental groups. Previous studies suggest that perceptions may be related to socialization tendencies of parents.

Parental socialization is an adult-initiated process for helping children develop habits and values congruent with their culture (Baumrind 1980). Children learn through insight, training, and imitation. Parental socialization research, often couched in social learning theory (Bandura and Walters 1963), implies that parental socialization is not a one-way process. As an example, parents may use parent-child relationships to fulfill emotional needs (Grossbart and Crosby 1984). Hence, parental socialization tendencies may be indicators of parents' efforts to meet their own emotional needs (Becker 1964; Strauss and Brown 1978).

Parents influence the development of children by serving as role models and by providing purposive training and opportunities to learn (Ward, Wackman, and Wartella 1977), but most socialization occurs through subtle interpersonal processes (Ward 1980). As Carlson and Grossbart (1988) note, socialization methods differ among groups employing distinct parenting "styles." Parental socialization theory has been used to explain parental reactions to food advertising (Crosby and Grossbart 1984; Grossbart and Crosby 1984) and toy-based programs (Carlson, Laczniak, and Muehling 1994). Hence, suggesting that parental socialization tendencies may be related to regulatory options for children's television seems plausible.

Parental Socialization Styles

Parental methods of relating to children have been classified according to parental styles (Baumrind 1968). Extensive work by Baumrind

(1991a) suggests that four parental types are prevalent: neglecting, indulgent, authoritarian, and authoritative. In comparison with the other parental styles, neglecting parents are more detached from their children. They neither seek or exert much parental control. Being low in restrictiveness and warmth, neglecting parents do not monitor or encourage children's autonomous development. Essentially, they give their children little attention. Because of their low participation in the socialization process, little is known about neglecting parents' effects on their children. The children may be influenced more by other socialization agents.

Indulgent parents tend to be more permissive than restrictive and warm rather than cold when interacting with their children. They attempt to remove as many environmental constraints as possible without endangering their children's welfare (Baumrind 1978). They also tend to provide children with adult rights but not adult responsibilities.

In contrast, authoritarian parents are more restrictive than permissive when interacting with children. They tend to discourage verbal exchanges and maintain high levels of control over youngsters. Children are expected to obey rather than question parental authority. Also, authoritarians tend to be more hostile than warm toward children (Crosby and Grossbart 1984).

Authoritative parents are most likely to balance parents' and children's rights and responsibilities (Gardner 1982). In comparison with authoritarians, authoritatives are warmer and encourage self expression (Baumrind 1968). However, authoritatives are quite restrictive. They expect children to act maturely and in accordance with family rules. As children grow, authoritatives tend to expand children's boundaries and promote autonomous development (Baumrind 1978).

Hypotheses

Parental Responsibility

Parental responsibility is manifested in the role parents play in the mediation and monitoring of their children's television viewing. Some of those efforts focus on setting and enforcing rules related to children's consumption of television. Restrictive parents are inclined to enforce rules, expect obedience, and demand compliance in matters such as manners and care of family possessions (Becker 1964). Authoritative and authoritarian parents, who are restrictive, are likely to exhibit such tendencies in regulating their children's television viewing. They may be willing to deal directly with their children. Monitoring of television viewing also implies that parents are involved with their children's consumption of programs and advertising. For example, they may keep tabs on the types of programs children watch and may observe children's reactions to commercials. Such monitoring actions are more consistent with the authoritative and authoritarian parental styles.

Parental responsibility is manifested in interactions with children about television programming and advertising. Activities may include parents watching and discussing television programs and advertising with their children. Such activities suggest open communication patterns between parents and children, which are most apt to be present in parent-child relationships characterized by a higher degree of warmth (Carlson, Grossbart, and Stuenkel 1992). Warmth tends to be more prevalent in authoritative and indulgent parent-child relationships than in neglecting and authoritarian ones. In addition to projecting more warmth, authoritative and indulgent parents appear to be more concerned with the *consumer socialization* of their children. They tend to participate actively in the socialization process rather than expecting obedience. Hence, authoritative and indulgent parents seem likely to advocate parental participation in children's use of television.

Overall, authoritative parents, who exhibit restrictiveness and warmth, are most likely to set rules and interact with children about television consumption. They therefore would be the strongest supporters of parental mediation of children's television.

H1a: Authoritative mothers are more likely to agree that parents should participate actively in attempting to mediate the effects of television on children than authoritarian, indulgent, and neglecting mothers.

Indulgent parents, who are relatively high on the socialization dimension of warmth, may be somewhat supportive of parental efforts to mediate the effects of children's television. Authoritarian parents, who are more restrictive than permissive, are likely to favor the rule-setting and enforcement aspect of parental mediation. However, because they are more cold than warm, they would not be inclined to interact with children in mediation of television. Indulgent parents, who are higher on warmth and less restrictive than authoritarians, may support the interaction aspect of parental responsibility, but not the rule enforcement aspect of it. Given their less restrictive tendency, indulgent parents would be somewhat supportive of parental mediation of children's television. Finally, neglecting parents, who are less restrictive and less warm, would be the least likely to support the role of parental responsibility.

H1b: Indulgent and authoritarian mothers are more likely to agree that parents should participate actively in attempting to mediate the effects of television on children than neglecting mothers.

Government Regulation

If parents perceive that television may interfere in their lives and relationships with their children, they may favor government regulation of children's television. Authoritarian parents who see television as marketplace interference with the proper upbringing of children (Carlson, Laczniak, and Muehling 1994) may want to remove that interference. Because they do not communicate openly with their children, authoritarians may look to an established vehicle such as the government to help accomplish that goal. Though they may resist outside influence in family matters, they may feel that regulation of children's television by government officials is not interference but proper action taken under authority granted to officials. In effect, government laws and regulations may be seen as rules necessary for orderliness in society. Baumrind (1968) observed similar tendencies. She noted that authoritarian parents believe in the development of respect for authority and preservation of traditional structures and order. Hence, authoritarians would view government regulation of television more favorably than other parents.

Indulgent parents, in contrast, may view governmental regulation as a means to do what they themselves would rather not do—deny children's requests stemming from television viewing. Such parents are concerned about their children's environment, but tend to avoid setting and enforcing rules. Indulgent parents would rather have a supportive environment for children without the potential conflict associated with denying children's requests. Hence, they would welcome governmental regulation enacted to mediate children's TV.

Authoritative parents are likely to address the issue of children's television directly by monitoring their children's viewing and are apt to participate in their children's socialization to television. They would not be likely to view television as a potential threat to their relationships with their children, and would have little expectation or need for government regulation.

Neglecting parents, like authoritarian parents, are lower in warmth and nurturance than indulgent and authoritative parents. Unlike authoritarian parents, they tend be permissive by default. They place little emphasis on strictness, enforcement of rules, and value conformity (Walsh 1991). They exercise minimal control over children and do little monitoring of their activities. With so little interest and involvement in their children's activities, they would be indifferent to governmental regulation.

H2: Authoritarian and indulgent mothers are more likely to agree that governmental regulation is needed to mediate the effect of television on children than authoritative and neglecting mothers.

Independent Organization

The parental style groups are likely to hold the same perspectives of regulation by an independent organization as they do of government regulation. Indulgent parents support a child-centered environment but tend to look to others to set the rules. Authoritarian parents also show signs of wanting a more regulated environment for children. As long as an independent agency does not directly interfere in family matters and is regarded as a respectable body, authoritarians are apt to support its efforts to mediate children's television.

Authoritative and neglecting parents are the least likely to support an independent agency's effort. Authoritative parents tend to assume full responsibility for their children's consumer socialization, including consumption of television. They are unlikely to expect outsiders to control the marketing activities directed toward children. Because of their indifference toward children, neglecting parents would show little interest in regulation from any source.

> H3: Authoritarian and indulgent mothers are more likely to agree that an independent organization is needed to mediate the effect of television on children than authoritative and neglecting mothers.

Broadcasters

Indulgent parents want a good TV environment for their children, but do not want to have to confront their children. They are likely to look to others to make the rules because having others assume responsibility for setting and enforcing rules for children's television is better than doing nothing. Authoritative and authoritarian parents, who are high on restrictiveness, may appreciate some responsible action on the part of broadcasters. However, both groups may lack trust in broadcasters and may suspect they are more interested in marketing to children than in providing a healthy and supportive environment for raising them. Therefore, they may not be inclined to credit broadcasters' efforts. Neglecting parents would show little concern about regulation of children's television, no matter what the source.

> H4: Indulgent mothers are more likely to agree that broadcasters should assume responsibility in mediating the effects of television on children than authoritative, authoritarian, and neglecting mothers.

Method

___

Sample

Self-administered questionnaires were distributed to students in grades 3 through 6 in two elementary schools in medium-size towns (one in the southeastern United States and the other in the Midwest). The school in the Southeast is public, whereas the school in the Midwest is parochial. Children were asked to take the questionnaires home and have caretakers (preferably their mothers) complete them. Research suggests that mothers know about the marketplace and its relation to children (Aldous 1974), act as the mediators of various consumer socialization agents' influence (Abrams 1984), and are believed to have a longitudinal effect on children's choices (Alsop 1988). We therefore considered mothers to be appropriate respondents for our study. Mothers were asked to complete questionnaire items with respect to their youngest school-age child to avoid multiple responses from the same family. The schools were paid one dollar for each returned questionnaire.

Data Collection Procedure

Children returned 209 questionnaires (a 48% response rate from a total distribution of 435). Of those returned, 151 were deemed usable (i.e., 35% of 435 parents completed all items). The response rates of 52% from the midwestern school and 47% from the southeastern school are similar to those in previous research with similar data collection procedures (cf. Carlson and Grossbart 1988; Carlson, Laczniak, and Muehling 1994). Incomplete items appeared to be random; we found no significant differences across the study variables between mothers who did and those who did not complete all items. Because mothers' responses across the two schools also appeared to be similar (i.e., we found no significant differences for the dependent variables), results are reported for the entire sample rather than for each geographic subsample. Demographic data for the sample are reported in Table 6.1.

TABLE 6.1 Selected Demographic Data for the Study Sample

	Head of Household			
	Female		Male	
	Frequency	%	Frequency	%
Education Level				
Some high school	0	0	3	2.0
High school graduate	5	3.3	3	2.0
Some college	26	17.2	8	5.3
College graduate	70	46.4	38	25.2
Advanced degree	47	31.1	90	59.6
Missing	3	2.0	9	6.0
Total	151	100	151	100
Age				
26-30	3	2.0	3	2.0
31-35	31	20.5	10	6.6
36-40	52	34.4	48	31.8
41-45	49	32.5	52	34.4
46-50	12	7.9	27	17.9
51 or over	1	.7	4	2.6
Missing	3	2.0	7	4.6
Total	151	100	151	100

Household Income	Frequency	%
$5,000—$9,999	2	1.3
10,000-14,999	2	1.3
15,000-19,999	1	.7
20,000-24,999	4	2.6
25,000-29,999	6	4.0
30,000-34,999	14	9.3
40,000-49,999	22	14.6
50,000-74,999	54	35.8
75,000-99,999	44	29.1
Missing	2	1.3
Total	151	100

Dependent Measures

Parental perceptions of who should participate and what is needed to mediate the effects of television on children were gathered on multiple-item scales. All perception items were measured on 5-point scales anchored by "strongly disagree" (1) and "strongly agree" (5). Table 6.2 summarizes the descriptive statistics of the dependent variables.

The parent responsibility measure consisted of the following seven items. As the scale appeared to be internally consistent ($\alpha = .76$), responses to the items were summed to form PARENTRE perception scores, which were used to test H1a and H1b.

- ◆ Parents should play a large role in determining what kids watch on TV.
- ◆ Children should be taught by parents about the difference between TV ads and programs.
- ◆ Parents should watch television with their children.
- ◆ Parents need to discuss TV programs and commercials with their children.
- ◆ Parents should carefully monitor children's viewing of TV programs intended for adult audiences.
- ◆ Family rules are absolutely necessary to control what kids watch on television.
- ◆ Parents should be aware of the television programs their children watch.

The following nine items tapped mothers' perceptions of the need for government regulation to address the children's television advertising controversy. An index (GOVREG) created by summing the responses to the items ($\alpha = .89$) was used to test H2.

- ◆ New laws should be enacted to create a better television environment for children.
- ◆ Further government regulation is needed to improve television programs directed toward children.
- ◆ Laws should be passed to provide more hours of educational viewing for children.

TABLE 6.2 Descriptive Statistics of Dependent Variables for Entire Sample

	Items	Mean	SD	Scale Midpoint
PARENTRE	7	30.75	3.44	21
GOVREG	9	27.88	7.90	27
INDORG	5	17.93	3.97	15
BROADCAS	9	33.59	5.06	27
Descriptive Statistics of Other Measures				
QUALTV	3	7.18	2.40	9
TVAD	5	16.16	3.90	15

✧ Television commercials directed at children should be banned.

✧ Lack of adequate government control of television allows advertisers to take advantage of kids.

✧ Commercials that use popular program characters to sell products to kids should be banned.

✧ Government's regulation of television programming for children is in the best interest of kids.

✧ Legal regulations need to be imposed upon broadcasters to improve children's television.

✧ The government should pose limits on the time devoted to commercials during children's viewing times.

The following five items reflected mothers' views toward the need for an independent organization to mediate children's television. An index (INDORG) formed by summing the responses to the items (α = .84) was used to test H3.

✧ An independent organization is needed to rate the educational level of children's TV programs.

✧ An independent organization of parents, educators, and broadcasters should be formed to control children's TV.

✧ Parent groups should be formed to improve children's television programs.

✧ Monitoring of children's TV by an independent organization is needed.

✧ Television advertising directed at children needs to be regulated by people who are *NOT* directly involved with the selling of products to children.

The mothers' views of broadcasters assuming responsibility for children's television were collected with the following nine items. Responses were summed to form BROADCAS scores ($\alpha = .81$), which were used to test H4.

✧ Broadcasters should make clear distinctions between children's TV programs and commercials.
✧ Broadcasters should increase viewing options for children.
✧ Television networks should control Saturday morning programs for children.
✧ Television networks should prohibit "host selling" (i.e. using the same characters in ads that are shown during a TV program about the character).
✧ Television broadcasters need to have standards so that program needs of children are fulfilled.
✧ Networks should offer more hours of educational programming for children.
✧ Broadcasters should set standards which regulate children's television program content.
✧ Broadcasters should be responsible for improving the content of children's television programming.
✧ Television executives should develop guides for developers of children's television programs.

Other Measures

In addition to the dependent measures, data were collected on mothers' overall attitude toward children's television programming. The following three items were measured on 5-point scales anchored by "strongly disagree" (1) to "strongly agree" (5). Responses were summed to form a quality of television (QUALTV) scale ($\alpha = .81$). Descriptive statistics for the measures are reported in Table 6.2.

✧ The quality of children's TV programs is excellent.
✧ Children's TV programs are "tasteful."

✧ The educational level of children's TV programs is excellent.

A measure of mothers' perceptions of television advertising directed toward children (TVAD, α = .82) consisted of five items:

✧ Children's television is nothing but commercials.
✧ TV commercials directed toward children are unethical.
✧ TV advertising takes advantage of children's inability to understand selling techniques.
✧ Television commercials directed toward children use fair selling techniques to promote products. (reverse coded)
✧ TV commercials with the same characters as in television programs should NOT be allowed during the program (e.g., Power Ranger toys during a Power Ranger episode).

Development of Parental Styles

Previous research shows that parental styles can be depicted by either a two- (cf. Baumrind 1991a, b; Carlson, Laczniak, and Muehling 1994) or a three-dimensional (cf. Armentrout and Burger 1972; Becker 1964; Carlson and Grossbart 1988) orthogonal array. Factors identified by researchers using three-dimensional measures include (1) warmth versus hostility, (2) restrictiveness versus permissiveness, and (3) calm detachment versus anxious-emotional involvement. Most two-dimensional depictions use the warmth versus hostility and restrictiveness versus permissiveness dimensions. Recognizing the possibility that either dimensional array might describe our sample's parental styles, we collected data for enough indicators (seven) to accommodate either a two- or a three-dimensional solution.

In all, seven potential measures were used to determine parental styles. Table 6.3 describes the scale used for each measure, by dimension. As in previous work (Carlson, Laczniak, and Muehling 1994), three variables loaded on the warmth versus hostility dimension of parental style: nurturance, parents' willingness to listen and share feelings and experiences with children; avoidance of communication, parents' tendencies to discourage children from discussing child trouble with parents; and encouraging verbalization, the extent to which parents invite children to talk to them about all issues.

TABLE 6.3   Independent Variables: Indicators of Parental Style
Dimensions

Parental Style Dimension and Indicators	No. of Items	Scale[a]	Original Source
Restrictiveness vs. Permissiveness			
Values conformity	3	mc	Baumrind (1971)
Firm enforcement	2	mc	Baumrind (1971)
Authoritarian	6	mc	Baumrind (1971)
Strictness	3	sa/sd	Schaefer and Bell (1958)
Warmth vs. Hostility			
Nurturance	7	sa/sd	Rickel and Biasatti (1982)
Encouraging verbalization	4	sa/sd	Schaefer and Bell (1958)
Avoidance of communication	3	sa/sd	Schaefer and Bell (1958)

a. Scales: mc = multiple choice; sa/sd = 5-point, strongly agree/strongly disagree.

Previously identified measures for the restrictiveness versus permissiveness dimension include strictness, the degree to which parents hold children to firm rules; authoritarianism, acceptance of the nonequal status of parents and children; values conformity, parents' approval of children obeying rules formed outside the home (e.g., school); and firm enforcement, parents' perception that their discipline attempts are very firm.

On the basis of factor analysis results, we summed the independent indices to form two overall indicators: warmth versus hostility and restrictiveness versus permissiveness. We checked for correlation of measures with Crowne and Marlow's (1964) social desirability scale (SD) to determine whether mothers' perceptions of their parenting practices might be influenced by their desire to respond in a socially desirable way. SD was not significantly correlated with either of the study's independent variables (warmth with SD = .04, p > .66, restrictiveness with SD = −.04, p > .55).

Generally following the procedures of Lamborn et al. (1991) and Maccoby and Martin (1983), we developed four parental socialization styles by dichotomizing the sample on each of two independent variables (warmth and restrictiveness). *Authoritative* mothers (n = 26) had scores above the median for both the warmth and restrictiveness dimensions. *Neglecting* mothers (n = 37) had scores below the median for both of those dimensions. *Authoritarian* mothers (n = 41) had scores below the median on the warmth dimension but above the median on the restrictiveness dimension. Finally, mothers above the median on the warmth dimension but below the median on the restrictiveness dimension were categorized as *indulgent* (n = 47).

Results

MANOVA Results

We conducted a MANOVA to control for potential interrelation among the four dependent variables used in the study. The results were significant (Wilks' lambda = .79, approximate F = 2.83; d.f. = 12,362; *p* =.001), indicating the appropriateness of investigating differences on each of the dependent measures across parental styles.

ANOVA Results

Table 6.4 reports the results of the hypothesis tests. H1a posits that authoritative mothers are more likely than the other parental style groups to agree that parents should participate in mediating the effects of television. H1b adds that authoritarian and indulgent mothers are more likely to agree than neglecting mothers. Though we find strong agreement among most respondents that parental mediation is needed (the overall mean response is 30.75, which is well above the scale midpoint of 21.00), the univariate PARENTRE F is significant (F = 4.42; *p* = .005), indicating differences among parental style groups. Planned comparisons indicate partial support for H1a and H1b. The mean for authoritative mothers (32.27) is higher than the means for neglecting (29.50) and authoritarian (30.26) mothers but not the mean for indulgent mothers (31.36). Indulgent mothers have a higher mean than neglecting mothers. However, we find no differences between authoritarian and neglecting mothers.

TABLE 6.4　Comparisons of Dependent Measures Across Parental Styles

	Neglecting (n = 37)	Indulgent (n = 47)	Authoritarian (n = 41)	Authoritative (n = 26)	F-Ratio	F-Probability
PARENTRE	29.50^{ab}	31.36^{a}	30.26^{c}	32.27^{bc}	4.42	.005
GOVREG	26.68	29.74^{a}	28.84^{b}	24.69^{ab}	2.88	.038
INDORG	17.03^{a}	19.11^{ab}	18.53^{c}	16.15^{bc}	4.32	.006
BROADCAS	32.00^{a}	35.32^{ab}	33.61	32.69^{b}	3.49	.017

abc. Superscripts designate significant differences between groups in hypothesized direction.

H2 posits that authoritarian and indulgent mothers favor more governmental regulation than the other two groups. Unlike PARENTRE, GOVREG has a sample mean (27.88) near the scale midpoint (27) and the F (2.88) is significant ($p = .038$). As predicted, authoritarian (mean = 28.84) and indulgent (mean = 29.74) mothers were more favorable toward government regulation than authoritative mothers (mean = 24.69) but not more favorable than neglecting mothers (mean = 26.68). Hence, H2 is partially supported.

H3, that authoritarian and indulgent mothers are more likely to support independent organizations than the other two groups, is also partially supported (INDORG, F = 4.32; $p = 006$). Indulgent (mean = 19.11) and authoritarian (mean = 18.53) mothers were more supportive of independent organizations than authoritative mothers (mean = 16.15). However, only indulgent mothers were more favorable toward independent organizations than neglecting mothers (mean = 17.03). We find no differences between authoritarian and neglecting mothers. The sample mean (17.93) is somewhat higher than the scale midpoint (15).

H4, that indulgent mothers (mean = 35.32) are more apt than the other groups to agree that broadcasters should assume more responsibility in mediating the effects of television on children (BROADCAS, F = 3.49; $p = .017$), is partially supported. Indulgent mothers were more supportive of broadcasters than neglecting (mean = 32.00) and authoritative (mean = 32.69) mothers, but not different from authoritarian mothers (mean = 33.61). As in the case of PARENTRE, the overall sample mean (33.59) is noticeably higher than the scale midpoint (27).

Other Measures

To gain a better understanding of mothers' attitudes toward children's television programming and commercials, we collected data on two other measures, QUALTV and TVAD. QUALTV tapped mothers' general perceptions of the overall quality of TV programs directed at children. TVAD captured mothers' views of the effects of TV advertising on their children. The results suggest that the mothers hold somewhat negative attitudes toward the quality of television programming (mean = 7.18, scale midpoint = 9), but not overwhelmingly negative attitudes toward programming quality or toward television advertising directed to children (TVAD, mean = 16.16, scale midpoint = 15).

Discussion and Limitations

We examined mothers' preferences for regulation of children's television programming. Despite the variety of opinions on parental wishes and responsibilities in mediating the effects of such programming on children, discussions of the issue have been devoid of parental input. Very little is known about what parents believe to be appropriate interventions for children's programming. Such knowledge is important because children's programming is constantly changing. For example, 900-number advertising and programs that have toy characters as their central focus are recent additions to children's programming. Such offerings are also indicative of the overlap between programming and advertising.

Because prior research has suggested that mothers' reactions to phenomena such as toy-based programming and 900-number ads are not uniform (cf. Carlson, Laczniak, and Muehling 1994; Laczniak, Muehling, and Carlson 1995), we examined the types of regulators that mothers might prefer for programs and advertising targeting children. In addition, using parental socialization theory as our conceptual foundation, we sought to ascertain whether perceptions of and preferences for children's programming regulation are related to identifiable groups of mothers. We hypothesized that certain segments of mothers, identified by their overall socialization tendencies (i.e., parental styles), would have similar feelings about regulating children's television. Such an examination has been specifically advocated by Laczniak, Muehling, and Carlson (1995). However, future research should investigate specific parental preferences for regulating advertising versus programming.

Our findings must be considered in light of our sample. As indicated in Table 6.1, it consisted of highly educated and older parents: 77.5% of the female and 84.8% of the male heads of household held college and advanced degrees, 75.5% of the women and 86.7% of the men were 36 years of age or older, and 64.9% of the respondents reported household income of $50,000 or more. No racial data were collected, but the sampling frame was primarily Caucasian.

Our findings incorporated with previous results indicate that parental styles hold promise for comprehending how and why mothers differ on the issue of children's programming regulation. For instance, the results for our first hypothesis indicate that authoritative mothers, who are both restrictive and warm, are more likely to support parental responsibility and family guidance to mediate the effects of television on children than neglecting and authoritarian mothers, but not more likely to do so than indulgent mothers. Because authoritative mothers are not significantly different from indulgent mothers, the results may offer insights related to the warmth versus restrictiveness socialization dimensions. Both groups that are higher on warmth appear to prefer programming interventions that incorporate inputs and views from family members, rather than approaches strictly dictated and enforced by parents. Those tendencies may reflect parents who are "child-centered" and who score higher on the warmth dimension (see Becker 1964).

The results of hypothesis testing do not provide a clear picture of the role of restrictiveness. For example, authoritarian mothers who are restrictive but not warm are not significantly different from neglecting mothers who exhibit less of either tendency. If warmth plays a role, differences between indulgent and authoritarian mothers' preferences would be expected. However, we observed few significant differences between the two groups on the issues studied.

The second and third hypotheses, positing that authoritarian and indulgent mothers favor governmental and/or independent organizational regulations more than the other two groups, are partially supported. In both cases, authoritative mothers were the least supportive of governmental or organizational interventions. Such mothers are the most attuned to their children's development and how the marketplace may be affecting children (Carlson and Grossbart 1988). In addition, they show overall concern about children's advertising (Carlson and Grossbart 1988) and specific types of ads (cf. Crosby and Grossbart 1984; Carlson, Laczniak and Muehling 1994). Authoritative mothers tend to use consumer information more than other parental style groups (Carlson and Grossbart 1988).

The results for the fourth hypothesis might be explained by indulgent mothers' tendencies to avoid setting restrictions on their children. In spite of their concern for their children's environment, they appear to want others to set and enforce the rules. They may not care who provides help with this task. Hence, indulgent mothers may be willing to have broadcasters assume responsibility. In comparison, authoritarian mothers, who are assumed to favor respect for authority, may be less inclined to give broadcasters more responsibility for children's television. Such mothers probably would be suspicious of broadcasters' motivations for taking on responsibility for mediating children's television. Broadcasters' motivations and subsequent behaviors might conflict with authoritarian mothers' desires for obedience and deference to authority from their children. However, our findings do not support a difference between authoritarian and indulgent mothers.

In general, our findings are consistent with the notion that authoritative mothers prefer to rely on themselves to teach their children about consumption. They tend to show more support for parental responsibility and less for third-party mediation of children's television than the other groups. Indulgent mothers assume some responsibility and consistently look to others for mediation of children's television. Authoritarian mothers seem to favor more governmental or independent regulation. Finally, neglecting mothers favor parental responsibility the least and they give mixed feedback about the other options.

Conclusions

Groups of mothers in our sample are inconsistent in their views of who should assume responsibility for children's television and advertising, but are relatively consistent in their opinions of the quality of children's TV programming. To gain a better understanding of how parents' attitudes relate to their behaviors, additional research is needed. For instance, if parents are dissatisfied with children's television, what behaviors will they exhibit? Are they likely to (1) urge more government or independent regulation, (2) join child-advocate groups in criticizing network offerings, or (3) encourage children to use other media?

Parents who tend to assume responsibility for monitoring and controlling their children's media habits have more options available today than they did in the past. Such parents may choose substitutes for network programming and advertising such as videos, VCRs for recording programs, interactive TV systems (Riha 1995), CD-ROMS, computer games, chatrooms, on-line exploration, and "edutainment" software (Katz 1997). Also, with the greater number of channels and new technologies such as the V-chip, parents have more alternatives for directly mediating the effects of television programming and advertising on their children. Some of those options may be seen as positive rather than negative methods for guiding children in their media use. As an example, parents can offer children computer games instead of denying them time in front of the TV. In other words, recent developments in computer technology and software for children may be affecting the ways in which parents are able to monitor and control advertising and programming directed to children. How parents view those options and the extent to which they are using them should be explored.

Parents who tend to look outside the home for help in regulating children's advertising and programming may find information and forums from a variety of child-advocate groups. Newspaper articles (cf. Farhi 1995) indicate that many organizations, such as the American Academy of Pediatrics, the American Association of School Administrators, the National Institute for Mental Health, and the American Psychiatric Association, have publicly criticized TV advertising and programming directed at children. Marks (1995) claims that such organizations represent 59 million people who believe that broadcasters are doing nothing for children and are just trying to sell them more toys. Even Ann Landers (1991) has voiced negative concerns about the lack of quality in TV programming for youngsters. Other organizations such as the United Methodist Church, the National PTA, the Southern Baptists, and Junior League have sponsored and promoted media literacy programs designed to help viewers make informed decisions about children's television viewing. What influence such organizations and programs are having on parents is another issue that should be examined.

Instead of waiting to see what parents do and what government regulations are forthcoming, marketers and broadcasters may find it advantageous to take a more proactive approach to ensuring quality offerings to children, whether it be in programming or advertising. The rationale for such an approach was outlined by Ward (1972). Whether the current generation of parents are receptive and appreciative of marketers who provide quality programming and promote industry codes, program classification, and technologies such as V-chips that empower parents remains to be seen.

References

Abrams, Bill (1984), "TV Ads, Shows Struggle to Replace Bygone Images of Today's Mothers," *Wall Street Journal* (October 5), 27.

Aldous, Joan (1974), "Commentaries on Ward, 'Consumer Socialization,' " *Journal of Consumer Research,* 1 (September), 15-16.

Alsop, Ronald (1988), "Mom Leaves Her Mark in Loyalty to Products," *Wall Street Journal* (January 19), 1.

Armentrout, James A. and Gary K. Burger (1972), "Factor Analysis of College Student's Recall of Parental Child-Rearing Behaviors," *Journal of Genetic Psychology,* 121 (September), 155-161.

Armstrong, Gary M. and Merrie Brucks (1988), "Dealing with Children's Advertising: Public Policy Issues and Alternatives," *Journal of Public Policy & Marketing,* 7, 99-113.

Bandura, A. and R. H. Walters (1963), *Social Learning and Personality Development,* New York: Holt.

Baumrind, Diana (1968), "Authoritarian vs. Authoritative Parental Control," *Adolescence,* 3 (Fall), 255-272.

——— (1971), "Current patterns of Parental Authority," *Developmental Psychology Monograph,* 4, 1-103.

——— (1978), "Parental Disciplinary Patterns and Social Competence in Children," *Youth and Society,* 9 (March), 239-276.

——— (1980), "New Directions in Socialization Research," *American Psychologist,* 35 (July), 639-652.

——— (1991a), "Parenting Styles and Adolescent Development," in *The Encyclopedia on Adolescence,* R. Lerner, A. C. Peterson, and J. Brooks-Gunn, eds., New York: Garland, 746-758.

—— (1991b), "The Influence of Parenting Style on Adolescent Competence and Substance Use," *Journal of Early Adolescence*, 11 (1), 56-95.

Becker, Wesley C. (1964), "Consequences of Different Kinds of Parental Discipline," in *Review of Child Development Research*, Vol. 1, Martin L. Hoffman and Lois W. Hoffman, eds., New York: Russell Sage, 169-204.

Brucks, Merrie, Gary M. Armstrong, and Marvin Goldberg (1988), "Children's Use of Cognitive Defenses Against Television Advertising: A Cognitive Response Approach," *Journal of Consumer Research*, 14 (March), 471-482.

Carlson, Les and Sanford Grossbart (1988), "Parental Style and Consumer Socialization of Children," *Journal of Consumer Research*, 15 (June), 77-94.

——, ——, and J. Kathleen Stuenkel (1992), "The Role of Parental Socialization Types on Differential Family Communication Patterns Regarding Consumption," *Journal of Consumer Psychology*, 1 (1), 31-52.

——, Russell N. Laczniak, and Darrel D. Muehling (1994), "Understanding Parental Concern About Toy-Based Programming: New Insights From Socialization Theory," *Journal of Current Issues and Research in Advertising*, 16 (2), 59-72.

Crosby, Lawrence and Sanford L. Grossbart (1984), "Parental Style Tendencies and Concern About Children's Advertising," in *Current Issues and Research in Advertising*, James H. Leigh and Claude R. Martin, Jr., eds, Ann Arbor, MI: Division of Research, Graduate School of Business Administration, 43-63.

Crowne, Douglas and David Marlowe (1964), *The Approval Motive: Studies in Evaluative Independence*, New York: Wiley.

Farhi, Paul (1995), "Turning the Tables on TV Violence," CD News Bank Comprehensive, *Washington Post* (June 21), F1.

Gardner, Howard (1982), *Developmental Psychology: An Introduction*, 2nd ed., Boston: Little, Brown.

Goldberg, Marvin E. (1990), "A Quasi-Experiment Assessing the Effectiveness of TV Advertising Directed to Children," *Journal of Marketing Research*, 27 (4), 445-54.

Greenfield, Patricia M., Emily Yut, Mabel Chung, Deborah Land, Holly Kreider, Naurice Pantoja, and Kris Horsley (1990), "The Program Length Commercial: A Study of Effects of Television/Toy Ties-Ins on Imaginative Play," *Psychology & Marketing*, 7 (4), 237-255.

Grimm, Matthew (1989), "Santa '900' Lines Mix Fantasy and Reality to Woo Kids," *Adweek's Marketing Week*, 30 (December 18), 5.

Grossbart, Sanford L. and Lawrence A. Crosby (1984), "Understanding the Bases of Parental Concern and Reactions to Children's Food Advertising," *Journal of Marketing*, 48 (Summer), 79-92.

Gunther, Marc (1995), "FCC Won't Require More Educational Kids' TV Shows," CD News Bank Comprehensive, *Knight-Ridder Washington Bureau* (November 1).

Huston, Aletha C., Bruce A. Watkins, and Dale Kunkel (1989), "Public Policy and Children's Television," *American Psychologist*, 44 (2), 424-433.

Jensen, Elizabeth (1995), "Violence Floods Children's TV, New Study Says," *Wall Street Journal* (September 20), p. B1.

Katz, Jon (1997), "Old Media, New Media and a Middle Way," *New York Times* (January 19), Section 2, p. 1+.

Kunkel, Dale (1997), "Why Content, Not the Age of Viewers, Should Control What Children Watch on TV," *Chronicle of Higher Education* (January 31), B4-B5.

—— and Walter Gantz (1992), "Children's Television Advertising in the Multichannel Environment," *Journal of Communication*, 42 (3), 134-152.

Laczniak, Russell N., Darrel D. Muehling, and Les Carlson (1995), "Mothers' Attitudes Toward 900-Number Advertising Directed at Children," *Journal of Public Policy & Marketing,* 14 (1), 108-116.

Lamborn, Susie D., Nina S. Mounts, Laurence Steinberg, and Sanford M. Dornbusch (1991), "Patterns of Competence and Adjustment Among Adolescents From Authoritative, Authoritarian, Indulgent, and Neglectful Families," *Child Development,* 62 (5), 1049-1065.

Landers, Ann (1991), "Something Can Be Done to Curb Violence on TV," *Des Moines Register* (July 15), 2T.

Maccoby, Eleanor E. and John A. Martin (1983), "Socialization in the Context of the Family: Parent-Child Interaction," in *Handbook of Child Psychology,* 4th ed., Paul H. Mussen, ed., New York: Wiley, 1-101.

Marks, Alexandra (1995), "FCC Head Fights for Quality TV," CD News Bank Comprehensive, *Christian Science Monitor* (November 6), 12.

Minow, Newton N. and Craig L. LaMay (1995), *Abandoned in the Wasteland,* New York: Hill and Wang.

Muehling, Darrel D., Les Carlson, and Russell N. Laczniak (1992), "Parental Perceptions of Toy-Based Programs: An Exploratory Analysis," *Journal of Public Policy & Marketing* (Spring), 63-71.

Raju, P. S. and Subhash C. Lonial (1990), "Advertising to Children: Findings and Implications," *Current Issues and Research in Advertising,* 12 (2), 231-274.

Rickel, Annette U. and Lawrence L. Biasatti (1982), "Modification of the Block Child Rearing Practices Report," *Journal of Clinical Psychology,* 38 (January), 129-134.

Riha, Carol Ann (1995), "Test of Interactive TV Set in Oregon," *Marketing News,* 29 (January 2), No. 1, 17.

Roberts, Donald F. (1983), "Children and Commercials: Issues, Evidence, Interventions," in *Rx Television: Enhancing the Preventive Impact of TV,* Joyce Sprafkin, Carolyn Swift, and Robert Hess, eds., New York: Hawthorne Press.

Schaefer, Earl S. and Richard Q. Bell (1958), "Development of a Parental Attitude Research Instrument," *Child Development,* 29 (3), 339-361.

Seiter, Ellen (1995), *Sold Separately,* New Brunswick, NJ: Rutgers University Press.

Strauss, Murray A. and Bruce W. Brown (1978), *Family Measurement Techniques: Abstracts of Published Abstracts 1935-1974,* Minneapolis: University of Minnesota Press.

Walsh, Ann D. (1991), "Intergenerational Similarities, Socialization and Mother's and Adolescent's Marketplace Orientations," unpublished doctoral dissertation, University of Nebraska.

Ward, Scott (1972), "Kids' TV—Marketers on Hot Seat," *Harvard Business Review,* (July-August), 16-28+.

——— (1980), "Consumer Socialization," in *Perspectives in Consumer Behavior,* Harold H. Kassarjian and Thomas S. Robertson, eds., Glenville, IL: Scott Foresman.

———, Daniel B. Wackman, and Ellen Wartella (1977), *How Children Learn to Buy,* Beverly Hills, CA: Sage.

The guidelines lead one to assume that to provide complete information about the advertised product/service, children's advertising would contain more disclosures than adult-oriented advertising and the disclosures would be more clearly and conspicuously presented to help reduce the possibility that children will confuse and/or misunderstand the advertising claims. We examined that assumption by comparing the prevalence of disclosures in children's and prime-time TV advertisements and assessing the potential effectiveness and "fairness" of in-ad disclosures directed at children. However, rather than investigating disclosures in general, we focused on one particular type of disclosure—the "fine-print" disclosure.

The use of fine print in television advertising has been, and continues to be, a hotly debated and often criticized advertising practice (King 1990; Muehling and Kolbe 1997; Ono 1997). Because of the general impression that advertisers "do not intend to communicate" when using fine print or do so with "the intent to deceive," pejorative statements such as "The large print [or off-screen voiceover] giveth, and the small print taketh away" (Flotron 1995; Foxman, Muehling, and Moore 1988) have become commonplace. In our recent study of practitioners' views of fine print in television advertising (Muehling and Kolbe 1997), the majority of respondents representing the nation's leading advertisers, agencies, regulators, and media firms agreed that consumers "do not," "cannot," and/or "do not attempt to" read the fine print in advertising, and many respondents agreed that "most fine-print statements are probably placed in ads with the intention of their not being seen." Of particular relevance is the fact that 73% of the respondents agreed that "advertisers should not be allowed to use fine-print statements in advertising directed at children." The need for "adequate disclosure" (as articulated by the networks and other regulatory bodies), coupled with our survey evidence, suggests that though disclosures in children's TV advertising may be prevalent, the use of fine-print disclosures should be relatively limited (especially in comparison with their use in adult-oriented prime time advertising).

The prevalence of fine-print disclosures in children's TV advertising is important, but the placement, duration, and informational characteristics of the disclosures (in comparison with those in prime-time ads) also must be considered. If advertisers are expected to communicate important product/service information to their young viewers, one would assume that ads directed to children would be more likely than adult-oriented ads to contain statements worded and placed in such a way as to facilitate young viewers' understanding of the advertised claims. Knowing the general content of the disclosures (i.e., whether they augment or limit/restrict points made elsewhere in the ad), as well as the means by which they are communicated (e.g., where and when in the ad they are placed and for how long), would be beneficial in assessing their potential usefulness and their ability to communicate product/service information.

Though several studies have examined the incidence and relative effectiveness of disclosures in television advertising, no study to date has made a direct comparison of children's and prime time advertising disclosure practices, especially in the context of fine-print disclosures. We designed our study to help fill that research void.

Background Literature

Since the 1970s, several content analysis studies have documented the use of audio and verbal disclaimers (disclosures) in children's advertising. For example, Atkin and Heald (1977) noted that 31% of toy ads sampled in 1972/1973 contained either a visual disclaimer or a visual and verbal disclaimer. Data collected in 1971 and 1975 by Barcus (1975, 1977) set the incidence rate between 33 and 41% for weekend and after-school ads directed at children, a rate similar to that reported by Stern and Harmon (1984) from a more recent study of children's advertising disclaimers. Studies in the 1990s by Klebba, Stern, and Tseng (1994), Kolbe and Muehling (1995), and Murray (1995) suggest that the use of in-ad disclosures has grown (they are estimated to appear in 60 to 80% of children's television advertising).

That development is surprising, given the reported ineffectiveness of advertising disclaimers directed at children. Liebert et al. (1977) were among the first researchers to document that standard disclaimers (such as "some assembly is required") may be more difficult for young children to understand than more simply worded disclaimers (such as "it must be put together before you can play with it"). They found that the standard disclaimer used in two different test commercials was totally ineffective in communicating to children in the age range for which it was intended.

Similarly, an empirical study by Stern and Resnik (1978) showed that disclaimers were ineffective in altering young children's visual perceptions of product attributes. Children exposed to a "Digger the Dog" ad containing the disclaimer "pull Digger's string and he'll walk five feet" were just as likely to overestimate the toy's walking distance (at 26 feet) as were children exposed to ads containing no such disclaimer.

A more recent study of children by Stutts and Hunnicutt (1987) provides additional evidence of the ineffectiveness of advertising disclaimers, suggesting that viewer age is likely to influence understanding. Five-year-olds gave more correct responses to questions about disclaimer content than four- and three-year-olds, though most respondents in the study gave incorrect responses, corroborating previous findings about the communication limitations of disclosures in children's advertising.

Hypotheses

We sought to determine whether children are indeed treated differently in the advertising marketplace. To explore the differential use and characteristics of fine-print disclosures, we developed hypotheses based on children's abilities and the standards for disclosures established by the networks, self-regulatory bodies, and the FTC.

Recognizing that children (particularly preschool-age children) have limited abilities, we might expect advertisers to communicate with that audience differently than they do with prime-time audiences. We would expect that if advertisers were adhering to the regulatory and self-regulatory guidelines established to protect children, and functioning in accord with our 1997 survey findings, they would use an information format other than fine-print disclosures to communicate product information to their young viewers. Accordingly:

H1:   The incidence of fine-print disclosures is lower for ads appearing during children's programming than for ads appearing during prime-time programming.

Ideally children should be able to read and understand all disclosures (fine print or otherwise). However, reading may be more critical for certain types of disclosures than for others. For instance, informational and advisory disclosures attempt to guide and inform, whereas restrictive disclosures delimit advertisers' claims (the more negative "giving and taking away" message). Though restrictive disclosures technically clarify the selling message for the viewer, if unread those selling points may mislead children about potentially critical aspects of the advertised product. Consequently, we might expect advertisers to use informational/advisory rather than restrictive disclosures in children's ads to avoid charges of misleading or deceptive advertising practices.

H2:   The content of fine-print disclosures in ads appearing during children's programming is different (more informational and less restrictive) from that in ads appearing during prime-time programming.

Children's comprehension of fine-print disclosures is likely to differ significantly from that of other audiences because of their limited ability to process such information. Children need more time to execute cognitive processes (e.g., memorial processes, spatial skills, and reasoning) than adults (Kail 1986). In addition, young children read more slowly than older children or adults. First and second graders, for example, read between 80 and 115 words a minute (Harris and Sipay 1990), which is well below the 200 to 300 word-per-minute reading speed of the average adult (Smith 1988). Most preschoolers cannot be expected to have more than a rudimentary ability to read. Consequently, because of the differential cognitive processing and reading skills of the younger audience, fine-print disclosures used in ads directed to children would be expected to have fewer words and appear on the screen longer than disclosures in adult ads.

H3:   The number of words in a fine-print disclosure is smaller in ads appearing during children's programming than in ads appearing during prime-time programming.

H4:   The length of time a fine-print disclosure appears on the screen is greater in ads appearing during children's programming than in ads appearing during prime-time programming.

Where the disclosure is positioned on the screen and when it appears in the ad may also affect attention and comprehension. Analysis of children's visual attention to the television screen indicates that children typically attend to the optical center of the screen (approximately one eighth above the physical center of the screen). Information presented in the upper part of the screen is more likely to be seen than that placed elsewhere (e.g., at the bottom of the screen). Attention and recall may depend on when the message appears within the ad. Research suggests that attention is best for messages appearing in the beginning of the ad (primacy effect), whereas recall may be best for messages appearing at the beginning and end of the ad (recency and primacy effects). Again, on the assumption that advertisers would make an effort to enhance young viewers' understanding of ad material, the findings pertaining to the spatial and temporal presentation of information lead to the following hypothesis:

H5:   A fine-print disclosure is more likely to appear near the beginning of an ad and in the top third of the screen in ads appearing during children's programming than in ads appearing during prime-time programming.

Finally, because many young children cannot read, advertisers who use fine-print disclosures would be expected to present the disclosure simultaneously in both the audio and video parts of the ad to enhance viewer attention and recall (a "Clear and Conspicuous" Standard recommendation). Research has found that simultaneous audio/video presentations substantially increase children's attention to television programs (Rolandelli et al. 1991) and recall of ad messages (Atkin 1975). If advertisers followed that reasoning, we would expect a larger proportion of disclosures with accompanying voiceovers in children's ads than in prime-time ads.

H6: A fine-print disclosure is more likely to be accompanied by an oral announcement of the disclosure in ads appearing during children's programming than in ads appearing during prime-time programming.

To test the hypotheses, we used a content analysis methodological framework to compare children's ad disclosure practices with prime-time ad disclosure practices.

Method

Data for the content analysis were collected by sampling ads appearing in programming periods we believed to be representative of children's and general adult TV viewing: Saturday morning programming (7:00 a.m.—11:00 a.m.) for children and prime-time (8:00 p.m.—11:00 p.m.) programming for adults. Much consideration was given to the "appropriate" days, weeks, and months from which to sample prime-time and children's programming to arrive at a representative sample of children's and prime-time television ads. For example, if we had elected to sample children's programming solely in November or December, ads for toys and others gifts might have been overrepresented in our children's sample because of the holiday season. We were less concerned about, but nonetheless sensitive to, seasonal variations in prime-time advertising. We also contemplated sampling after-school and Sunday programming for children, but because of the number of adult-oriented network talk shows, infomercials, and local programming appearing during those time periods, we elected to concentrate on Saturday morning children's programming only. In addition, the Fox television network was considered for both children's and prime-time programming, but because Fox has no network programming in the 10:00 p.m. to 11:00 p.m. time period (see, e.g., *Advertising Age* 1997) and has less well-defined children's programming periods than the other major networks, we chose to sample programs and ads from the NBC, ABC, and CBS networks only. For a similar reason, programming on cable stations was not considered. Further, to facilitate statistical comparisons, we wanted the numbers of ads sampled from the two programming groups (children's and prime time) to be relatively similar.

We therefore decided to videotape all programs and ads appearing from 8:00 p.m. to 11:00 p.m., Monday through Friday, in a week in early February to represent the prime-time television group, and all programs and ads appearing from 7:00 a.m. to 11:00 a.m. on the first Saturday of every other month throughout the year (i.e., February, April, June, etc.) to represent the children's television group. The data for both samples were collected in 1990. Though the sampling procedures for the two groups were different, we believe the ads selected for analysis are representative of ads appearing in children's programming periods and prime-time programming periods and are therefore consistent with the purpose of our study—to compare disclosure practices in ads directed at children with those in ads directed at more mature audiences.

As we were interested only in the ads (and not the programs) aired during the designated programming periods, we edited the videotapes so that only the ads remained. To facilitate the independent coding and evaluation of ad contents, we logged and edited the ads onto individual tapes, separated according to the network on which they were aired. Excluding local ads, public service announcements, and ads duplicated within a network, we obtained a sample of 582 prime-time and 552 children's ads. Because of historical evidence that the three networks sometimes treat identical ads differently (i.e., one network may require a lengthy disclosure, a second network may require a brief disclosure, and a third network may not require a disclosure at all), we elected to include ads that were duplicated across networks in our final sample.

As recommended in the content analysis literature (e.g., Kolbe and Burnett 1991), two different pairs of trained judges coded study-relevant information about each ad for each sample of ads. In the few cases of disagreements, a third independent judge mediated the differences in coding. We did not code the ads ourselves. All ads containing fine-print disclosures were considered for inclusion in the study. We adopted the following definition of fine print (from Kolbe and Muehling 1992, p. 48):

> Any part of an advertisement that appears in type size noticeably smaller than the headline or dominant ad copy, designed to augment, document, clarify, or delimit the selling message, offer advice, identify the product manufacturer, and/or provide supplemental information to the viewer.

Judges were first asked to determine whether or not an ad contained a fine-print disclosure. We found no evidence that coders had any difficulty interpreting and applying our "noticeably smaller" operationalization of "fine print" in their coding tasks, as they were nearly unanimous in agreement (i.e., more than 95%) on the ads they designated as containing fine-print disclosures. When an ad was deemed to contain such a disclosure, further judgments were made about the contents, placement, and other executional features of the disclosure.

Fine-print disclosures were classified as fitting into one of six content categories: general advisory, specific advisory, restrictive, informational, corporate, and citation messages. Appendix B provides definitions and examples of each category. In addition, the number of words per disclosure, the length of time a disclosure appeared on the screen (in seconds), where (top, middle, bottom third of the screen) and when (beginning, middle, or end of the ad) the fine-print disclosure appeared, and whether the visual (written) disclosure was accompanied by an off-screen verbal announcement were coded and used in the analyses. Interjudge reliability coefficients, calculated by Perreault and Leigh's (1989) method, ranged from .86 to .99 for the study variables, indicating a satisfactory level of agreement between judges on a variety of the coded items.

As the data were mostly nominally and ordinally scaled, we used chi-square and Z-statistic analytical procedures to test the hypotheses. In the cases where a mean could be calculated (e.g., the average number of words per disclosure), t-tests were conducted.

Results

Our samples of prime-time and children's programming contained numerous ads with fine-print disclosures. More than two-thirds (69.1%, n = 402) of the 582 prime-time ads contained a fine-print message,

TABLE 7.1 Prevalence of Disclosure Types[a]

	Children's Ads		Prime-Time Ads	
Disclosure Type	Frequency	%	Frequency	%
General advisory	13	1.9	106	14.8
Specific advisory	10	1.5	13	1.8
Restrictive	126	18.4	163	22.8
Informational	171	25.0	194	27.1
Corporate	364	53.1	229	32.0
Citation	1	0.1	11	1.5
Total	687[b]	100	716[b]	100

a. Difference in distributions of disclosure types between children's ads and prime-time ads is $\chi^2 =$ 117.88, $p < .001$.
b. Column totals exceed number of ads in sample because many of the ads had more than one disclosure and many of the fine-print disclosure statements contained more than one disclosure type. The column total for children's ads also contains two public relations disclosures, which were not included in the chi-square calculation. There were no public relations disclosures in the prime-time ads.

whereas 62.5% (n = 345) of the 552 children's ads contained such a message. Those proportions are different (Z = 2.36; $p < .05$), suggesting that fewer children's ads than prime time ads contain fine-print disclosures, and supporting H1.

The type of fine-print disclosure (i.e., advisory, restrictive, etc.) also was different for children's ads than for prime-time ads ($\chi^2 = 117.88$; $p < .001$; H2). Children's ads were more likely (Z = 8.12; $p < .001$) to contain corporate identifiers (i.e., identification of a corporate name, brand name, or trademark) than prime-time ads (53.1% and 32.0%, respectively), and were less likely to contain general advisory (e.g., "use only as directed"; Z = 8.60, $p < .001$) and restrictive disclosures (e.g., "void where prohibited"; Z = 2.04, $p < .05$; refer to Table 7.1). However, contrary to H2, children's ads were no more likely to contain informational (e.g., "no purchase necessary") fine-print messages than prime-time ads (Z = .91, $p > .15$). For the remaining disclosure categories, no significant differences were found.

To provide additional insight about ad disclosure practices, we examined the disclosure types across product categories and programming periods (see Table 7.2). Because the ad level frequencies (reported in the table) were not independent (i.e., individual ads often contained more than one fine-print disclosure and disclosure type), chi-square

TABLE 7.2 Incidence of Disclosure Types by Product Category

Sample/Product Category (n of Ads)	Disclosure Type						Total No. of Disclosures	Mean No. of Disclosures per Ad
	General Advisory	Specific Advisory	Restrictive	Informational	Corporate	Citation		
Children's Saturday Morning Advertisers	(n = 13)	(n = 10)	(n = 126)	(n = 171)	(n = 364)	(n = 1)	(n = 687)[a]	1.99
Toys (n = 130)	1	1	39	65	95	0	201	1.55
Breakfast foods (n = 76)	0	5	11	49	109	0	174	2.29
Fast food restaurants (n = 59)	11	3	61	30	71	0	176	2.98
Snack foods (n = 24)	0	1	12	7	26	1	47	1.96
Candy and gum (n = 18)	0	0	0	13	22	0	35	1.94
All other products (n = 38)	1	0	3	7	41	0	54[b]	1.42
Prime-Time Advertisers	(n = 106)	(n = 13)	(n = 163)	(n = 194)	(n = 229)	(n = 11)	(n = 716)[a]	1.78
Food and snack (n = 88)	2	0	2	36	66	0	106	1.20
Drugs and medicine (n = 66)	59	8	0	22	23	2	114	1.73
Automobiles and accessories (n = 62)	15	0	64	42	20	9	150	2.30
Hotels/restaurants/retailers (n = 50)	5	1	61	20	28	0	115	2.30
Personal and beauty (n = 43)	20	1	11	22	21	0	75	1.74
All other products (n = 93)	5	3	25	52	71	0	156	1.68

a. Row totals exceed number of product categories in sample because many ads had more than one disclosure and many fine-print disclosure statements contained more than one disclosure type.
b. Row total includes two public relations disclosures.

analyses were not conducted on the within- or between-sample data. The data in Table 7.2 provide interesting comparisons.

Perhaps not surprisingly, a large proportion of the children's ads containing fine-print disclosures were for toys (38%), breakfast foods (22%), and fast food restaurants (17%). Most prime-time ads containing fine-print disclosures were for food and snacks (22%), drugs and medicine (16%), and automobiles and accessories (15%). Excluding corporate identifying disclosures (which were most prevalent for both ad groups and many of the products advertised), we found that informational disclosures were most likely to appear in children's ads for toys, breakfast foods, and candy and gum, whereas restrictive disclosures were most likely to appear in children's fast food restaurant and snack food ads. For prime-time advertising, general advisory disclosures were the type often used in drug/medicine ads, whereas restrictive disclosures were the type often found in ads for automobiles and accessories and hotels/restaurants/retailers.

The number of words in the fine-print disclosures ranged from a low of one (a single word in both prime-time and children's ads) to as many as 29 (in the children's ads) and 57 (in the prime-time ads). In support of H3, we found that the average number of words per fine-print disclosure was smaller ($t = 2.27, p < .05$) for children's ads (mean $= 6.24$) than for prime-time ads (mean $= 6.89$). In addition, the average length of time the fine-print disclosures appeared on the screen was greater ($t = 7.10, p < .01$) for the children's ads (mean $= 2.34$ seconds) than for the prime-time ads (mean $= 1.94$; H4). The average prime-time ad had a fine-print disclosure rate of 211 words per minute, whereas the average children's ad had a fine-print disclosure rate of 160 words per minute.

Contrary to H5, where the disclosures appeared on the screen did not differ between prime-time and children's ads ($\chi^2 = 5.38, p > .05$). For both samples, the bottom of the screen was the predominant location for disclosures (see Table 7.3). We found differences between the two samples in when the disclosures appeared in the ad ($\chi^2 = 11.81$, $p < .005$). However, that finding does not suggest that disclosures appeared more often at the beginning of children's ads than prime-time ads (as predicted in H5), but rather that the differences occurred in the "middle of the ad" category (32.4% vs. 23.2% for prime-time and children's ads, respectively; $Z = 3.41, p < .001$).

TABLE 7.3 Executional Aspects of Fine-Print Disclosures

	Children's Ads		Prime-Time Ads	
Coding Category	Frequency	%	Frequency	%
Where Disclosure Appeared[a]				
Top of screen	24	4.6	47	7.8
Middle of screen	8	1.5	13	2.2
Bottom of screen	486	93.8	542	90.0
When Disclosure Appeared[b]				
Beginning of ad	160	30.9	162	26.9
Middle of ad	120	23.2	195	32.4
End of ad	238	45.9	245	40.7
Was Disclosure Repeated by Off-Screen Announcer?[c]				
Yes	91	26.4	55	13.7
No	254	73.6	347	86.3

a. $\chi^2_2 = 5.38, p > .05$.
b. $\chi^2_2 = 11.81, p < .001$.
c. $\chi^2 = 19.03, p < .001$.

Our finding that fine-print disclosures in children's ads were more likely to be accompanied by an off-screen vocal announcement than those in prime-time ads supports H6. More than a quarter (26.4%) of the fine-print disclosures in the children's ads but only 13.7% of those in prime-time ads were accompanied by a vocal announcement ($\chi^2 = 19.03, p < .001$).

Discussion

We sought to determine whether the fine-print disclosure practices in children's advertising are substantially different from those in prime-time advertising. Our expectation was that if the child audience is truly treated differently in the advertising marketplace, the differences would be apparent in the incidence rate and executional features of the disclosures in ads targeted to the two groups. At the extreme, we might expect that none of our sample of children's ads would contain fine-print disclosures because of the inherent difficulties children (especially preschool-age children) would have in seeing, reading, and interpreting the meaning of the disclosures. Such an expectation acknowledges the inherent differences between children and adults in terms of their processing abilities and other cognitive skills, and the necessity for advertisers and others (either voluntarily or in adherence to established regulations) to acknowledge the needs and inadequacies of the youthful viewer. However, even a cursory examination of advertising suggests that some children's advertising contains fine-print disclosures. The question addressed in our study, therefore, was: To what extent is that advertising practice being used in children's advertising in comparison with adult-oriented prime-time advertising, and how is it being used differently in the two groups?

Consistent with our expectations, we found the fine-print disclosures in children's ads (1) were less prevalent, (2) contained fewer words, (3) were on the screen longer, (4) were more often repeated by an off-screen announcer, and (5) were less restrictive than those in prime-time ads. However, contrary to expectations, we found the fine-print disclosures in children's ads to be no more informatively oriented than disclosures in prime-time ads, and no more likely to be near the beginning of the ad or in the top part of the television screen (where they might facilitate viewer attention and comprehension) than prime-time ad disclosures.

The conclusions from the data may lead us to believe that advertisers are generally responding to children's needs, but the data must be judged in a relative sense. "Statistically" significant differences between the two samples on many of the variables should not be interpreted to mean that children will be able to process the information contained in fine-print disclosures; rather, an alternative interpretation of the results might suggest just the opposite. For example, though we found that disclosures in children's ads generally contained fewer words presented for a longer time, the average fine-print disclosure in the children's sample would require a 160-word-per-minute reading speed—which most young children do not have, even under ideal reading conditions (Dechant and Smith 1977). Such a finding suggests that we look beyond the "statistically" significant to examine the "meaningful" differences between the two samples. For example, more than half (over 62%) of all children's ads in our sample contained a written disclosure appearing in fine print, with 18% of those disclosures classified as "restrictive" (i.e., limiting the primary selling point). In addition, though off-screen announcements reinforcing the contents of the fine-print disclosures were more prevalent in the children's ads than in the prime-time ads, nearly three-fourths of all children's ads with disclosures *did not* contain such an announcement—a rather disappointing finding, considering the television networks' and self-regulatory agencies' encouragement to the contrary.

Just as important is the fact that all of the disclosures examined in our study were *fine-print* disclosures. By definition the messages had print size that in most cases was very small, thereby calling into question the likelihood that young children would even see the disclosures, let alone be able to understand their content. That point is crucial when we consider the potential relevance of the message contained in the disclosure. Whether advisory, informational, or restrictive, a disclosure (of any size) presumably is placed in an ad to aid a young viewer's interpretation and understanding of an advertiser's selling point. Without an opportunity to attend to and comprehend the disclosure statements (because of the size or duration of the disclosure, or the inherent processing limitations of young viewers), children are not given full information about the manufactured good's or service's characteristics. Hence, children's impressions of the advertised item are likely to be somewhat different from reality. Whenever the viewer's interpretation of reality differs from actual product performance because of his/her inability to obtain the clarifying information, concerns about deception arise (Richards 1990).

Two competing conclusions can be drawn from our study. One is that, in the use of fine-print disclosures, advertisers treat children differently than they treat adults. The statistically significant differences in many of our comparisons between children's advertising practices and prime-time advertising practices bear that out. However, an alternative conclusion is that advertisers have not been as sensitive to the needs of young viewers as they should (or could) be. One could argue that, if advertisers were truly interested in giving children information in ads, they would eschew the use of fine-print disclosures and instead use an alternative means of providing the needed information.

In either case, our findings suggest that fine-print disclosure practices in television ads may need to be reconsidered by advertisers, advertising agencies, media, and public policy administrators. Coupled with our 1997 survey results indicating that advertisers do not assume the average viewer reads or can read fine-print disclosures and children should not be the targets of fine-print disclosure advertising, the findings reported here show that a call for action is warranted.

One public policy response to our findings would be a total ban on the use of fine print in children's advertising. Such a regulation, though extreme (but apparently consistent with the opinions of a majority of advertising practitioners and regulators), would not only require advertisers and their agencies to develop alternative information disclosure techniques/strategies, but also necessitate public policy statements/ guidelines recommending a potentially useful alternative strategy that could be employed by advertisers. Implementation and enforcement of such a policy, though not impossible, may be difficult. More important, it is unclear whether such a policy would satisfy its ultimate objective— to enhance the information-providing function of advertising to young children.

Some observers might argue that stronger adherence to current policy guidelines is all that is needed. The FTC's "Clear and Conspicuous" Standard, the broadcasting standards of the major networks, and self-regulatory guidelines (e.g., the Council of Better Business Bureaus' Self-Regulatory Guidelines for Children's Advertising) all provide directives for effective communication with children. However, our findings suggest that advertisers are not strictly adhering to those general rules and regulations (or being monitored and held accountable by regulatory and self-regulatory agencies and media groups). Advertisers may be adhering to the letter of the law in some cases, but not producing ads consistent with the law's intent. Closer scrutiny of enforcement policies and the ad review process is warranted, and a better understanding of the impetus behind advertisers' and agencies' adherence (or nonadherence) to disclosure practices—especially as they pertain to children's advertising—is needed.

An additional remedy may be the creation of new regulations specifically designed to address concerns about children's in-ad disclosure. In our opinion, current guidelines for in-ad disclosures (e.g., the FTC's "Clear and Conspicuous" Standard) could be modified and applied to children's disclosure issues. The new guidelines/

recommendations would address children's advertising issues, but would be much more specific in their discussion of application and enforcement. Replacing the vague terminology of current guidelines with specific, objectively verifiable measures and terminology would be a noticeable improvement. We envision the disclosure guidelines as including, but not being limited to, type size, format, placement, duration, and language used.

The positive outcome of the recommendations (in addition to a better-informed consumer) might be a consumer less cynical and distrustful of advertising and business in general. In his commentary on fine-print disclosures, Best (1989) suggested that, if left unchecked, advertisers' use of such strategies may undermine consumers' notions about the legal standards for advertising and sales transactions, and ultimately may negatively affect their beliefs about and interactions with companies and their agents. If children come to believe that the "truth" is in the unreadable fine print, the number of future adults with jaundiced views about advertising is likely to increase, which can only be detrimental to the advertising industry in the long run. Our results indicate a need to examine critically the future use of in-ad disclosures in children's television advertising and to re-examine the mechanisms currently used to address the use (or misuse) of that advertising practice.

Limitations and Extensions

We examined fine-print disclosures in children's and prime-time television advertising. Other disclosures (e.g., disclosures appearing in larger print or audio-only disclosures) were not examined. Future research on advertising disclosure practices—especially those used in children's advertising—should consider the other disclosure types and broaden the sampling frame to include ads appearing in other time periods and on other networks and cable stations. An investigation of disclosures in other media (e.g., magazines) may also be worthwhile. Finally, as our data were collected in the early part of this decade, research is needed to monitor developing trends in fine-print practices, especially given the current regulatory environment as it pertains to children's advertising/marketing issues.

We acknowledge that content analysis techniques preclude direct conclusions about the effects and effectiveness of various advertising phenomena. Our review of the literature uncovered a few empirical studies that have examined the processing tendencies and outcomes of children viewing ads with or without disclosures, but more empirical work remains to be done. Future research should test various ad disclosure formats (types, duration, etc.) on children of different ages and cognitive abilities. Results of such studies may prove useful to public policy makers and media personnel who are entrusted with developing, monitoring, and enforcing advertising guidelines designed to encourage a more informative and less deceptive advertising environment.

Appendix A

Federal Trade Commission's "Clear and Conspicuous" Standard

- The disclosure should be presented simultaneously in both the audio and video portions of the television advertisement.

- The video portion of the disclosure must contain letters of sufficient size so that it can be easily seen and read on all television sets, regardless of picture tube size.

- The video portion of the disclosure should contain letters of a color or shade that readily contrast with the background, and the background should consist of only one color or shade.

- No other sounds, including music, should be presented during the audio portion of the disclosure.

- The video portion of the disclosure should appear on the screen for a sufficient duration to enable it to be completely read by the viewer.

- The audio and video portions of the disclosure should immediately follow the specific sales representations to which they relate and should occur each time the representation is presented during the advertisement. In cases where a disclosure is required, but is not linked to a specific representation, it should appear in immediate conjunction with the major sales theme of the advertisement.

SOURCE: *Trade Regulation Reporter* (1971, 12, 166).

Appendix B
Fine-Print Disclosure Types

- *General Advisory:* Recommendation or other guidance offered by the advertiser suggesting some general action be taken by the viewer.

  Examples: "Part of a nutritious breakfast"
  "Caution. May contain small parts"

- *Specific Advisory:* Detailed recommendations or other guidance offered by the advertiser suggesting some specific action be taken and the necessary information to carry out this action.

  Examples: "Call 1-800-xxx-xxxx for more information"
  "See package for details"

- *Restrictive:* Notations to inform consumers that limitations exist with regard to the offers, claims, or inferences made in the advertisement.

  Examples: "Some restrictions may apply"
  "Batteries not included"

- *Informational:* Statements which augment or clarify without delimiting offers, claims, or inferences offered in the advertisement.

  Examples: "Each sold separately"
  "No purchase necessary"

- *Corporate:* Identification of corporate names, brand names, and trademarks (including those of competitors).

  Examples: "Nabisco Brands"
  "© 1990 Mattel"

- *Citation:* Annotations of sources of information presented in ad.

  Example: "January 1996 Nielsen Ratings"

References

ABC (1992), *Children's Advertising,* ABC Department of Broadcast Standards and Practices (March), 1-7.

Advertising Age (1997), "1997-98 Broadcast TV Ad Rates," table (September 15), 18.

Atkin, Charles (1975), "The Effects of Television Advertising on Children: First Year Experimental Evidence," Lansing: Department of Communications, Michigan State University.

———— and Gary Heald (1977), "The Content of Children's Toy and Food Commercials," *Journal of Communication*, 27 (Winter), 107-114.

Barcus, F. Earle (1975), *Weekend Commercial Children's Television*, Newton, MA: Action for Children's Television.

———— (1977), *Children's Television: An Analysis of Programming and Advertising*, New York: Praeger Publishers.

Best, Arthur (1989), "The Talismanic Use of Incomprehensible Writings: An Empirical and Legal Study of Words Displayed in TV Advertisements," *St. Louis University Law Journal*, 33 (Winter), 285-329.

CBS (undated), *CBS Television Network Advertising Guidelines*, New York: CBS Department of Broadcast Standards and Practices.

Children's Advertising Review Unit (1983), "Self-Regulatory Guidelines for Children's Advertising," New York: Council of Better Business Bureaus, Inc.

Dechant, Emerald V. and Henry P. Smith (1977), *Psychology in Teaching Reading*, Englewood Cliffs, NJ: Prentice Hall.

Flotron, John (1995), "The Large Print Giveth, But the Small Print Taketh Away!" *St. Louis Journalism Review*, 24 (April), 12.

Foxman, Ellen R., Darrel D. Muehling, and Patrick A. Moore (1988), "Disclaimer Footnotes in Ads: Discrepancies Between Purpose and Performance," *Journal of Public Policy & Marketing*, 7, 127-137.

Harris, Albert J. and Edward R. Sipay (1990), *How To Increase Reading Ability: A Guide to Developmental and Remedial Methods*, New York: Longman.

Kail, Robert (1986), "Sources of Age Differences in Speed of Processing," *Child Development*, 57 (August), 969-987.

King, Thomas R. (1990), "In More TV Ads, Fine Print Gets Evil Eye," *Wall Street Journal* (July 12), B1, B5.

Klebba, Joanne M., Bruce L. Stern, and Douglas Tseng (1994), "Disclaimers in Children's Television Advertising Revisited: A Decade Makes a Difference," in *Proceedings of the 1994 Conference of the American Academy of Advertising*, Karen Whitehill King, ed., Athens, GA: Henry W. Grady College of Journalism and Mass Communication, University of Georgia, 50-57.

Kolbe, Richard H. and Melissa S. Burnett (1991), "Content Analysis Research: An Examination of Applications with Directive for Improving Research Reliability and Objectivity," *Journal of Consumer Research*, 18 (September), 243-250.

———— and Darrel D. Muehling (1992), "A Content Analysis of the 'Fine Print' in Television Advertising," *Journal of Current Issues and Research in Advertising*, 14 (2), 47-61.

———— and ———— (1995), "An Investigation of the Fine Print in Children's Television Advertising," *Journal of Current Issues and Research in Advertising*, 17 (2), 77-95.

Liebert, Diane E., Joyce N. Sprafkin, Robert M. Liebert, and Eli A. Rubinstein (1977), "Effects of Television Commercial Disclaimers on the Product Expectations of Children," *Journal of Communication*, 27 (Winter), 118-124.

Muehling, Darrel D. and Richard H. Kolbe (1997), "Fine Print in Television Advertising: Views From the Top," *Journal of Advertising*, 26 (3), 1-15.

Murray, Keith B. (1995), "Early Findings of a Longitudinal Prevalence Study of In-Advertising Disclosure by Product Category in Cartoon Programming: There's Something Funny Going on in the Commercials, Too," in *Marketing and Public Policy Conference Proceedings*, Vol. 5, Pam Scholder and Patrick J. Kaufman, eds., Atlanta: Georgia State University, 108-127.

NBC (undated), *Advertising Standards,* New York: NBC Broadcast Standards and Practices Department.

Ono, Yumiko (1997), "Fine Print in Drug Ads Sparks a Debate," *Wall Street Journal* (April 1), B1, B7.

Perreault, William D., Jr. and Laurence E. Leigh (1989), "Reliability of Nominal Data Based on Qualitative Judgments," *Journal of Marketing Research,* 26 (May), 135-148.

Raju, P.S. and Subhash C. Lonial (1990), "Advertising to Children: Findings and Implications," *Current Issues & Research in Advertising,* 12 (1 & 2), 231-274.

Richards, Jef I. (1990), *Deceptive Advertising: Behavioral Study of a Legal Concept,* Madison: University of Wisconsin Press.

Rolandelli, David R., John C. Wright, Aletha C. Huston, and Darwin Eakins (1991), "Children's Auditory and Visual Processing of Narrated and Nonnarrated Television Programming," *Journal of Experimental Child Psychology,* 51 (February), 90-122.

Smith, Frank (1988), *Understanding Reading,* 4th ed., Hillsdale, NJ: Lawrence Erlbaum Associates.

Stern, Bruce L. and Robert R. Harmon (1984), "The Incidence and Characteristics of Disclaimers in Children's Television Advertising," *Journal of Advertising,* 13 (2), 12-16.

—— and Alan J. Resnik (1978), "Children's Understanding of a Televised Commercial Disclaimer," in *Research Frontiers in Marketing: Dialogues and Directions,* Subhash C. Jain, ed., Chicago: American Marketing Association, 332-336.

Stutts, Mary Ann and Garland G. Hunnicutt (1987), "Can Young Children Understand Disclaimers in Television Commercials?" *Journal of Advertising,* 16 (1), 41-46.

——, Donald Vance, and Sarah Hudelson (1981), "Program-Commercial Separators in Children's Television: Do They Help a Child Tell the Difference Between Bugs Bunny and The Quik Rabbit?" *Journal of Advertising,* 10 (2), 16-48.

Trade Regulation Reporter (1971), " 'Clear and Conspicuous' Disclosure," Chicago: Commerce Clearing House, Inc. [CCH 7569.09], 12, 166.

Van Evra, Judith (1990), *Television and Child Development,* Hillsdale, NJ: Lawrence Erlbaum Associates.

Ward, Scott, Daniel B. Wackman, and Ellen Wartella (1977), *How Children Learn to Buy,* Beverly Hills, CA: Sage.

The Beauty Myth and the Persuasiveness of Advertising

A Look at Adolescent Girls and Boys

MARY C. MARTIN
JAMES W. GENTRY
RONALD PAUL HILL

Physical attractiveness is a phenomenon unique to neither a culture nor its time in history. However, the importance of physical attractiveness is prevalent in almost every aspect of our lives, beginning in infancy. Langlois et al. (1987) found preferences for physically attractive people among infants as young as two months, who looked longer at attractive faces in contrast to an unattractive face. Dion (1973) found that preschoolers (aged 3 to 6) exhibited stereotyping based on facial attractiveness. These children showed significant preferences for attractive children as potential friends and inferred that attractive children were more likely to behave prosocially while unattractive children were more likely to display antisocial behaviors. Such beliefs can be traced back to philosophers such as Plato (see Hatfield and Sprecher 1986).

More recently, Foucault (1978) stated that in Western cultures one's body has been interpreted as a material sign of the moral character "within."

The importance consumers place on physical attractiveness results largely from cultural messages they receive from a variety of sources. For example, Thompson and Hirschman (1995, p. 150) propose that

> the social world in which each consumer is embedded operates to enforce and reinforce this system of bodily meanings and practices. The result is a form of socialization that inspires a deeply internalized duty to discipline and normalize one's body. To be thinner, more toned, less gray, and less wrinkled, and to hide a variety of imperfections are acts of self-care that serve to discipline the body that has, without conscious consent, deviated from valued cultural norms of appearance.

As Eagly et al. (1991, p. 112) wrote, "In children's television and books, the wicked witch and evil giant are ugly and the heroic prince and virtuous princess are attractive. In advertising, attractive endorsers appear in positive settings (e.g., in happy crowds, as the object of admiration) and with valued possessions (e.g., fancy cars, fashionable clothes)." A content analysis of television commercials by Downs and Harrison (1985) revealed that some form of attractiveness message was observed in 1 out of every 3.8 commercials.

Wolf (1992, p. 10) enlivened the debate over the media's role by suggesting that advertisers promote harmful standards of physical attractiveness, causing a "violent backlash against feminism that uses images of female beauty as a political weapon against women's advancement." She (1992, pp. 4-5) notes that this "beauty myth" is

> an employer saying to a woman engineer, "we can't hire you because you're so pretty you'll keep the men from doing their work," . . . a People magazine "health" feature in which a young actress says that she knows it's time to eat when she passes out on the set, . . . and a male student telling a female classmate that she got a scholarship only because of her looks.

This beauty myth, thus, is a "generalized atmosphere" in which images of beauty in advertising and mass media exercise control over women.

Despite these criticisms, advertisers continue to use these "idealized images" (Richins 1991) to promote products because, in general, practitioners and researchers tend to agree that physically attractive communicators have a positive impact on the effectiveness of an advertising message (Belch, Belch, and Villarreal 1987; Benoy 1982). However, our review of the literature will show that an unequivocal explanation as to why the physical attractiveness of models influences consumers' evaluations of ads and products is lacking.

The purpose of this chapter is to investigate the nature of the beauty myth in the domain of advertising. Specifically, the potential persuasive effects of using physically attractive models in advertising for female and male adolescents are assessed. The focus was on adolescents for two reasons. First, adolescence is a period in our lives when we strive to stabilize our conceptualization of the "self," a concept heavily affected by our self-perceptions of physical attractiveness. Thus, adolescents are likely to be more sensitive to the effects of physically attractive models in ads (Martin and Gentry 1997; Martin and Kennedy 1993). Second, adolescents appear to be more susceptible to persuasion by advertisements in general (e.g., Linn, Delucchi, and deBenedictis 1984; Moschis and Churchill 1979; Ross et al. 1984) and may also be more susceptible to persuasion by aspirational reference groups (e.g., models in ads). This chapter first reviews literature that suggests that girls, in particular, may be susceptible to advertising with physically attractive models. Then, one explanation as to why physically attractive models may be persuasive, particularly for girls, is reviewed and tested empirically.

The Beauty Myth and Persuasion

Boys face different norms for physical attractiveness and, at the same time, go through different processes during puberty than girls. According to Franzoi (1995), females tend to view their bodies critically as "object," where their physical beauty determines how they and others judge their overall value. Thus, self-perceptions of physical attractiveness are decidedly more negative among female adolescents than male adolescents (Harter 1993; Rosenberg 1986) and are more significant determinants of self-esteem for female adolescents (Harter 1993).

The desire for thinness appears to be widespread before and during puberty in females. For example, Collins (1991) developed and administered a pictorial instrument in a cross-sectional survey of body figure perceptions and preferences among children in grades one through three; bias toward thinness among females occurred across all levels of age, weight, race, and school/community setting, with 42% desiring thinner figures. For girls, this emphasis on thinness is particularly confusing, as they face weight gain in puberty.

Males, on the other hand, tend to view their bodies as "process," where power and function are more important criteria for evaluating their physical self. Consistent with this notion, Lerner, Orlos, and Knapp (1976) found that female adolescents' self-concepts derived primarily from body attractiveness while male adolescents' self-concepts were more strongly related to perceptions of physical instrumental effectiveness. Wadden et al. (1991), in a survey of high school sophomores, found that weight and figure are of primary concern to adolescent females relative to other issues, such as looks, popularity, and relationships with the opposite sex. Male adolescents, on the other hand, are not weight-preoccupied. Similarly, Franzoi and Herzog (1987) found that female college students' body esteem is largely determined by weight, while male college students' body esteem is largely determined by upper body strength.

The Beauty Myth and Girls' and Boys' Ad and Brand Attitudes

This difference in body orientation results in a more culturally salient ideal of attractiveness for females (Franzoi 1995; Rozin and Fallon 1988). The prevalence of this ideal has been demonstrated through studies showing that female adolescents are exposed to a greater number of messages and images in advertising related to physical attractiveness than male adolescents. For example, Ogletree et al. (1990) analyzed commercials from Saturday morning cartoon programming for the number of male/female main and supporting characters, sex of narrator, sex of intended consumer, and appearance enhancement of person, doll, or animal. As expected, a high percentage of the commercials was for food products (60.6%) and appealed equally to both boys and girls. Most important, the majority of commercials for appearance-enhancement products was targeted toward girls. The authors concluded by saying:

> Because of the heavy emphasis on various food products in television advertising and, for girls, an emphasis on appearance enhancement, children's commercials may be one factor contributing to less than ideal eating attitudes and habits in females. Although certainly individual and familial variables are important in explaining eating disorders, socio-cultural forces may also contribute to the dramatic male/female differences in these disorders. The present study provides supporting evidence that the media differentiates between males and females, not in the emphasis on food, but in the importance of appearance for the female; this differential emphasis may start in the childhood years and may affect females', compared to males', higher incidence of eating disorders. (Ogletree et al. 1990, p. 796)

Andersen and DiDomenico (1992) examined the 10 most commonly read magazines by young men and young women (ages 18-24) for advertisements and articles promoting weight loss or shape change.[1] They found that the women's magazines contained 10.5 times as many advertisements and articles promoting weight loss as did men's magazines. Andersen and DiDomenico (1992) reported that "this ten-fold difference in diet-promoting content is almost identical to the difference in prevalence of females versus males with eating disorders" (p. 285), and they conclude that "the comparative frequency of eating disorders in males versus females is more closely related to the differing extent of gender-related reinforcement of related dieting behavior than any known biological parameter" (p. 283). In an analysis of *Seventeen,* Guillen and Barr (1994) found that models' body shapes were less curvaceous than those in magazines for adult women, and that the hip to waist ratio decreased from 1970 to 1990. As these authors point out, this magazine is "referred to as the 'the best friend' of high school girls. With a total circulation of 1.75 million, *Seventeen* has the potential to influence a substantial proportion of the adolescent female population" (Guillen and Barr 1994, p. 465).

Boys and men, on the other hand, do not face the same types of attractiveness-related messages and probably do not have the same aspirations. Fischer and Halpenny (1993) found that the idealized images of men in advertising do, in fact, differ from those of women and that men's reactions to these images are dissimilar. For example, Thompson and Heinberg (1992) argue that men are less likely to make upward comparisons with male models, as their bodies have less socio-cultural importance than females' bodies.

Given the differences in body orientation and the pervasiveness and nature of attractiveness messages and images for females, there is a greater likelihood that females will be impacted by the feminine ideal than men will be by the masculine ideal (Franzoi 1995). In particular, females with low self-esteem and/or who have poorer body images may be especially susceptible to physically attractive models in advertising (Martin and Kennedy 1993; Stephens, Hill, and Hanson 1994). For example, Martin and Kennedy (1993) found that the tendency of female pre-adolescents and adolescents to compare themselves to models in ads is greater for those with lower self-perceptions of physical attractiveness and/or self-esteem. Stephens and colleagues (1994) proposed that women who are more dissatisfied with their bodies are also less able to resist peer pressure. Thus, they are more likely to be persuaded by physically attractive endorsers and to evaluate ads and socially conspicuous products in ads more positively than those women who have better body images. Therefore, the following hypotheses are suggested:

H1a: Adolescent girls who have poorer (better) body images will have higher (lower) attitudes toward ads and products when promotions feature physically attractive female endorsers.

H1b: Adolescent boys will not differ in these attitudes according to body image.

The Beauty Myth and Girls' and Boys' Ascription of Socially Desirable Traits to Models

Various theoretical perspectives have been proposed and/or tested in an attempt to explain the persuasiveness of physically attractive endorsers in advertisements, including social adaptation theory (Kahle and Homer 1985; Kamins 1990), attribution theory (Kamins 1990;

Miller 1970), and elaboration likelihood theory (Pallak 1983). Empirically, physical attractiveness has been found to have main effects on the persuasion process (Kahle and Homer 1985; Petroshius and Crocker 1989), to act as a mediator (Debevec, Madden, and Kernan 1986), and to interact with other variables such as the sex of respondents (Baker and Churchill 1977; Caballero and Pride 1984; Caballero and Solomon 1984; Debevec and Kernan 1984) and product type (Baker and Churchill 1977; Caballero and Solomon 1984; Kamins 1990; Parekh and Kanekar 1994). However, despite the extensive research that exists in this area, an unequivocal explanation is lacking as to why the physical attractiveness of endorsers influences consumers' ad and brand attitudes.

One possible explanation is that consumers make positive inferences about physically attractive endorsers, and this attribution of "socially desirable traits" enhances their persuasiveness (Brumbaugh 1993; Maddux and Rogers 1980). This notion is consistent with the "what is beautiful is good" stereotype (Dion 1986; Dion, Berscheid, and Walster 1972) "whereby physically attractive individuals are believed to possess a wide variety of positive personal qualities" (Eagly et al. 1991, p. 109), otherwise known as a "halo effect." These socially desirable traits may include social competence, adjustment, potency, intellectual competence, integrity, and a concern for others (Eagly et al. 1991). Once again, the empirical results of these investigations are inconsistent. Brumbaugh (1993) found that personality inferences concerning a physically attractive endorser positively affected consumers' attitudes toward the product. For example, models who were perceived as capable and poised received positive evaluations of their clothing from consumers. Maddux and Rogers (1980), on the other hand, found that consumers who assigned socially desirable traits to physically attractive communicators did not necessarily agree with their message.

In order to make sense of such conflicting findings, Stephens et al. (1994) proposed that the assignment of socially desirable traits to endorsers in ads may be more common in women who are dissatisfied with their bodies than women who are satisfied with their bodies. For example, Mintz and Betz (1988) found that those female college students more likely to be dissatisfied with their bodies tended to agree with "what is beautiful is good" stereotypes (e.g., "attractive people are more poised and outgoing"). On the other hand, researchers found that people with moderately high or high self-perceptions of physical attractiveness hold more stereotyped views based on attractiveness than those with moderately low or low self-perceptions (Downs and Abshier 1982; Downs and Currie 1983; Downs et al. 1982).

Female adolescents, in particular, may be more likely to ascribe socially desirable traits to physically attractive models in ads because they serve as an aspirational reference group (Richins 1991). For example, Martin and Kennedy (1994) found that female preadolescents and adolescents have aspirations to be models. Using a projective test, one fourth grader wrote, "Susie is daydreaming about what she would be like if she was a model. Susie is reading the magazine to get some beauty tips. Susie is thinking she could be a model some day. Susie will become very beautiful and become a model." Other research suggests that aspirations to be models do not exist for males (Fischer and Halpenny 1993). As Wolf (1992, p. 58) suggests, "men are exposed to male fashion models but do not see them as role models."

Therefore, one explanation is that physically attractive models enhance the effectiveness of an ad since adolescents attribute socially desirable traits to them. However, girls are much more likely to be affected given the pervasiveness of attractiveness-related images and messages targeted to them and the more culturally salient ideal of attractiveness for females. Consistent with the suggestion by Stephens et al. (1994), it is proposed that girls dissatisfied with their bodies will attribute socially desirable traits to models in ads. Specifically, the following hypotheses are suggested:

H2a: Girls with poorer (better) body images will be more (less) likely to ascribe socially desirable traits to physically attractive female endorsers.

H2b: Girls will be more likely to ascribe socially desirable traits to physically attractive same-sex endorsers than boys.

Methodology

Experimental Design

To test the proposed effects, the experiment was a 2 (ad exposure) × 2 (level of perceived body image) × 2 (sex) between-subjects mixed model design. The first factor represents the types of ads to which a subject was exposed; a subject was exposed either to a series of ads with same-sex models or to a series of ads with no models. The second factor is categorical, where subjects were divided into two groups (high and low) with respect to body image. The final factor is categorical, representing the sex of the subject.

In a study to "learn about how people respond to advertising," subjects were exposed to a series of three ads for socially conspicuous products. Following exposure to an ad, subjects gave ratings of their attitudes toward the ad, attitudes toward the advertised product, and their beliefs regarding same-sex models socially desirable traits.

Subjects

Female (n = 226) and male (n = 190) adolescents in grades five (n = 143), seven (n = 157), and nine (n = 116) from a public school system in the Midwest participated in the study (total sample size of 416). The public school system is located in a county in which 98% of the population is white and the median family income is $31,144. As an incentive, the subjects who participated were entered in a drawing for two prizes of $50.00 each. In addition, a $500.00 donation was made to the public school system. Parental permission was obtained for all subjects.

Experimental Procedures

Classroom teachers administered the questionnaires at the schools during an hour of class time. They were required to complete the following tasks:

✧ Pass out the survey instruments to all students. Each packet contained two separate booklets. Booklet #1 consisted of the measure for body image. The teachers were instructed to read Booklet #1 for the students as they completed the scales.

✧ Collect the completed materials of Booklet #1.

✧ Instruct students to read and follow the instructions contained in Booklet #2, stressing that they should not interact with other students during the completion of this task. This booklet included the ads and appropriate measurement instruments for socially desirable traits and ad and brand attitudes.

The assignment to treatments was randomized by giving each classroom a random assortment of the two types of questionnaires.

Advertising Stimuli

Four sets of three ads were chosen from magazines that contained a large number of promotions for socially conspicuous products: *Teen, Seventeen, YM, Sassy, GQ,* and *Esquire.* For girls, ads for skin cleanser, makeup, and jeans were included. For boys, ads for sunglasses, jeans, and exercise machines were included. Respondents in the model conditions were shown three ads that included same-sex models. The control group saw ads for the same products, but no models were included. Full-color copies were made of the ads and inserted into the survey booklets.

For subjects who saw ads with models, their perceptions of the models' attractiveness were measured to ensure that they perceived them as attractive. Three 7-point scales from "very unattractive, ugly" to "very attractive, beautiful," from "very fit, in shape" to "very unfit, out of shape," and from "very thin" to "very fat" were used. While the boys' ratings were lower than the girls' ratings, results demonstrated that both female and male subjects did perceive the models to be attractive as the means for each model fell above 11, the midpoint on the scale. For girls, the models' mean ratings were 17.8, 16.7, and 17.3, respectively. For boys, the models' mean ratings were 13.6, 13.7, and 15.4, respectively.

Independent and Dependent Variables

Body Image

Three items measured body image. Prior to exposure to a set of ads, subjects were asked to rate themselves in relation to all girls (boys) they know on seven-point scales from "very unattractive, ugly" to "very attractive, beautiful," from "very fit, in shape" to "very unfit, out of shape," and from "very thin" to "very fat" (adapted from Grubb, Sellers, and Waligroski 1993). Responses on these items were summed to form a score on the scale. Coefficient alpha was .77. A subject was then assigned to either the high or low category after a median split of the measure of perceived body image was conducted.

Attitude Toward the Ad

A five-item instrument was used to assess attitude toward the ad. For each ad, seven-point scales from "ordinary" to "different," "happy" to "sad," "boring" to "interesting," "convincing" to "unconvincing," and "good" to "bad" were used (adapted from Baker and Churchill 1977). These items were summed to form a score for each ad. The scores for each ad were then summed to form an overall attitude toward the ad score. Coefficient alphas were .70, .69, and .74, respectively, for the three ads.

Attitude Toward the Product

A three-item instrument was used to assess attitude toward the advertised product. For each ad, subjects responded to the statement, "My overall attitude toward using the product I just saw in the ad is," on seven-point scales from "favorable" to "unfavorable," "bad" to "good," and "wise" to "foolish" (MacKenzie, Lutz, and Belch 1986). These items were summed to form a score for each ad, and the scores were then summed to form an overall attitude toward the product score. Coefficient alphas were .88, .90, and .90, respectively, for the three products.

Socially Desirable Traits

For those subjects who saw ads with models, five items were used to assess the subjects' ascription of socially desirable traits to the models in the ads. For each ad, subjects were asked to rate the model on a seven-point scale from "warm, caring" to "cold, insensitive," "sad" to "happy," "friendly/nice" to "unfriendly/mean, rude," "bashful/shy" to "outgoing," and "smart" to "dumb." Responses to the items for each model were summed to form an overall score for each trait.

The five items were based on previous work that has assessed the "what is beautiful is good" stereotype (Brumbaugh 1993; Debevec and Kernan 1984; Downs and Currie 1983; Downs et al. 1982; Maddux and Rogers 1980). Consistent with Eagly et al. (1991), the items correspond to different categories of traits: "warm, caring" indicates concern for others; "happy" indicates adjustment; "smart" indicates intellectual competence; and, "friendly/nice" and "outgoing" indicate social competence.

Results

Analyses of variance were used to test the hypotheses. In the analyses, the regression approach to partitioning variance was employed to control for nonorthogonality due to unequal cell sizes (Keppel 1991). Given that past research has found differences in response to gendered ads in this age range (Martin and Gentry 1997), grade was included as an independent variable in the analyses; however, its inclusion did not explain significantly more variance.

To test Hypotheses 1a and 1b, a three-way analysis of variance was conducted for each dependent variable. Support for hypotheses would be demonstrated by a significant three-way interaction as well as two-way analyses conducted for each sex. Finally, significant interactions would result in additional testing for simple main effects (Keppel 1991).

Effects of Ad Exposure on
Attitude Toward the Ads

The three-way interaction was significant when attitude toward the ads served as the dependent variable ($F_{1,378} = 12.4$, $p < .01$). Two-way analyses of variance were then conducted for each sex. For boys, neither the type of ad exposure (model or not) nor their level of body image affected attitude toward the ads. For girls, the ad exposure by level of body image interaction was significant ($F_{1, 218} = 12.3$, $p < .01$). Subsequent simple main effects tests indicated significant ad exposure effects within high body image ($F_{1, 218} = 5.7$, $p < .05$), ad exposure effects within low body image ($F_{1, 218} = 6.6$, $p < .05$), and no-model exposure effects between high and low body image ($F_{1, 218} = 15.1$, $p < .01$).

Those girls with poorer body images liked ads with models significantly more (mean of 68.0 vs. mean of 62.2), while those with better body images liked ads with models less (mean of 65.7 vs. mean of 71.9). The latter difference rules out the alternative explanation that the mere presence of a model makes an ad aesthetically more appealing and enhances attitudes toward ads. Thus, Hypothesis 1a was supported, since ads with physically attractive female models have more effect on girls with poorer body images than they do on girls with better body images. Hypothesis 1b was also supported: Exposure to physically attractive male models had no effect on boys' attitude toward the ads. The results of the analysis of variance are presented in Table 8.1.

Effects of Ad Exposure on Attitude Toward the Products

The three-way interaction was significant when attitude toward the products served as the dependent variable ($F_{1, 344} = 7.5$, $p < .01$). Two-way analyses of variance were then conducted for each sex. For females, the ad exposure by level of body image was significant ($F_{1, 199} = 4.6$, $p < .05$). Subsequent simple main effects tests indicated significant ad exposure within low body image ($F_{1, 199} = 4.0$, $p < .05$) and level of body image within no-model exposure ($F_{1, 199} = 10.8$, $p < .01$). For males, the ad exposure by level of body image was not significant ($F_{1, 145} = 3.1$, $p > .05$).

Consistent with the results in the previous subsection, girls with poorer body images liked products promoted using models significantly more (mean of 42.0 vs. 37.7), while those with better body images liked products promoted using models less (means of 42.8 vs. 45.1). Thus, Hypothesis 1a was supported. Hypothesis 1b was also supported, as exposure to male endorsers had no effect on boys' liking of the products between body image categories. It is interesting to note that the pattern

TABLE 8.1   Effects of Physically Attractive Same-Sex Endorsers on Females' and Males' Attitude Toward the Ad[a]

	Body Image		
	Low	High	Treatment Means
Girls			66.9
Ads with models (n = 119)	68.0 (11.4)*	65.7 (12.4)*	
Ads without models (n = 103)	62.2 (12.3)**	71.9 (14.3)	
Boys			59.9
Ads with models (n = 88)	57.8 (12.6)	64.6 (13.8)	
Ads without models (n = 76)	58.2 (11.3)	58.4 (13.7)	
Treatment means	62.3	65.5	

a. Standard deviations are reported in parentheses.
* Significantly different from girls who saw ads without models (with same level of body image) at $p <$ .05.
** Significantly different from girls with high body image (exposed to the same type of ad) at $p <$ .05.

of results for boys was just the opposite of the one for girls. Though not significant, the ads without male endorsers affected all boys similarly in terms of liking the product (means = 37.1 and 36.7, respectively), but the ads with male endorsers generated more favorable product attitudes among boys with better body images (mean = 33.0 vs. mean of 39.1 for those with poorer body images). The results of the analysis of variance are presented in Table 8.2.

Ascription of Socially Desirable Traits to Ad Endorsers

To test Hypotheses 2a and 2b, a two-way analysis of variance (level of body image by sex) was conducted for each of the five socially desirable traits, with only subjects who saw ads with models used in the analyses. For Hypothesis 2a, support would be demonstrated by a significant interaction and subsequent significant differences between levels of body image of girls. For Hypothesis 2b, support would be demonstrated by a significant main effect for sex. A significant main effect would be interpreted following a significant interaction only if that interaction was determined to be ordinal (Keppel 1991).

TABLE 8.2 Effects of Physically Attractive Same-Sex Endorsers on Females' and Males' Attitude Toward the Product[a]

| | Body Image | | |
	Low	High	Treatment Means
Girls			41.8
Ads with models (n = 107)	42.0 (10.8)*	42.8 (10.6)	
Ads without models (n = 96)	37.7 (11.4)**	45.1 (11.0)	
Boys			36.4
Ads with models (n = 83)	33.0 (11.7)	39.1 (10.6)	
Ads without models (n = 66)	37.1 (8.9)	36.7 (13.0)	
Treatment means	37.9	41.2	

a. Standard deviations are reported in parentheses.
* Significantly different from girls who saw ads without models (with same level of body image) at $p < .05$.
** Significantly different from girls with high body image (exposed to the same type of ad) at $p < .05$.

When the five traits were analyzed separately (see Table 8.3), none of the interaction terms was significant, indicating that Hypothesis 2a was not supported. In all five cases, sex was significant, as girls rated models more positively with respect to the socially desirable traits ($p < .01$, except for "outgoing," where $p < .05$). Thus, Hypothesis 2b was supported; girls rated models as warmer, happier, friendlier, more outgoing, and smarter than boys did. In addition, for all five traits, both boys and girls with better body images rated the models more favorably, and significantly ($p < .05$) for "warm, caring," "friendly/nice," and "outgoing."

Discussion

The results of this study suggest that exposure to ads for socially conspicuous products featuring physically attractive female endorsers may raise girls' with poorer body images attitudes toward ads and brands when compared to girls with better body images. Boys' attitudes, however, may not be affected in this way. At the same time, girls with

TABLE 8.3   Females' and Males' Ascription of Socially Desirable Traits to Same-Sex Endorsers[a]

Socially Desirable Trait	Body Image		Treatment Means
	Low	*High*	
Warm, caring[b]			
Girls (n = 118)	15.8 (3.4)	16.4 (3.7)	16.1*
Boys (n = 90)	10.5 (4.0)	12.0 (3.5)	11.3
Treatment means	13.6**	14.9	
Happy[c]			
Girls (n = 118)	18.1 (2.6)	18.4 (2.3)	18.3*
Boys (n = 89)	13.1 (4.4)	14.6 (4.1)	13.9
Treatment means	16.0	16.8	
Friendly, nice[d]			
Girls (n = 119)	16.5 (3.2)	17.3 (3.1)	16.9*
Boys (n = 91)	11.8 (4.5)	13.5 (4.3)	12.7
Treatment means	14.5**	15.6	
Outgoing[e]			
Girls (n = 118)	15.7 (4.2)	16.3 (3.7)	16.0*
Boys (n = 91)	13.9 (4.5)	15.6 (4.0)	14.8
Treatment means	14.9**	16.0	
Smart[f]			
Girls (n = 119)	16.3 (3.4)	16.3 (3.5)	16.3*
Boys (n = 90)	11.3 (3.7)	12.6 (4.5)	11.9
Treatment means	14.1	14.7	

a. Standard deviations are reported in parentheses.
* Significantly different from boys at $p < .05$.
** Significantly different from those with high body image at $p < .05$.
b. Main effect for sex significant: $F_{1,204} = 92.4, p < .01$. Main effect for level of body image significant: $F_{1,204} = 4.2, p < .05$. Interaction not significant: $F_{1,204} = 1.0, p > .05$.
c. Main effect for sex significant: $F_{1,203} = 89.2, p < .01$. Main effect for level of body image not significant: $F_{1,203} = 3.4, p > .05$. Interaction not significant: $F_{1,203} = 1.4, p > .05$.
d. Main effect for sex significant: $F_{1,206} = 65.4, p < .01$. Main effect for level of body image significant: $F_{1,206} = 5.8, p < .05$. Interaction not significant: $F_{1,206} = 1.0, p > .05$.
e. Main effect for sex significant: $F_{1,205} = 4.6, p < .05$. Main effect for level of body image significant: $F_{1,205} = 4.1, p < .05$. Interaction not significant: $F_{1,205} = 1.1, p > .05$.
f. Main effect for sex significant: $F_{1,205} = 68.4, p < .01$. Main effect for level of body image not significant: $F_{1,205} = 1.4, p > .05$. Interaction not significant: $F_{1,205} = 1.5, p > .05$.

poorer body images may not have greater tendencies to ascribe socially desirable traits to endorsers than girls with better body images. Nonetheless, while the notion of "what is beautiful is good" was not supported by the data from females alone, across-sex data reveal that girls may have a greater tendency to ascribe socially desirable traits to same-sex endorsers than boys.

It is interesting to note that the attributions of socially desirable traits to models in ads made by girls and boys with better body images occurred with respect to two of the four categories of traits: concern for others and social competence. In comparison to the categories of adjustment and intellectual competence, these categories are other-directed. That is, they represent the subjects' evaluations of how the models feel about and interact with others. In contrast, adjustment and intellectual competence are inner-directed and represent subjects' evaluations of how the models themselves feel and the models' personal abilities.

One explanation for the relationship between body image and the ascription of socially desirable traits to models is that of perceived similarity. Respondents with better body images may have seen themselves as more similar and, feeling good about themselves, assigned corresponding evaluations to the models. Those respondents with poorer body images may have perceived themselves as dissimilar to the models, whom they believed to be physically attractive.

These findings, as well as the differential responses across sexes among those with better body images, provide much "food for thought" for advertisers. Handsome models are attributed socially desirable traits by boys with better body images, but these attributions have little impact upon subsequent ad/product evaluations. Girls with better body images attribute socially desirable traits to beautiful models, but actually prefer ads and products advertised without models. On the other hand, the pattern is just the opposite for girls with poorer body images. Herein lies the danger of the "beauty myth": Girls with better body images are not particularly susceptible to the use of physically attractive models in ads; girls with poorer body images view the models similarly, but find the ads more appealing and effective in creating desires for products. Thus, it appears that ads with physically attractive female models are most effective (persuasive) in situations where they may contribute to harming a person's self-worth (girls with poor body images).

Future Research Opportunities

We interpret the results of this study to indicate that the most vulnerable young females in our society are differentially affected by the portrayal of physically attractive, same-sex endorsers in advertisements. These findings are potentially damning when one considers the conflict between social norms for young females ("thinner is better") and nature ("bigger is inevitable"). However, possible solutions to this dilemma may exist through additional research using a critical theory perspective (see Murray and Ozanne 1991; Murray, Ozanne, and Shapiro 1994).

Embedded within this framework is the ideal of the emancipation of individuals from existing cultural forces that coerce or belittle them. Ozanne and Murray (1995, p. 8) use Habermas's theory of communicative competence to ground this work within a marketing context. This theoretical domain posits an archetype of "general symmetry," which "refers to a situation in which all people have an equal opportunity to engage in discourse unconstrained by authority, tradition, or dogma." Thus, consumers may become reflexively defiant through personal contemplation, and they may choose to rebel against societal norms such as those associated with unrealistic standards for thinness.

One way to examine this possibility may involve empowering at-risk youths by providing them with a better understanding of societal norms and their potentially harmful consequences. Giroux (1992, p. 174) suggests that education is the appropriate mechanism to create this understanding so that those who are vulnerable have "the opportunity to engage in systematic analyses of the ways in which the dominant culture creates borders saturated in terror, inequality, and forced exclusions." Future research might look at ways to arm young women with the insights necessary to undermine cultural stereotypes through consumer education that demands personal reflection. As Martin and Gentry (1997) note, the timing of consumer education may be critical. In their research, they found different emics for body image to exist between fourth and sixth grade girls. For fourth graders, the ideal body image was bigger than their self-perceived image, while the opposite was true for sixth graders. Thus, Martin and Gentry (1997) found that the instillation of a downward self-enhancement motive resulted in less body satisfaction for fourth graders; apparently they still held a "bigger is better" perspective, and encouragement to denigrate the beauty of models in ads was seen as a threat to their own futures. No such effect was found for sixth grade girls.

Of course, education alone may not be enough. The advertising community needs to take responsibility for its actions beyond its ability to create exchanges. One possibility that may allow advertisers to meet the needs of their clients as well as society would be to continue to use attractive endorsers, but modify female consumers' motives for social comparisons with models in ads. Martin and Gentry (1997) found that the effects of social comparisons with physically attractive models (self-perceptions, self-esteem) are significantly better when self-improvement or self-enhancement motives are used rather than the self-evaluation motive. Regardless, the key to solving this problem is consumer recognition of its pervasive nature within our culture, including advertising messages.

Note

-----

1. Although the subjects in this study are younger than 18, we have included this information since adolescent women often read magazines targeted to young adults.

References

Andersen, Arnold E. and Lisa DiDomenico (1992), "Diet vs. Shape Content of Popular Male and Female Magazines: A Dose-Response Relationship to the Incidence of Eating Disorders?" *International Journal of Eating Disorders,* 11 (April), 283-287.

Baker, Michael J. and Gilbert A. Churchill, Jr. (1977), "The Impact of Physically Attractive Models on Advertising Evaluations," *Journal of Marketing Research,* 14 (November), 538-555.

Belch, George E., Michael A. Belch, and Angelina Villarreal (1987), "Effects of Advertising Communications: Review of Research," *Research in Marketing,* 9, 59-117.

Benoy, W. Joseph (1982), "The Credibility of Physically Attractive Communicators: A Review," *Journal of Advertising,* 11 (3), 15-24.

Brumbaugh, Anne M. (1993), "Physical Attractiveness and Personality in Advertising: More Than Just a Pretty Face?" in *Advances in Consumer Research* (Vol. 20), Leigh

McAlister and Michael L. Rothschild, eds., Provo, UT: Association for Consumer Research, 159-163.

Caballero, Majorie J. and William M. Pride (1984), "Selected Effects of Salesperson Sex and Attractiveness in Direct Mail Advertisements," *Journal of Marketing*, 48 (Winter), 94-100.

———— and Paul J. Solomon (1984), "Effects of Model Attractiveness on Sales Response," *Journal of Advertising*, 13 (1), 17-23.

Collins, M. Elizabeth (1991), "Body Figure Perceptions and Preferences Among Preadolescent Children," *International Journal of Eating Disorders*, 10 (2), 199-208.

Debevec, Kathleen and Jerome B. Kernan (1984), "More Evidence on the Effects of a Presenter's Physical Attractiveness," in *Advances in Consumer Research* (Vol. 11), Thomas C. Kinnear, ed., Provo, UT: Association for Consumer Research, 127-132.

————, Thomas J. Madden, and Jerome B. Kernan (1986), "Physical Attractiveness, Message Evaluation, and Compliance: A Structural Examination," *Psychological Reports*, 58, 503-508.

Dion, Karen K. (1973), "Young Children's Stereotyping of Facial Attractiveness," *Developmental Psychology*, 9 (2), 183-188.

———— (1986), "Stereotyping Based on Physical Attractiveness: Issues and Conceptual Perspectives," in *Physical Appearance, Stigma, and Social Behavior: The Ontario Symposium* (Vol. 3), C. Peter Herman, Mark P. Zanna, and E. Tory Higgins, eds., Hillsdale, NJ: Lawrence Erlbaum, 7-21.

————, Ellen Berscheid, and Elaine Walster (1972), "What Is Beautiful Is Good," *Journal of Personality and Social Psychology*, 24, 285-290.

Downs, A. Chris and G. R. Abshier (1982), "Conceptions of Physical Appearance Among Young Adolescents: The Interrelationships Among Self-Judged Appearance, Attractiveness Stereotyping, and Sex-Typed Characteristics," *Journal of Early Adolescence*, 2, 255-265.

———— and Marie V. Currie (1983), "Indexing Elementary School-Age Children's Views of Attractive and Unattractive People: The Attitudes Toward Physical Attractiveness Scale—Intermediate Version," *Psychological Documents*, 13, 23 (Ms. No. 2579).

———— and Sheila K. Harrison (1985), "Embarrassing Age Spots or Just Plain Ugly? Physical Attractiveness Stereotyping as an Instrument of Sexism on American Television Commercials," *Sex Roles*, 13 (1/2), 9-19.

————, Mary A. Reagan, Celia Garrett, and Pery Kolodzy (1982), "The Attitudes Toward Physical Attractiveness Scale (ATPAS): An Index of Stereotypes Based on Physical Appearance," *Catalog of Selected Documents in Psychology*, 12, 44 (Ms. No. 2502).

Eagly, Alice H., Richard D. Ashmore, Mona G. Makhijani, and Laura C. Longo (1991), "What Is Beautiful Is Good, But . . .: A Meta-Analytic Review of Research on the Physical Attractiveness Stereotype," *Psychological Bulletin*, 110 (1), 109-128.

Fischer, Eileen and Kate Halpenny (1993), "The Nature and Influence of Idealized Images of Men in Advertising," in *Gender and Consumer Behavior, Proceedings of the Second Conference*, Janeen Arnold Costa, ed., Salt Lake City, UT: University of Utah Printing Service, 196.

Foucault, Michel (1978), *The History of Sexuality: An Introduction*, Vol. 1, New York: Vintage.

Franzoi, Stephen L. (1995), "The Body-as-Object Versus The Body-as-Process: Gender Differences and Gender Considerations," *Sex Roles,* 33 (5/6), 417-437.

———— and Mary E. Herzog (1987), "Judging Physical Attractiveness: What Body Aspects Do We Use?" *Personality and Social Psychology Bulletin,* 13 (March), 19-33.

Giroux, Henry (1992), *Boarder Crossings: Cultural Workers and the Politics of Education,* New York: Routledge.

Grubb, Henry J., Marie I. Sellers, and Karen Waligroski (1993), "Factors Related to Depression and Eating Disorders: Self-Esteem, Body Image, and Attractiveness," *Psychological Reports,* 72, 1003-1010.

Guillen, Eileen O. and Susan I. Barr (1994), "Nutrition, Dieting, and Fitness Messages in a Magazine for Adolescent Women, 1970-1990," *Journal of Adolescent Health,* 15, 464-472.

Harter, Susan (1993), "Visions of Self: Beyond the Me in the Mirror," in *Developmental Perspectives on Motivation,* Nebraska Symposium on Motivation, Vol. 40, Janis E. Jacobs, ed., Lincoln: University of Nebraska Press, 99-144.

Hatfield, Elaine and Susan Sprecher (1986), *Mirror, Mirror . . . The Importance of Looks in Everyday Life,* Albany: State University of New York Press.

Kahle, Lynn R. and Pamela M. Homer (1985), "Physical Attractiveness of the Celebrity Endorser: A Social Adaptation Perspective," *Journal of Consumer Research,* 11 (March), 954-961.

Kamins, Michael A. (1990), "An Investigation Into the 'Match-Up' Hypothesis in Celebrity Advertising: When Beauty May Be Only Skin Deep," *Journal of Advertising,* 19 (1), 4-13.

Keppel, Geoffrey (1991), *Design and Analysis: A Researcher's Handbook,* 3rd ed., Englewood Cliffs, NJ: Prentice Hall.

Langlois, Judith H., Lori A. Roggman, Rita J. Casey, Jean M. Ritter, Loretta A. Rieser-Danner, and Vivian Y. Jenkins (1987), "Infant Preferences for Attractive Faces: Rudiments of a Stereotype?" *Developmental Psychology,* 23 (3), 363-369.

Lerner, Richard M., James B. Orlos, and John R. Knapp (1976), "Physical Attractiveness, Physical Effectiveness, and Self-Concept in Late Adolescents," *Adolescence,* 11 (43), 313-326.

Linn, Marcia C., Kevin L. Delucchi, and Tina deBenedictis (1984), "Adolescent Reasoning About Advertisements: Relevance of Product Claims," *Journal of Early Adolescence,* 4 (Winter), 371-385.

MacKenzie, Scott B., Richard J. Lutz, and George E. Belch (1986), "The Role of Attitude Toward the Ad as a Mediator of Advertising Effectiveness: A Test of Competing Explanations," *Journal of Marketing Research,* 23 (May), 130-143.

Maddux, James E. and Ronald W. Rogers (1980), "Effects of Source Expertness, Physical Attractiveness, and Supporting Arguments on Persuasion: A Case of Brains Over Beauty," *Journal of Personality and Social Psychology,* 39 (2), 235-244.

Martin, Mary C. and James W. Gentry (1997), "Stuck in the Model Trap: The Effects of Beautiful Models in Ads on Female Pre-Adolescents and Adolescents," *Journal of Advertising,* 26 (Summer), 19-33.

———— and Patricia F. Kennedy (1993), "Advertising and Social Comparison: Consequences for Female Pre-Adolescents and Adolescents," *Psychology and Marketing,* 10 (November/December), 513-530.

———— and ———— (1994), "Social Comparison and the Beauty of Advertising Models: The Role of Motives for Comparison," in *Advances in Consumer Research* (Vol.

21), C. T. Allen & D. Roedder John, eds., Provo, UT: Association for Consumer Research, 365-371.

Miller, Arthur G. (1970), "Role of Physical Attractiveness in Impression Formation," *Psychonomic Science,* 19 (4), 241-243.

Mintz, Laurie B. and Nancy E. Betz (1988), "Prevalence and Correlates of Eating Disordered Behaviors Among Undergraduate Women," *Journal of Counseling Psychology,* 35, 463-471.

Moschis, George P. and Gilbert A. Churchill, Jr. (1979), "An Analysis of the Adolescent Consumer," *Journal of Marketing,* 43 (Summer), 40-48.

Murray, Jeff B. and Julie L. Ozanne (1991), "The Critical Imagination: Emancipatory Interests in Consumer Research," *Journal of Consumer Research,* 18 (September), 129-144.

———, ———, and Jon M. Shapiro (1994), "Revitalizing the Critical Imagination: Unleashing the Crouched Tiger," *Journal of Consumer Research,* 21 (December), 559-656.

Ogletree, Shirley M., Sue W. Williams, Paul Raffeld, Bradley Mason, and Kris Fricke (1990), "Female Attractiveness and Eating Disorders: Do Children's Television Commercials Play a Role?" *Sex Roles,* 22 (11/12), 791-797.

Ozanne, Julie L. and Jeff B. Murray (1995), "Uniting Critical Theory and Public Policy to Create the Reflexively Defiant Consumer," *American Behavioral Scientist,* 38 (4), 516-525.

Pallak, Suzanne R. (1983), "Salience of a Communicator's Physical Attractiveness and Persuasion: A Heuristic Versus Systematic Processing Interpretation," *Social Cognition,* 2 (2), 158-170.

Parekh, Hetal and Suresh Kanekar (1994), "The Physical Attractiveness Stereotype in a Consumer-Related Situation," *The Journal of Social Psychology,* 134 (3), 297-300.

Petroshius, Susan M. and Kenneth E. Crocker (1989), "An Empirical Analysis of Spokesperson Characteristics on Advertisement and Product Evaluations," *Journal of the Academy of Marketing Science,* 17 (3), 217-225.

Richins, Marsha L. (1991), "Social Comparison and the Idealized Images of Advertising," *Journal of Consumer Research,* 18 (June), 71-83.

Rosenberg, Morris (1986), "Self-Concept From Middle Childhood Through Adolescence," in *Psychological Perspectives on the Self* (Vol. 3), J. Suls and A. G. Greenwald, eds., Hillsdale, NJ: Lawrence Erlbaum, 107-136.

Ross, Rhonda P., Toni Campbell, John C. Wright, Aletha C. Huston, Mabel L. Rice, and Peter Turk (1984), "When Celebrities Talk, Children Listen: An Experimental Analysis of Children's Responses to TV Ads With Celebrity Endorsement," *Journal of Applied Developmental Psychology,* 5, 185-202.

Rozin, P. and A. E. Fallon (1988), "Body Image, Attitudes to Weight and Misperceptions of Figure Preferences of the Opposite Sex: A Comparison of Men and Women in Two Generations," *Journal of Abnormal Psychology,* 97, 342-345.

Stephens, Debra Lynn, Ronald Paul Hill, and Cynthia Hanson (1994), "The Beauty Myth and Female Consumers: The Controversial Role of Advertising," *The Journal of Consumer Affairs,* 28 (Summer), 137-153.

Thompson, Craig J. and Elizabeth C. Hirschman (1995), "Understanding the Socialized Body: A Poststructuralist Analysis of Consumers' Self-Conceptions, Body Images, and Self-Care Practices," *Journal of Consumer Research,* 22 (September), 139-153.

Thompson, J. Kevin and Leslie J. Heinberg (1992), "Social Comparison: Gender, Target Importance Ratings, and Relation to Body Image Disturbance," *Journal of Social Behavior and Personality,* 7 (2), 335-344.

Wadden, Thomas A., Gary Brown, Gary D. Foster, and Jan R. Linowitz (1991), "Salience of Weight-Related Worries in Adolescent Males and Females," *International Journal of Eating Disorders,* 10 (4), 407-414.

Wolf, Naomi (1992), *The Beauty Myth: How Images of Beauty Are Used Against Women,* Garden City, NY: Anchor.

Selling Food to Children

Is Fun Part of a Balanced Breakfast?

BONNIE B. REECE

NORA J. RIFON

KIMBERLY RODRIGUEZ

There is considerable evidence that children ages two to 11 do not eat a well-balanced diet (Munoz et al. 1997). Moreover, there has been an increase in obesity in the United States in the past 20 years, with 12% to 22% of children six to 17 reported as being overweight (Finholm 1997). During this same period, there have been increases in the amount of nutrition information available to consumers, partly due to the revised nutrition labels required on all packaged foods. Two-thirds of parents of children 12 or younger noticed the changes in labeling information, and more than half had changed a purchase intention as a result of reading the labels ("Super Parents" 1995).

In light of this improved nutrition information environment, it is surprising that children's eating habits are inconsistent with government recommendations and that so many children are obese. A number of factors have been suggested as influencing this information-outcome gap. This study will focus on one of those factors, food advertising. A number of studies have reviewed food-oriented television commercials directed to children; however, they have focused almost exclusively on the types of foods advertised, and their samples of ads have typically been drawn only from Saturday morning. The study presented here examines the types of foods advertised to children. It also evaluates the nutrition and thematic content of the messages as well as the executional techniques used to attract and hold children's attention.

Background

Children's Eating and Television Viewing Habits

Findings of the U.S. Department of Agriculture's survey of food intakes by children indicate that only 1% of children meet guidelines set forth in the Food Guide Pyramid (Munoz et al. 1997). Although children ages two to 11 consume adequate amounts of dairy products, most consume too few fruits, vegetables, and grains. They also consume too many foods that are high in fat and sugar, which can lead to obesity. Childhood obesity is a significant risk factor for adult obesity. There is an association between obesity and cardiovascular disease, diabetes, and cancer (National Institutes for Health 1985). In addition to these long-term health consequences, obesity lowers children's self-esteem and affects their relationships with peers (Summerfield 1990). As noted above, the percentage of children considered to be obese has increased since the late 1970s (Finholm 1997). Thus it is important to investigate the factors that influence this situation.

Several contributory factors have been suggested. One, sedentary lifestyles (cuts in physical education classes or recess, time spent watching television or using computers) mean that children may burn fewer calories now than did children of earlier generations (Elmer-Dewitt 1995; Finholm 1997). Two, parents may plan well-balanced meals for their children, but they cannot control what their children actually eat, especially when children are at school or parents are at work. School lunches may be part of the problem, because many of them exceed federal guidelines for fat, saturated fat, and sodium ("Soft Drinks and School Lunchrooms" 1994). Three, some parents may not set a very good example for their children. There are indications that many people pay little attention to portion size, or they view eating reduced-fat foods as a license to eat the whole package of food (Elmer-Dewitt 1995; Fabricant 1994). Fourth, nutrition experts and parents have blamed television advertising for children's preferences for foods that are not wholesome (Brown 1977; Cotugna 1988; Grossbart and Crosby 1984; Gussow 1972; Kotz and Story 1994).

The average amount of TV viewing by children and adolescents has consistently been estimated at two to four hours per day for about 20 years (Sylvester, Achterberg, and Williams 1995). More recently, Webster (1997) reported that children continue to watch TV about 20 hours per week. The average child spends as much or more time watching TV during a year as he or she spends in the classroom. Rates of obesity are higher for children who watch television frequently, in part because they expend few calories and often consume high-calorie snacks while watching (Summerfield 1990). This implies that the average obese child watches more than 20 hours of TV per week. Theories and empirical studies suggest the importance of information content and executional elements of food advertising in determining its potential impact on children's preferences and behaviors.

Theories of Influence

Much of the early work on children and television advertising was based on Piaget's theory of cognitive development, which suggests that there will be age-related differences in children's ability to attend to, process, and remember things (Flavell 1977; Ginsberg and Opper 1979). These differences result from qualitatively different methods of thinking by children of different ages. Younger children have more limited communication abilities than older children, and they tend to focus on a single, perceptually salient feature of an object or event. As children get older, they decentrate their perceptions, understand concepts of class inclusion (e.g., product categories), and use various quantitative skills.

An alternative theoretical approach, social learning theory, has also been applied to studies dealing with consumer socialization of children. Social learning theory, sometimes referred to as observational learning, focuses on the processes involved in learning (Bandura 1977). Characteristics of the model, the observer, and the behavior itself determine the amount of attention given to a modeled behavior. A child's verbal abilities and his or her familiarity with rehearsal strategies facilitates retention, which is the symbolic coding and subsequent storage of the modeled behavior. The physical capabilities of the observer and the availability of component skills needed to initiate an overt performance influence motoric reproduction. External reinforcement, vicarious reinforcement, or self-reinforcement can provide motivation, the incentive to perform the behavior.

Empirical Studies of the Impact of Food Ads on Children's Behavior

A number of studies have linked children's exposure to certain kinds of food ads with their food preferences. Galst and White (1976) found a positive relationship between a child's attention to commercials in an experimental setting and the number of purchase influence attempts (PIAs) the child made on a later trip to a supermarket. Television exposure at home was also correlated with PIAs. The single most frequently requested items were cereals, 8% of total PIAs. If cookies, candy, gum, and snacks were combined, however, this category would have the most PIAs (22%). Many parents have said that their children request snack foods that are heavily advertised on TV (Grossbart and Crosby 1984).

Atkin (1976) found that exposure to advertising facilitated responses by young people to advertised cereals. Goldberg, Gorn, and Gibson (1978) found that children's snack preferences were influenced by the types of foods they saw advertised. Children who saw commercials for sugared snacks and cereals were significantly more likely to say they preferred highly sugared products than children who saw public service announcements for wholesome foods or children in a control group. Those who saw a pro-nutrition TV program chose fewer sugared snacks than the control group. Gorn and Goldberg (1982) exposed children at a summer camp to commercials for either candy, fruit, or pro-nutrition messages. Those who saw candy commercials were less likely to choose fruit or orange juice as snacks than children in the other conditions.

Scammon and Christopher (1981) reviewed a number of experimental studies dealing with the impact of televised food-oriented messages on children. Overall they found that exposure to these messages affected behavior. Pro-nutrition messages increased children's knowledge of desirable health behaviors, while exposure to ads for sugared products increased children's preference for sugared foods and led to greater consumption of sugared products. More recently, Signorielli and Lears (1992), in a survey of fourth and fifth graders, found a strong positive relationship between TV viewing and poor eating habits, even when several sociodemographic variables were held constant. They also found a positive relationship between TV viewing and unhealthy conceptions of food and proper nutrition.

Scammon and Christopher (1981) suggest that young children (less than age 6 or 7) are more likely to learn from an ad's concrete images than from its conceptual verbalizations. They also note that the structure of TV commercials (simple, attention getting, and repetitious) seems to match the cognitive abilities of young children. Other research suggests that even young children understand what advertisers want them to do (Wackman, Ward, and Wartella 1979).

Children appear to learn from and respond to television advertising. They develop beliefs consistent with the content of TV advertising and act consistently with those beliefs. There is some evidence that the strength of a child's commitment to the behavior is a function of his or her attention to the ad. Hence, the content of food ads and the executional elements associated with that content are salient to children's development of a preference for foods and their actual eating habits.

Previous Content Analyses

Several previous studies conducted by nutrition experts have described the types of products advertised on programming directed to children. Gussow's (1972) study evaluated the ads in 29 hours of children's programming over a whole week, while the others focused only on Saturday morning programs (Brown 1977; Cotugna 1988; Kotz and Story 1994). Food-oriented advertising, including vitamins and "drive-in" restaurants, accounted for 54% to 82% of all advertising in the earlier studies.

The specific results vary a bit across the four studies, but in general the most frequently advertised product was cereal, and the vast majority of these cereals were high in sugar; that is, sugar provided more than 20% of the product's total calories (Brown 1977). The second most frequently advertised products were cookies, candy, gum, and snacks, which Brown (1977) characterized as high-calorie foods of poor nutritional value. The authors of these papers criticized the foods that were advertised for their poor nutrition ratings and their emphasis on sweetness, chocolate, and fun. Details of the breakdown of product categories are presented later in this chapter for comparison with the current study.

Only one of the studies presented information about message themes and the presence of nutrition claims (Kotz and Story 1994). The most frequently used themes were taste, premium offers, and fun. The most common health or nutrition claim was "part of a complete/nutritious/balanced breakfast," found in almost all cereal commercials. Although this phrase was stated verbally in the ads, the authors characterized it as merely an implicit health or nutrition message (Kotz and Story 1994). These authors also presented limited data about the style and characters in the ads, but there was no context for this information. In addition, the nutrition environment has changed, warranting reexamination of children's food advertising.

Marketing and Regulatory Environment

The Nutrition Labeling and Education Act (1990) resulted in changes in the content and format of nutrition labels, which are now required on almost all packaged foods. Guidelines issued by the Food and Drug Administration (FDA) in 1993 standardized the meanings of certain descriptive terms used by food marketers, and the Federal Trade Commission requires food advertising using these descriptors or making health claims to conform to the same standards set by the Food and Drug Administration.

Studies show that consumers have become more aware of diet and health and that many consumers are aware of the Nutrition Facts label (Silverglade 1996). Many of those who are aware of the label have changed their buying habits. Furthermore, marketers have introduced hundreds of new products that have reduced levels of fat or are fat free. Between 1987 and 1994 there were changes in print food ads directed at adults, including an increase in the number of ads making health or nutrition claims and the provision of more explicit nutrient information (Reece, Sheffet, and Rifon 1997).

The Children's Advertising Review Unit (CARU) was established in 1974 by the National Advertising Review Council to encourage responsible children's advertising (Better Business Bureau 1997). One of the CARU guidelines deals explicitly with food. It states that food ads should encourage good nutritional practices, that ads representing mealtimes should show the product within the framework of a balanced diet, and that snacks should not be represented as a substitute for meals (Better Business Bureau 1997, "Product Presentations and Claims," item 8).

Research Questions

The background data presented above suggest two possible scenarios for what we might expect to find in recent food advertising directed to children. In one scenario, the introduction of so many new lower fat products and the changes in the content of food advertising directed to adults could be echoed by changes in food advertising addressed to children. We might expect to see a difference in the types of foods advertised or in the general themes of those ads. Even if the types of foods advertised to children have not changed, it is possible that nutrition information presented in the commercials will highlight for children the proper role for these products in a well-balanced diet. Thus we might expect to see more nutrition information in children's food ads than in Kotz and Story's (1994) study. Some of this information may be presented in response to the CARU guidelines.

On the other hand, there is secondary data showing that children's eating habits are not ideal and that rates of obesity have increased. Empirical evidence supports a theoretical link between children's television viewing and certain behavioral outcomes, including food preferences. In the second scenario, if children are eating nutritionally poor foods and television advertising contributes to this pattern, we would expect to see no change in the types of foods advertised or perhaps a change for the worse. Theory also suggests that children, especially young ones, remember and respond to only one central message of an advertisement. Given the poor eating habits of children, we might expect that nutrition is not the main theme of most food advertising, either because the products are not nutritionally sound or because advertisers believe that other themes are more effective.

These conflicting scenarios lead to the following research questions:

1. What types of foods are advertised during children's programming? Have the types of foods advertised to children changed since previous studies?
2. What types of nutrition information are presented in this advertising?
3. When nutrition information is presented, is it the main theme of the advertising or is it a secondary theme?
4. What executional techniques do advertisers use to capture children's attention and encourage them to retain the message?

Method

Sampling of Ads

The data in this study come from a census of ads taped during programs identified as being attractive to advertisers targeting children. We used two techniques to identify appropriate programming from which to draw the sample. First, we looked for times when children are overrepresented in the TV audience. Second, we looked for programs labeled for children in *TV Guide*. We taped both types of programming and included in the study all food ads appearing during this programming.

Children two to 11 represent about 15.5% of the U.S. population above the age of two. In general, children make up more than 15.5% of the audience from 7 a.m. to 1 p.m. on Saturday, from 7 a.m. to 1 p.m. on Sunday, and from 3 p.m. to 6 p.m. Monday through Friday. The Nielsen data to which we had access were not the detailed program ratings; rather they were ratings by program type and by daypart. We also found references to network and daypart ratings in a trade ad for Nickelodeon (1997). Children's ratings actually peak between 8 p.m. and 9 p.m. (EST), but children represent only 12% of the total TV audience at this time (Nielsen 1997). Advertisers are unlikely to target children specifically when they are underrepresented in the audience, and our own experiences suggest that commercials directed at children seldom appear then.

With these time periods as a starting point, we reviewed program listings in *TV Guide* to select specific networks and blocks of time for videotaping. Generally, the programs that we selected were those labeled as either "children" or "cartoon" in the *TV Guide* listings on networks with children's ratings of 1.5 or higher. Nielsen ratings sometimes justified taping programs not specifically identified as being for children, for example, syndicated programs such as situation comedy reruns that are scheduled on weekday afternoons after 5:00 p.m. In other instances we recorded programs outside the specified time blocks because they were labeled as "children" or "cartoon." We included a syndicated episode of *The Simpsons* that ran at 6:00 p.m. on weekdays because it is highly rated with children. Nickelodeon programming for children extends beyond 6:00 p.m. on weekdays, and one of its most popular shows runs at 7:30 p.m., so we recorded this network from 2:00 p.m. to 8:00 p.m.

After identifying appropriate programming, we videotaped one example of all of the time blocks and networks noted through this procedure. For example we taped one Saturday morning on ABC, one Saturday morning on CBS, one weekday afternoon on Fox, etc. The result was 43 hours of programming on tape. Early in the taping process we noticed considerable commercial repetition. Thus we opted to spread the taping over several weeks to locate a wider variety of commercials than might be seen if all of the taping had been done in a single week.

We made a log of all the commercials that were recorded. We tallied all product ads and public service announcements (PSAs), but not station or network promotional messages. From this list we identified those commercials that were food related; that is, ads for food products or PSAs that dealt with eating or nutrition. One example of each food-related commercial was then copied onto another tape to facilitate coding of more detailed information.

Coding

We developed a preliminary coding sheet and tested it on a sample of 10 commercials. As a result of this test, we added several new items as well as some additional categories of responses to existing items. For comparisons with previous studies of child-directed food commercials, we collected data on product category. We used a detailed list of product categories but collapsed these later to match the earlier studies, with two exceptions noted in the Results section below. Because contextual features of ads (attractive models in attractive settings, upbeat music, quick cuts, etc.) influence their effectiveness (Goldberg, Gorn, and Gibson 1978), we included information about some of these aspects of the ads as well. We focused on objective measures of ad characteristics rather than subjective assessments of things like attractiveness.

Social learning theory suggests that model characteristics help to attract attention. We collected data on the age groups and genders of characters in each commercial, as well as whether the characters were real or animated. Special presenters such as celebrities or ad-created central characters influence brand recall (Rossiter and Percy 1997, p. 222), so we wanted to know whether a celebrity appeared in the ad. Male voices attract attention better than female voices and are perceived as being more objective (Rossiter and Percy 1997, p. 266). Thus, we compiled information about the presence and gender of a voiceover announcer in the commercials. Background music may enhance the effectiveness of commercials, and jingles may increase brand recall (Rossiter and Percy 1997, pp. 222 and 282). Consequently, we noted whether a jingle or background music appeared in the commercial.

We were also interested in the type of behavior being modeled in the food commercials. We instructed judges to record whether characters consumed the food and, if so, when the eating incident occurred (mealtime or between meals). They also noted the setting of the ad so we could assess whether eating occurred in a typical "eating place" such as a kitchen, dining room, or restaurant or whether it occurred someplace else. We also wanted to know the major themes for each ad; judges could select up to two themes from a list. Finally, because of the special research questions of this study, we asked judges to note the type of nutrition information included, if any, as well as the format of that information (audio or video) and the length of time that the nutrition information appeared.

After a brief training session judges, who were only aware of the general purpose of the study, coded the ads. At least two judges coded each ad. When judges disagreed about how to code an item, the issue was resolved through discussion or, as a last resort, the senior author served as tie-breaker. Intercoder reliability (I_r) was assessed with Perreault and Leigh's (1989) measure. Reliability estimates ranged from .74 to .98.

There were three categories that posed particular problems for coders. The first dealt with when food was consumed ($I_r = .74$). This was not always obvious, and the disagreements usually occurred because one coder made inferences about when the food was being eaten and another circled the "can't tell" response. Another problem area was main character's age ($I_r = .75$), where coders were unable to agree on whether someone was a child or a teenager. The final coding difficulty was for ad theme ($I_r = .86$); in this case there was often agreement about one of an ad's themes but not about a second.

Results

The Sample of Food Ads

More than 900 commercials aired during the 43 hours of children's programming taped for this study, an average of 21.1 ads/hour. It appears that the number of ads/hour has risen since the previous studies,

TABLE 9.2 Types of Foods Advertised as a Percentage of Total Food-Related Ads

Product Category	1972[a] Percentage	1976[b] Percentage	1987[c] Percentage	1992[d] Percentage	1997[e] Percentage
Cereal	38.5	41.0	31.0	38.7	39.2
Candy/Cookies/Gum/ Snacks	17.0	37.0	34.0	19.2	21.4
Vitamins	15.0	0	0	0	0
Beverages	8.0	7.0	7.0	9.1	4.8
Other Breakfast Foods	7.5	3.0	4.0	3.3	4.6
Canned/Boxed Pasta	5.0	2.0	5.0	5.0	2.4
Canned Desserts/Frozen Dinners/"Drive-ins"/ Peanut Butter/Oranges	9.0	5.0	13.0	—	—
Other	—	5.0	6.0	10.0	4.3
Restaurants[f]	—	—	—	10.6	21.6
PSAs	—	—	—	1.7	1.9

a. Data from Gussow (1972); N = 319.
b. Data from Brown (1977) collected in September, 1976; N = 107.
c. Data from Cotugna (1988) collected in January, 1987; N = 160.
d. Data from Kotz and Story (1994) collected in October, 1991, January, 1992, and February, 1992; N = 574 when nutrition-oriented PSAs are included.
e. Data collected in February and March, 1997; N = 416.
f. Because of the large number of restaurant ads in the 1992 and 1997 samples, a separate category was created for these commercials. Restaurants were part of the "Canned Desserts, etc." category in the previous studies. Cotugna reported that 95% of the ads in this category in 1987 were for fast food restaurants.

The primary themes for children's food ads were fun and excitement or taste, either as single themes or in combination with another theme (see Table 9.3). Notable exceptions included seven PSAs that focused exclusively on nutrition. Their topics included the nutrition label, fruits and vegetables, a balanced breakfast, and the food pyramid. Another exception was a Kellogg's Rice Krispies commercial that focused entirely on what a balanced breakfast would look like, with the brand itself subordinated to the nutrition theme.

Executional Techniques

The prototypical ad featured real people or animals, with both males and females the same age or slightly older than the target.

TABLE 9.3   Modeled Behavior and Nutrition Information

Type of Information	Number
Food Consumed During Commercial	
Yes	71[a]
Time of Consumption	
Mealtime	17
Between meals	28
Can't tell	26
Presentation of Nutrition Information	
Yes	47
Type of Nutrition Information	
Part of a balanced breakfast	33
Nutrition label/balanced diet	8
Other	6
Type of Visual Presentation	
Illustration	39
Package	5
Words on screen	1
Primary Themes[b]	
Taste	40
Fun/excitement	37
Premium	15
Ingredients	12
Nutrition	9

a. Actual number of commercials from the unduplicated sample with this characteristic; N = 98.
b. An ad could have two primary themes, so numbers add to more than 98.

However, cartoon characters appeared, alone or with real people, in nearly half of the ads (see Table 9.4). When a single sex appeared in the ad, it was far more likely to be male than female. Likewise, voiceover announcers were almost always male. Thus it appears that characters in the commercials are indeed selected to be appealing to and effective with children.

Background music was very common, but jingles were not. Celebrities were rarely used, and they were as likely to be fictional characters such as Fred Flintstone or Timon (from *The Lion King*) as they were to

TABLE 9.4 Contextual Characteristics of Food Commercials

Characteristic	Number
Type of Performer	
Real people or animals	44[a]
Cartoon or clay people or animals	22
Real and cartoon characters	26
Anthropomorphized food	5
Gender of Performers	
Male only	38
Female only	5
Both genders	46
Age of Performers	
Children only	23
Teens only	21
Adults	17
Mixed age group	24
Type of Celebrity Performer	
Real actor or athlete	5
Fictional characters	6
Voice-over Announcer	
Male	70
Female	5
Type of Music	
Background	80
Jingle	14
Setting of Commercial	
Kitchen/dining room	7
Restaurant	4
Outdoors	29
Multiple locations	29
School/lab/factory	6
Other	13
Can't tell/no set	10

a. Actual number of commercials from the unduplicated sample with this characteristic; N = 98. Commercials coded as "Can't tell" or "Not applicable" are generally not included for a given category.

be well-known actors. A large number of commercials were set out-
doors, somewhat surprising for food products. An equally large number
of ads used multiple settings, which suggests the "quick cuts" techniques
noted earlier as being attention getting.

Discussion

Food advertising directed to children is ubiquitous. Although food ads
represent a smaller proportion of all ads on children's television than
in earlier studies, nearly half of the advertising during children's programming is food related, and this is true across all dayparts. The types
of foods advertised have changed. Vitamin pills, of course, disappeared
in the mid-1970s when manufacturers voluntarily took them off the air.
Restaurants, particularly those serving fast food known for being high
in fat, are now an important presence on children's programs. Cereals
continue to be heavily advertised.

Although most cereals advertised to children provide a brief nutrition message, we wondered just how nutritious they are. *Consumer
Reports* ("The Wizards of Oats" 1996) suggested that they are not very
nutritious, but we did our own check of the labels. We were able to find
data for 26 of the 27 cereals advertised on our tapes. As a whole, the
cereals were low in saturated fat (0.154 grams on average) and had no
cholesterol, so they could be considered heart healthy. According to
Consumer Reports, very nutritious cereals have at least five grams of
fiber and no more than three grams of fat. All but one of the cereals in
this study met the fat requirement, but only Kellogg's Frosted Mini
Wheats had enough fiber to be considered highly nutritious. In fact,
only two cereals had more than one gram of fiber, and many had none.

Previous content analyses of children's food ads noted that most of
the cereals were highly sugared; that is, sugar provided more than 20%
of total calories (Brown 1977). On average, the cereals in our study had
12.2 grams of sugar. With an average number of calories per serving of
120.8 and four calories per gram of sugar, the average cereal had 40%
of its calories coming from sugar. This is not surprising considering that
some commercials mention the chocolate taste or the marshmallow

shapes. The best cereal with respect to sugar percentage was Kellogg's Rice Krispies (3 grams, 10% of calories from sugar) and the worst was Kellogg's Smacks (formerly Sugar Smacks) at 15 grams of sugar, accounting for 60% of calories per serving.

The nutrition information presented in the ads in our study was generally that required by CARU. Almost all breakfast food commercials showed how the product fits into a complete or balanced breakfast. In a study by Stutts and Hunnicutt (1987), the majority of four- and five-year-olds gave a correct verbal response to a question about this disclaimer after a single exposure, although the percentage was lower for three-year-olds. Thus children might learn that juice, toast, and milk are part of a balanced breakfast, but the primary messages are that the foods taste chocolatey or fruity and they help you have fun. Because young children focus on a single message, the themes that fill the first 25 seconds of the ad are likely to be the ones that leave an impression.

What might children learn about nutrition based on the commercials they see? Children do have the opportunity to learn about nutrition from PSAs, and four of these ads featured celebrity spokescharacters to help get attention: Curious George read the nutrition label, and Disney's Timon and Pumbaa discussed the food pyramid. The use of associated visual cues such as a spokescharacter or a distinctive logo have been shown to improve information processing (Macklin 1996). However, these PSAs accounted for only eight of the 416 ads in our sample; with such a small share of voice, the message of the PSAs may be overwhelmed by other messages.

Most of these results were based on the analysis of 98 unduplicated ads. This is an easy way to summarize the types of themes, production characteristics, and nutrition content that advertisers use across an array of food products. However, it understates the potential impact of the advertising on children because it ignores the effects of repetition. For example, five fast food restaurants mentioned a premium in their commercials. These premium-oriented ads represent 16.8% of the 416 food commercials we recorded, including 24 repetitions for a McDonald's commercial that offered a hockey "puck cam" toy. These messages teach that an external reward should be provided for eating your food.

Overall there is a fairly large number of food ads targeted to children that contain some nutrition information, and advertisers should be commended for this. We did not, however, find the type of explicit nutrient information that has started to appear in ads targeted to adults. Moreover, the nutrition information may be overwhelmed by the even greater emphasis on other themes. Children are being taught that you eat certain foods because they taste "magically delicious" and they will help bring fun and excitement to your life, not because they fulfill your body's needs.

References

Atkin, Charles K. (1976), "Children's Social Learning From Television Advertising: Research Evidence on Observational Modeling of Product Consumption," *Advances in Consumer Research*, 3, 513-519.

Bandura, Albert (1977), *Social Learning Theory*, Englewood Cliffs, NJ: Prentice Hall, 22-29.

Better Business Bureau (1997), "The Children's Advertising Review Unit 1997 Self Regulatory Guidelines for Children's Advertising," http://www.bbb.org/advertising/caruguid.html.

Brown, Judith (1977), "Graduate Students Examine TV Ads for Food," *Journal of Nutrition Education*, 9 (3), 120-122.

Cotugna, Nancy (1988), "TV Ads on Saturday Morning Children's Programming— What's New?" *Journal of Nutrition Education*, 20 (3), 125-127.

Elmer-Dewitt, Philip (1995), "Fat Times," *Time* (January 16), 58-65.

Fabricant, Florence (1994), "Today's Foods May Be Lower in Fat, but Big Portions Still Make Big People," *New York Times* (October 19), B1 and B6.

Finholm, Valerie (1997), "Experts Worry About Overweight Kids," *Ann Arbor News* (May 7), C3.

Flavell, John H. (1977), *Cognitive Development*, Englewood Cliffs, NJ: Prentice Hall.

Galst, Joann Paley and Mary Alice White (1976), "The Unhealthy Persuader: The Reinforcing Value of Television and Children's Purchase-Influencing Attempts at the Supermarket," *Child Development*, 47, 1089-1096.

Ginsburg, Herbert and Sylvia Opper (1979), *Piaget's Theory of Intellectual Development*, 2d ed., Englewood Cliffs, NJ: Prentice Hall.

Goldberg, Marvin E., Gerald J. Gorn, and Wendy Gibson (1978), "TV Messages for Snack and Breakfast Foods: Do They Influence Children's Preferences?" *Journal of Consumer Research*, 5 (September), 73-81.

Gorn, Gerald J. and Marvin E. Goldberg (1982), "Behavioral Evidence of the Effects of Televised Food Messages on Children," *Journal of Consumer Research*, 9 (September), 200-205.

Grossbart, Sanford L. and Lawrence A. Crosby (1984), "Understanding the Bases of Parental Concern and Reaction to Children's Food Advertising," *Journal of Marketing*, 48 (3), 79-92.

Gussow, Joan (1972), "Counternutritional Messages of TV Ads Aimed at Children," *Journal of Nutrition Education,* 4 (2), 48-52.

Kotz, Krista and Mary Story (1994), "Food Advertisements During Children's Saturday Morning Television Programming: Are They Consistent With Dietary Recommendations?" *Journal of the American Dietetic Association,* 94 (11), 1296-1300.

Macklin, M. Carole (1996), "Preschoolers' Learning of Brand Names From Visual Cues," *Journal of Consumer Research,* 23 (December 1996), 251-261.

Munoz, K. A., S. M. Krebs-Smith, R. Ballard-Barbash, and G. E. Cleveland (1997), "Food Intakes of U.S. Children and Adolescents Compared With Recommendations," *Pediatrics,* 100 (3), 323-329.

National Institutes for Health (1985), *Health Implications of Obesity,* NIH Consensus Development Statement Online, February 11-13, 5 (9), 1-7.

Nielsen Media Research (1997), *NTI National Audience Demographics Report,* February 1997.

Nickelodeon (1997), "Nick > Broadcast," *Advertising Age,* 68 (No. 5, February 3), 23.

Nutrition Labeling and Education Act of 1990, P.L. 101-535, 104 Stat. 2353.

Perreault, William D., Jr. and Laurence E. Leigh (1989), "Reliability of Nominal Data Based on Qualitative Judgments," *Journal of Marketing Research,* 26 (May), 135-148.

Reece, Bonnie B., Mary Jane Sheffet, and Nora J. Rifon (1997), "The Nutrition Labeling and Education Act of 1990: Have Food Advertisements Changed Too?" presented at the 1997 Marketing and Public Policy Conference, Boston, May 15-17.

Rossiter, John R. and Larry Percy (1997), *Advertising Communications & Promotion Management,* New York: McGraw-Hill.

Scammon, Debra and Carole L. Christopher (1981), "Nutrition Education With Children via Television: A Review," *Journal of Advertising,* 10 (2), 26-36.

Signorielli, Nancy and Margaret Lears (1992), "Television and Children's Conceptions of Nutrition: Unhealthy Messages," *Health Communication,* 4 (4), 245-257.

Silverglade, Bruce A. (1996), "The Nutrition Labeling and Education Act: Progress to Date and Challenges for the Future," *Journal of Public Policy and Marketing,* 15 (1), 148-150.

"Soft Drinks and School Lunchrooms" (1994), *U.S. News & World Report* (May 9), 18.

Stutts, Mary Ann and Garland G. Hunnicutt (1987), "Can Young Children Understand Disclaimers in Television Commercials?" *Journal of Advertising,* 16 (1), 41-46.

Summerfield, Liane (1990), "Childhood Obesity," ERIC Digest, ED 328556.

"Super Parents Consider Nutritional Labeling When Buying Food," (1995), *Research Alert,* December 15, p. 5.

Sylvester, Gina Pazzaglia, Cheryl Achterberg, and Jerome Williams (1995), "Children's Television and Nutrition: Friends or Foes?" *Nutrition Today,* 30 (1), 6-15.

Wackman, Daniel B., Scott Ward, and Ellen Wartella (1979), "Comments on FTC Staff Report," in *Public Policy Issues in Marketing,* Cynthia J. Frey, Thomas C. Kinnear, and Bonnie B. Reece, eds., Ann Arbor: University of Michigan Press, 81-97.

Webster, Nancy (1997), "Winnowed Kids' TV Field Still Drawing Big Bucks," *Advertising Age,* 68 (No. 6, February 10), 28.

"The Wizards of Oats," (1996), *Consumer Reports,* 61 (10), 18-23.

PART

III

Advertising Directed to Children About
Cigarettes, Smoking, and Beer

How Do We Persuade
Children Not to Smoke?

LAURA A. PERACCHIO
DAVID LUNA

Youth tobacco consumption has been called the single most important public health issue of our era (Tuakli, Smith, and Heaton 1990). Every day in the United States, 3000 children and teenagers under the age of 18 years begin smoking (Light 1996). According to the U.S. Food and Drug Administration (FDA), at least 1000 of those children and teens will die eventually from a tobacco-related disease. Children and adolescents are the only group that continues to take up smoking in large numbers, causing the FDA to define smoking as a "pediatric disease." Nearly nine of 10 smokers begin in their childhood or teenage years (Light 1996; Tuakli, Smith, and Heaton 1990).

Given the high rate of smoking initiation among children and youth and the adverse health effects of smoking, discouraging young people

AUTHORS' NOTE: Reprinted from "The Development of an Advertising Campaign to Discourage Smoking Initiation among Children and Youth," *Journal of Advertising,* Vol. XXVII, Number 3, Fall 1998. Reprinted with permission.

The authors thank the American Cancer Society of Wisconsin for assistance with the research.

very large public high school in the Midwest. The school was chosen because its student body came from both urban and suburban areas and represented a diverse socioeconomic population that was felt to be representative of the target population. Twenty-five percent of the students at the school and of the study respondents were people of color.

Moderators. The four moderators were college students 20 to 21 years of age. They were selected to be several years older than the respondents to enhance credibility with the teen respondents (Grandstaff 1996). Two of the moderators were female and two were male. The moderators were trained extensively in techniques for moderating focus groups developed by Krueger (1988). They also received training in how to work with and elicit responses from teenagers.

Procedure. Respondents participated in the focus groups during a scheduled class period. They were asked to come to a lounge area/ classroom furnished with sofas. They were told that they would be discussing issues of interest to teens. Once in the lounge, they completed a screening questionnaire that asked about their smoking behavior. Respondents were then divided into four groups based on their gender and smoking behavior: female smokers, male smokers, female nonsmokers, and male nonsmokers. Five focus groups of each type were conducted for a total of 20 focus groups. Each focus group had an average of five to six members. Female moderators conducted groups with female respondents, and male moderators conducted groups with male respondents. Moderators remained with the same group type (e.g., female smokers) for the entire study to ensure internal consistency.

After the respondents had been divided into the four group types, moderators explained that the purpose of the study was to investigate teenagers' opinions about smoking. All focus group discussions were audiotaped. Respondents were informed that the tape recordings would be used to facilitate analysis of their responses. They were told that all responses would be reported in summary form and that no individuals would be identified by name. Moderators then asked the respondents if they had any questions.

Next, focus group discussions began on the topic of smoking and proceeded to specific issues, including the content of antismoking messages and the target audience for such messages. Following the procedure outlined by Krueger (1988), moderators drew their questions from a discussion guide that included general questions and specific probes. Each group discussion lasted approximately 50 minutes.

After completion of the focus groups, moderators transcribed the audiotapes and made additional notes. Typed transcripts were used in conjunction with the notes to prepare a summary of the focus group findings.

Results

The analysis of the focus group transcripts was conducted systematically according to procedures defined by Krueger (1988). Responses were analyzed by both gender and smoking behavior. Because responses were not moderated by gender, that variable is not discussed further. As suggested by Krueger (1988), the four focus group moderators assisted with the analysis of the transcripts. Clear trends and patterns emerged among the focus groups. In the following summary, all findings are illustrated with representative comments from the respondents.

Initiation of Smoking Behavior. Smokers reported that they began smoking as a means of group affiliation.

"If you see other people do it then you crave to join in the group."
"If you're in a group, it just kinda happens."
"I wanted to fit in with older people and everyone else was smoking."

Smokers reported that they continued to smoke as a perceived way to relieve stress and that they were unable to quit.

"If you're really stressed it seems [to] be relaxing, but constantly smoking doesn't seem relaxing after a while."
"It seems like it's supposed to relax you, but it really doesn't. It's tough to quit."
"I started to smoke because I thought it was cool, but now it's an addiction."

Nonsmokers felt a sense of support from others for their decision not to smoke.

"Some of my friends would be unbelievably mad at me if I even did start to smoke. It's like there is an opposite pressure almost, too."

"Well, so many people don't smoke and the people who do, a lot of people don't like that they do. There's a lot of nonsmokers. It's like you don't have any pressure to smoke because people may not like you if you do."

" . . . people I hang with don't smoke. I can choose my friends."

A major difference between smokers and nonsmokers appeared to be whether or not their peers smoked. Smokers indicated that they had begun smoking as a "social thing" and then found they "needed" to smoke regularly with or without peers. Several smokers also indicated that their parents as well as their peers smoked.

"My Mom smoked, so I always knew I would smoke."

"I think a lot of it starts off at the family level and I think that people who are raised in a family with smokers in it are a lot more inclined to smoke."

Negative Aspects of Smoking. The most commonly mentioned drawbacks of smoking were the bad smell and effect on eyes. They were mentioned universally by all nonsmokers and by the vast majority of smokers.

"It's a gross habit. It smells."

"Even just being around people who smoke, you know, my eyes start to water and burn."

"I hate the smell. I also have contacts and it kills my eyes."

"It stinks. It gets on your clothes. It gets on your breath."

Long-term health effects, such as lung cancer, were mentioned by nonsmokers as reasons for not smoking. Nonsmokers often paired the long-term health risks with the short-term effects of smoking.

"What probably makes me not smoke are all the health risks. Talking about lungs and can't breathe. Health hazards. It's not worth it."

"I don't smoke because I know what it does to your health. All that tar and your lungs turn black and decrepit."

"The fact that you can die from it is a turn-off, but also the fact that you smell like it especially when you are around others."

Smokers rarely addressed the long-term health effects of smoking. When probed about those effects, smokers commented:

"It's hard to imagine what is going on inside your body; hard to see the immediate effects; out of sight, out of mind."

"Maybe if I could imagine what it was really doing to my body."

Targeting Youth. Both smokers and nonsmokers agreed that antismoking messages should be directed to younger children. They indicated that attitudes toward smoking were already well formed by adolescence.

"They have to start really young. I mean, probably young enough that they really don't understand what smoking really is. I mean, if you wait until seventh or eighth grade, that's already the peak of when they start trying the stuff. I think they should start younger."

"I don't think they would convince anybody unless they start at elementary. By the time they get to high school, it's too late."

"If I was a smoker and I saw those pictures I'd be 'Oh yeah. Right.' But if I was a little kid and kept seeing those posters as I got older, that picture would stick in my mind in the long-run."

"At our age most teenagers think those ads are stupid. That's why I think they have to start younger. That's when they're not as prone to worry about what other people think."

Antismoking Message Content. Both smokers and nonsmokers offered advice on the content of an advertising message targeting children. A common theme throughout their comments was the "grossness" of smoking.

"It smells so gross."

"Gross thing to do."

"Gross. Smokers should get a life."

Both smokers and nonsmokers suggested a focus on the negative effects of smoking.

"It makes it hard to breathe."

"Getting sick from it."

"It's a dirty habit."

"How it really can affect your health."

"Takes so much out of you physically."

"Smoking bothers your eyes really bad."

holds. They attended a large public grammar school in the Midwest. Parents' permission was obtained for children to participate in the focus groups.

Moderators. The four moderators were the same college students who had conducted the focus groups in study 1 with one exception. The one new moderator was trained in the same way as the others. All moderators were given additional training in how to work with and elicit responses from children. As in study 1, the two female moderators worked with female respondents and the two male moderators worked with male respondents.

Smoking Prevention Ads. Three smoking prevention ads designed by BVK McDonald, an advertising agency, for use by the American Cancer Society were tested. One of the ads, "Sock," depicts a dirty, grimy sweatsock with the caption, "Gross," next to an ashtray full of cigarette butts with the caption, "Really gross." The analogy developed in the ad required that children create a simple association between the sock and the ashtray based on their similar surface features.

The second ad, "Insect," contains the following copy: "Every year nicotine is used to kill millions of insects and thousands of smokers. Considering they contain the same basic chemicals, smoking a cigarette is equivalent to spraying insecticide in your own face. And why would you want to do that?" Below the copy is a picture of a dead fly. The analogy was designed to be more complex than the one in the sock ad as it asks the child to abstract the relationships between smoking and the objects presented.

The third ad, "Tailpipe," reads, "Inhale a lethal dose of carbon monoxide and it's called suicide. Inhale a smaller amount and it's called smoking. Believe it or not, cigarette smoke contains the same poisonous gas as automobile exhaust. So if you wouldn't consider sucking on a tailpipe, why would you want to smoke?" Below the copy is a picture of a tailpipe. The ad was designed to be the most complex in the campaign. First, children had to comprehend the relationship between exhaust fumes and tailpipe and then draw a parallel to the relationship between smoke and cigarette. The analogy is particularly complex as it makes reference to abstract concepts (Small 1990). In addition, the illustration does not explicitly communicate the consequences of smoking, which must be inferred from the ad copy. Finally, children had to comprehend a second analogy that suggests exhaust fumes are as harmful to a person as smoking.

The three ads represent varying levels of analogical complexity. The sock ad offers the simplest analogy, the insect ad is more complex, and the tailpipe ad requires the most complex analogical reasoning. All of the ads feature situations familiar to children and indicate short-term negative consequences (e.g., sucking on a tailpipe). The ads then relate the short-term consequences to the long-term health effects of smoking.

Procedure. The procedure was similar to that used in study 1. Children participated in the focus groups during scheduled class time. They were asked to come to an empty classroom furnished with small tables and chairs for the younger children and larger tables and chairs for the older children. They were told they would be discussing issues of interest to kids. Once in the classroom, they completed a screening questionnaire that asked about the smoking behavior in their household. Respondents were then divided into four groups based on their gender and household smoking behavior: girls from smoking households, boys from smoking households, girls from nonsmoking households and boys from nonsmoking households. Four focus groups of each type were conducted for a total of 16 focus groups. Each group had an average of five to seven members. Moderators remained with the same group type (e.g., females from smoking households) for the entire study.

After the respondents had been divided into the four group types, the same introductory procedure used in study 1 was followed. Discussions focused on the sample ads. The children were shown the ads and asked to tell a story about what was happening in each one. Specific probes were used to assess the children's understanding of the individual elements and terminology in each of the ads. As in studies by Donaldson (1978) and Peracchio (1992), the ads were visible and available during the sessions to provide a context for the verbal discussions. The children frequently incorporated the ads into their responses, using words and gestures. Each group discussion lasted approximately 40 minutes. After completion of the focus groups, moderators transcribed the audiotapes and prepared a summary of the focus group findings.

Results

The analysis of the focus group transcripts was conducted in the same way as in Study 1. In accord with the study 1 findings, children's responses were not moderated by gender or household smoking behavior. A clear pattern of results emerged from the focus groups. In the following summary, the findings are illustrated with representative comments from the children.

Sock Ad. Even the youngest children understood that the sock ad was meant to portray the sock and the cigarette butts as "gross." Some of the younger children commented:

> "That's gross [pointing to the sock] and that's gross [pointing to the ashtray]."
> "They're both really smelly."
> "Ugly gross. Stink gross."

Children seven to 11 years of age indicated an understanding of the simple analogy and message in the sock ad.

Insect Ad. The youngest children, seven- and eight-year-olds, had difficulty understanding the insect ad. They commented:

> "Someone sprayed [the fly] with bug spray."
> "I don't think smoking is good for killing flies."
> "He's dead [the fly]. Cause of all that smoke."

Children nine to 11 years of age showed a deeper understanding of the ad.

> "Smoking and insecticides are the same thing. They both can kill you. You shouldn't smoke, you'll die."
> "I wouldn't spray insecticide on me. Why would I smoke?"

Tailpipe Ad. All but the oldest children had difficulty understanding the tailpipe ad. Most of the youngest children, seven to eight years of age, understood that exhaust fumes are harmful. However, they failed to relate the tailpipe and vehicle exhaust to smoking. They commented:

"Never stand behind a bus because you could get poisonous in your face."
"People sometimes get sick from exhaust."
"It's putting pollution in the air."

Children eight to 10 years of age showed some understanding of a connection between smoking and the tailpipe. They had a variety of hypotheses about the connection, but did not seem to completely comprehend the ad.

"About smoke, that it is turning the tailpipe into a cigarette."
"The person who's driving is smoking."
"No matter what kind of smoking it is, it can always make you sick."

Only the 11-year-olds had an adultlike understanding of the analogy between smoking and the tailpipe.

"You could hurt yourself with that stuff. The same stuff in car exhaust is in cigarettes . . . You should be warned about smoking."
"The tailpipe of a car is like the same as smoking and smoking could kill you . . . both of them could kill you."

Discussion

The results of Study 2 indicate age differences in children's understanding of advertising analogies designed to discourage smoking initiation. The youngest children, seven- and eight-year-olds, understood the smoking prevention message in only the most straightforward analogy based on surface features, the sock ad. That ad offers the least complex antismoking message as it is based on the analogy between smoking (the ashtray) and something undesirable to children (the grimy sock).

The insect ad presents a more complex analogy between cigarette smoke and insecticide. Seven- and eight-year-olds had difficulty comprehending the analogy as they attempted to connect the dead fly and the cigarette smoke in a literal way. They frequently suggested that cigarette smoke must have killed the fly. Older children, nine- to 11-year-olds, had a more complex understanding of the ad and were able to create an analogy between cigarette smoke and insecticide. For those children, the ad successfully conveyed the long-term effects of smoking in a concrete way by analogy to something familiar, insecticide.

Finally, the tailpipe advertising analogy was difficult to comprehend for all but the oldest children, the 11-year-olds. The seven- and eight-year-olds focused on a commonly known negative effect of car exhaust, pollution. They did not try to create an analogy between the ad and smoking. The nine- to 10-year-olds tried to develop some type of analogy between smoking and the tailpipe. They expressed a variety of hypotheses about the connections between vehicle exhaust and smoking (e.g., that the driver was smoking and that all smoke, presumably both from cigarettes and cars, makes you sick). Only the oldest children, the 11-year-olds, created an adultlike analogy between the effects of car exhaust and cigarette smoke. Like the insect ad, the tailpipe ad communicated the long-term effects of smoking concretely to those children by relating smoking to something they knew about, car exhaust.

Our findings are consistent with those on the development of inference-making ability and analogical reasoning in children (Gentner 1983; Gentner and Toupin 1986). As expected, the younger children did not efficiently use the strategies necessary to make inferences and comprehend analogies. Instead, they relied on surface features when performing analogical reasoning. The older children showed improved analogical abilities and were able to employ relational reasoning in their processing of analogies. Hence, in study 2, the development of analogical reasoning and inference making was evident. The youngest children, seven- to eight-year-olds, were able to understand only the simplest analogy presented in the sock ad. The nine- to 10-year-olds showed ability to understand the moderately complex analogy in the insect ad, but not the more complex analogy in the tailpipe ad. Apparently the nine- and 10-year-olds were undergoing a shift to relational reasoning and their ability depended on the complexity of the analogy presented. The oldest children, the 11-year-olds, comprehended even the most complex analogy based on relational reasoning presented in the tailpipe ad.

The research findings demonstrated that the three ads in the campaign target children in an age-appropriate way. The sock ad targets seven- to eight-year-olds, the insect ad targets nine- to 10-year-olds, and the tailpipe ad targets 11-year-olds. The ads were distributed as school posters that could be hung in or outside the classroom of the target age group. The sock ad was also produced as a billboard for use on outdoor signs near schools.

Conclusions

Youth smoking has become a dominant public policy issue as society has become aware of the negative health effects of smoking as well as the early initiation of smoking among young people (Andreasen 1993). Despite the importance of the issue, few studies have explored how to develop effective advertising message content to discourage youth smoking initiation (Pechmann and Ratneshwar 1994). We therefore examined young smokers' and nonsmokers' attitudes toward smoking and assessed children's ability to comprehend age-appropriate analogies to develop an advertising campaign that would discourage youth from beginning to smoke.

Our research makes several contributions to knowledge about youth smoking initiation. One contribution is the development of an advertising campaign to discourage youth smoking initiation. The ad campaign focuses on communicating the long-term health effects of smoking in a concrete way by creating analogies between the effects of smoking and things with which children are familiar, such as insecticide and vehicle exhaust. The objective of the campaign is to provide both potential smokers and nonsmokers with relevant and meaningful images and messages about the long-term effects of smoking.

Second, the research elucidates some of the attitudinal differences between teenage smokers and nonsmokers. The results indicate that teenage smokers do not have concrete internal images of the negative health effects of smoking, but nonsmokers do seem to have such images. If attempts to communicate the long-term negative health effects of smoking are to influence potential future smokers, they must portray those effects in a way to which children can relate. Care should be taken, however, to ensure that ads do not provoke high levels of arousal or anxiety, which may have a negative effect on persuasion (Keller and Block 1996; Henthorne, LaTour, and Nataraajan 1993). Finally, efforts to reduce youth smoking initiation should be directed to children

was administered. Participation was voluntary; no credit or reward was offered for participation. After the study, students were shown a video with an antismoking message to counter the positive effects, if any, of cigarette ad exposure.

Materials

Students were given a booklet containing four open-ended questions, a word association task, and demographic questions. The four open-ended questions, called the *Reading Profile* (Holt and Mulvey 1997), were designed to elicit the meanings of an ad: (1) What story is the ad telling? (2) Does this ad relate to your life? Why or why not? (3) What does the ad say about Camel (Marlboro) cigarettes? (4) Do you like the ad? Why or why not?

The use of these questions can be criticized, however, because they may lead to socially desirable answers. That is, students may feel pressured to write what they perceive is the "correct" answer to the questions: that they do not like cigarette advertising and do not smoke. Social desirability bias was reduced through the use of anonymous, written responses rather than oral responses that would reveal informants' answers to others. Informants also were assured of confidentiality at many different times during the study. In analyzing student responses, it appears that students were honest in their answers; they discussed their cigarette (and even drug) use, and emphatically listed what they liked and disliked about the ads used in the study.

To reduce social desirability bias further and to add another dimension to the study, a word association task also was used. Szalay and Deese (1978) report that word association reduces informants' rationalizations because it does not require them to state their intentions. This method also taps associations that are difficult to explain or express, and its time constraint reduces self-monitoring and conscious editing of responses. The word association method has been shown to provide consistent and rich cultural meanings for groups of informants (Phillips 1996b) and produces a cognitive map that summarizes the ideas collectively associated with each cigarette character. In addition, the cognitive map identifies the percentage of informants who mention a particular association, giving an idea of the relative importance of each association to the character's shared meaning (Phillips 1996a).

Procedure

All students completed a word association task and answered open-ended questions. In Part A of the study, students were randomly assigned to one of six word association groups. Three "camel" conditions were created: one group provided word associations for the word *camel,* one group responded to a black and white drawing of a realistic camel, and one group responded to a black and white drawing of Joe Camel. Three similar "cowboy" conditions were created for the Marlboro cowboy.

The method for word association outlined by Szalay and Deese (1978) was followed. Informants completed a practice word association task. Students had 60 seconds to write down any word that came to mind when viewing the practice word or image. After the practice task, one of the authors answered questions pertaining to the word association method, and then informants were given 60 seconds to complete the actual word association task.

The open-ended questions were answered in Part B of the study. Half of the students, who previously were assigned to any of the "cowboy" word association conditions, saw an ad with Joe Camel projected on a screen. The ad was an actual, full-page, color print ad and showed Joe Camel playing pool and smoking. The Surgeon General's warning on the ad stated, "Smoking causes lung cancer, heart disease, emphysema, and may complicate pregnancy." The other students, who previously were assigned to any of the "camel" conditions, saw an ad with the Marlboro cowboy. The Marlboro ad showed the Marlboro cowboy riding a horse in the country and smoking, with the same Surgeon General's warning. All informants answered the four questions after viewing the ad on the screen. Finally, informants answered demographic questions and questions regarding their smoking behavior.

Analysis

Informants' responses to the open-ended questions were independently analyzed by the authors using the grounded theory method (Strauss and Corbin 1990). Authors examined responses for the themes students identified in the ads, the relevance of each theme to students' lives, and students' critical perspectives about the ads. There was high initial agreement between the authors regarding the emerging meaning perspectives, and the authors returned to the data in an iterative process until 100% agreement was reached.

Informants' responses to the word association task for each of the six conditions were grouped into themes independently by each author. Initial agreement between the two researchers in identifying themes, as measured by the number of coding agreements divided by the number of coding decisions, was above 83% for five of the six conditions. For the Joe Camel condition, which was examined first, agreement was 60%. The authors returned to the data and reclassified the words for all of the conditions until they reached agreement. A third coder, who was unaware of the purpose of the study, was recruited to categorize the words into the themes for all conditions again; the agreement between the third coder and the authors, measured using Cohen's kappa, was above 80% for all conditions.

Results

Taken as a whole, the results of this study provide a detailed examination of the meanings of cigarette characters for junior high school students. First, the responses to the open-ended questions explain the themes that students identify in cigarette character ads, and students' connection to and liking for these ads. Next, responses to the word association task illustrate students' top-of-mind associations with cigarette characters. Students' smoking behavior is compared to their character perceptions in an attempt to identify the possible impact these characters have on smoking behavior. Finally, word association results are used to explore students' likely reactions to future cigarette appeals.

Interpretation of Cigarette Ads

Based on the responses to the written questions, 10 themes were identified in the Camel ad by students (presented in Table 11.1). The primary theme conveyed by the ad for 77% of informants was that

TABLE 11.1 Themes Identified by Informants in Joe Camel Ad

Theme	Number of Mentions (n = 79)	%
Smoking is cool	61	77
Smoking causes health problems	12	15
Smoking leads to better performance	7	9
Smoking leads to popularity	7	9
Smoking is fun	7	9
Smoking is relaxing	7	9
Smoking is normal	4	5
Smoking makes one look good	4	5
Camel is the best brand	3	4
Smoking is sexy	3	4

smoking is cool. This theme is exemplified by the responses of the following student:

> A cool guy walks into a billiard hall and he is a jock. He is smoking. He is wearing sunglasses because they are trying to make him look cool. If you smoke, then you are cool.

The next most-mentioned theme, *smoking causes health problems,* was identified by only 15% of the informants. These informants referenced the Surgeon General's warning as part of the ad's message. Each of the next four themes was identified by 9% of informants: *smoking leads to better performance* (i.e., success in playing pool); *smoking leads to popularity; smoking is fun;* and *smoking is relaxing.*

The seventh theme, *smoking is normal,* was identified by 5% of informants. An example of this theme was provided by a male informant in answer to the question, "What does the ad say about Camel cigarettes?"

> That they're normal. No big deal. An everyday part of life. The camel's not focused on the cigarette. He's focused on pool.

The last three themes, mentioned by 5% or fewer of the informants, are: *smoking makes one look good; Camel is the best brand;* and *smoking is sexy.*

The 11 themes that informants identified in the Marlboro ad are presented in Table 11.2. In contrast to the Camel ad themes, no Marlboro ad theme was identified by more than 50% of informants. In addition, while Camel ad themes focused on the positive effects of smoking, the Marlboro ad themes centered around the product user: *cowboys and country men smoke Marlboro* (48%); *tough, real men smoke Marlboro* (21%); and *hard-workers smoke Marlboro* (5%). For example, an informant answered the question, "What does the ad say about Marlboro cigarettes?" by responding:

> That it is a country cigarette and it's for hard-working cowboys out on the ranch. He seems to be enjoying them.

Two other themes appear to be related to the "cowboy" image (e.g., Lohof 1969) of this brand: *smoking makes one independent* (6%); *smoking relieves boredom* (3%).

A greater proportion of informants ($\chi^2 = 4.26$; $p < 0.05$) mentioned the theme *smoking causes health problems* for the Marlboro ad (29%) than for the Camel ad (15%). This could be because one primary theme was not evident for the Marlboro ad, leading students to rely on the Surgeon General's warning in interpreting the ad's message. The remaining Marlboro themes are similar to the Camel themes, such as *smoking is cool, smoking is relaxing, smoking is normal, Marlboro is the best brand,* and *smoking is sexy.* This pattern of results suggests that cigarette ads present common themes and benefits for their brands.

Based on these responses, it appears eighth grade students can easily identify themes presented in cigarette character ads. These themes are overwhelmingly positive, with less than 30% of students mentioning the health risks of smoking, even though the risks are printed on the ad. Given the themes identified, these two cigarette characters seem to be important tools for presenting a positive message about smoking to young adults.

TABLE 11.2 Themes Identified by Informants in Marlboro Cowboy Ad

Theme	Number of Mentions (n = 80)	%
Cowboys and countrymen smoke Marlboro	38	48
Smoking causes health problems	23	29
Tough, real men smoke Marlboro	17	21
Smoking is cool	13	16
Smoking is relaxing	10	13
Smoking is normal	9	11
Marlboro is the best brand	8	10
Smoking makes one independent	5	6
Hard-workers smoke Marlboro	4	5
Smoking relieves boredom	2	3
Smoking is sexy	2	3

Relevance of Cigarette Ads

The themes identified, however, only describe the message that informants perceive in the ad; they do not explain whether informants relate to or connect with the themes. To explore this issue, students were asked whether the ads related to their lives. Their responses are summarized in Table 11.3. The most important consideration informants used to identify whether or not the ad related to them was their smoking behavior. Almost half (49%) of informants who saw the Joe Camel ad rejected it as irrelevant. Similarly, 45% of informants rejected the Marlboro ad. These results translate into over three quarters of *nonsmokers* who stated the ads were not relevant to them. This lack of resonance was summarized by one informant when asked if the Marlboro ad related to her life:

No, because I'm not a smoker. I do not ride horses on ranches. Maybe the peaceful part might relate to my life. But everything else is not me.

TABLE 11.3 Does This Ad Relate to Your Life?

A. Joe Camel Ad (n = 79)

Yes . . .	Number of Mentions	%	No . . .	Number of Mentions	%
. . . because I smoke	7	9	. . . because I don't smoke	39	49
. . . because I play pool	16	20	. . . because I don't play pool	6	8
. . . because I am cool	4	5	. . . because I don't have to be cool	2	3
. . . because I wear Joe's type of clothing	2	3	. . . because I don't wear Joe's type of clothing	3	4
. . . because I like to relax	3	4	—	—	—
—	—	—	. . . because I'm not a camel	5	6

B. Marlboro Cowboy Ad (n = 80)

Yes . . .	Number of Mentions	%	No . . .	Number of Mentions	%
. . . because I smoke	9	11	. . . because I don't smoke	36	45
. . . because I ride horses	2	3	. . . because I don't ride horses	10	13
. . . because I live in the country	4	5	. . . because I don't live in the country	10	13
. . . because I like things to be peaceful	2	3	—	—	—
—	—	—	. . . because I'm not a cowboy or a country man	8	10

Surprisingly, a majority of smokers did not relate to the cigarette ads either; less than 11% of informants, or only one quarter of *smokers,* stated the ad was relevant to them because they smoked. Taken together, these findings indicate that although all students identified positive messages in the cigarette ads, a majority of them rejected the ads as irrelevant to their lives.

The responses to the open-ended questions also indicated that many students tended to be "literalists" who related the ad to their lives based on the images presented. For example, 20% of all Camel informants stated that they related to the Camel ad because Joe was playing pool, and 3% because of his clothes. Other students rejected the ad based on these signs:

> No, because I don't play pool, I don't smoke Camel Lights, and I'm not a camel.

This result suggests that the cigarette ad context may be more important in attracting underage smokers than initially thought. Joe Camel has been featured in various activities, such as playing the saxophone and fishing. It is possible that the relevance of these contexts to underage smokers may be more significant than the use of a specific character like Joe.

This finding is supported by the informants' responses to the Marlboro ad. Contrary to popular opinion that the Marlboro cowboy appeals to young adults as a symbol of independence (Pollay 1997), students tended to reject the ad based on their view of the product user. As shown in Table 11.3, informants stated that the ad did not relate to them because they do not ride horses (13%), do not live in the country (13%), and are not cowboys (10%).

Liking of Cigarette Ads

Beyond their personal connections with the ads, 20% of Camel informants and 13% of Marlboro informants spontaneously mentioned that these ads are trying to increase cigarette sales. Previous research supports the idea that eighth graders are aware of and can identify the persuasive intent of advertising; this sophistication is thought to lead to skepticism and adultlike coping strategies (Boush, Friestad, and Rose 1994). To explore this skepticism further, informants were asked to indicate whether or not they liked the cigarette ads and why. Responses to this question are presented in Table 11.4. Not surprisingly, students

TABLE 11.4 Do You Like the Ad?

A. Joe Camel Ad (n = 79)

Yes . . .	Number of Mentions	%	No . . .	Number of Mentions	%
. . . because I like the picture/colors	21	27	—	—	—
. . . because I like the camel	3	4	. . . because I don't like the camel	9	11
—	—	—	. . . because I don't like cigarettes	12	15
—	—	—	. . . because the ad is targeted toward children and teens	10	13
—	—	—	. . . because smoking causes health problems	8	10
—	—	—	. . . because the ad causes people to start smoking	7	9

B. Marlboro Cowboy Ad (n = 80)

Yes . . .	Number of Mentions	%	No . . .	Number of Mentions	%
. . . because I like the picture/colors	9	11	. . . because I don't like the picture/colors	17	21
. . . because I like cigarettes	1	1	. . . because I don't like cigarettes	12	15
. . . because I like the cowboy	1	1	. . . because I don't like the cowboy	10	13
. . . because I like the horse	4	5	—	—	—
—	—	—	. . . because smoking causes health problems	12	15
—	—	—	. . . because the ad is targeted toward children and teens	4	5
—	—	—	. . . because the ad causes people to start smoking	3	4

disliked the ads because they disliked cigarettes, smoking, and/or smoking-related illnesses.

Of greatest concern in the responses to the Camel ad is the finding that although 11% of informants actively disliked Joe Camel, 27% liked the picture and the colors used in the ad, regardless of their opinion of smoking in general. The problem with this high level of ad liking is that, for an adult target, ad liking has been shown to influence brand liking and eventually purchase intention for other product categories (Brown and Stayman 1992). If the same is true for young adults, a positive response to the Camel ad can transfer positive affect to the brand and to smoking behavior.

Countering this affect transfer is the finding reported in Table 11.4 that 13% of Camel informants disliked the ad because it was perceived as being targeted toward kids and teens. Clearly these students have been exposed to the debate about the ethics of Joe Camel. Several students insisted that their positive feelings toward the ad did not affect their behavior. For example, when asked if the ad related to his life, one informant replied:

> No, with the exception of people talking about how Joe Camel makes me smoke, which it doesn't. Only dumb-asses smoke because of a cartoon.

Another informant discussed whether he liked the ad in the following manner:

> Yeah, he's dressed cool and drawn nice, and I love Joe Camel, really. But he's not going to make me smoke.

These protestations of immunity from cigarette advertising are encouraging, but have to be tempered by the fact that many consumers fail to recognize the effect of ads on their behavior.

In contrast, far fewer students ($\chi^2 = 4.07$; $p < 0.05$) liked the Marlboro ad picture (11%) than liked the Camel ad picture (27%), and 21% of Marlboro viewers mentioned that they disliked the picture because it was "stupid," "boring," and "uninteresting." When asked if he liked the ad, one informant replied:

No, it's dumb. If they wanted to sell cigarettes, don't use a hick as the spokesperson; use someone cool.

Again, a few students (5%) indicated that they disliked the ad because it was perceived as being targeted toward kids and teens.

To summarize the results of the open-ended questions, eighth graders identify many common, positive themes in cigarette character ads. These positive themes are filtered through a student's life experience and skepticism. Many students reject cigarette ads as irrelevant because they do not smoke, but students may connect with the images and contexts used. Joe Camel ads appear to be liked more than Marlboro ads.

The above findings describe students' interpretations of cigarette character ads. But does this ad interpretation "stick" in students' minds? The next section provides a snapshot view of the top-of-mind associations surrounding cigarette characters.

Associations With Cigarette Characters

A word association task was used to develop the cognitive maps elicited by Joe Camel and the Marlboro cowboy (Figure 11.1). Although the word association results are presented after the findings of the open-ended questions in this chapter, informants actually completed the word association task first, before they viewed the cigarette ads or knew that cigarette ads would be studied. This ensured that top-of-mind associations would not necessarily be focused on smoking.

On average, Joe Camel elicited five words per student, while the Marlboro cowboy elicited only three. Compared to well-known images of cultural icons, such as a generic camel and cowboy that each elicited six words per student (Figures 11.2 and 11.3), the associations that surround the Marlboro cowboy are less numerous and less rich. The associative network surrounding the Marlboro cowboy therefore does not seem to be as well developed as the one surrounding Joe Camel.

Both cigarette characters are associated with smoking as well as negative, positive, and neutral characteristics. The negative characteristics of Joe Camel (48% of mentions) and the Marlboro man (44%

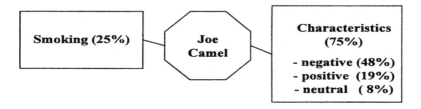

Percentages are based on 124 total mentions. The number of informants was 25.

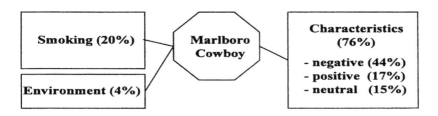

Percentages are based on 71 total mentions. The number of informants was 26.

Figure 11.1. Cognitive Maps for Joe Camel and the Marlboro Cowboy

of mentions) outweigh the positive characteristics (19% and 17%, respectively). Negative associations include negative descriptions of the characters (e.g., "stupid," "ugly") and negative descriptions of smoking behavior (e.g., "unhealthy," "stinky"). These findings support the results of the open-ended questions that suggest students may not like cigarette character ads despite being able to identify positive themes in them.

Although positive characteristics were mentioned less frequently, it is important to note that a positive characteristic, "cool," was the word mentioned most often (by 48% of informants) in response to the Joe Camel word association task. In contrast, just 19% of informants found the Marlboro cowboy "cool." Joe Camel was also viewed as "slick" and "smooth" while the Marlboro cowboy was described as "tough." These findings support the contention that Joe Camel is more appealing to students (i.e., cooler) than the Marlboro cowboy, especially given Joe's better-developed and richer associative network.

Camel to youth-enticing contexts, the image of the generic camel is already associated with smoking in the minds of some eighth graders.

A comparison between the cognitive maps elicited by two nonanimal characters (i.e., the Marlboro cowboy and a generic cowboy) also provides clues for the future of cigarette advertising. The cognitive map for the generic cowboy is shown in Figure 11.3. Students described the cowboy's clothes (e.g., "hat"), animals (e.g., "horse"), environment (e.g., "west"), and tools (e.g., "rope"). Students also were likely to mention neutral characteristics of cowboys, such as "man," "white," and "old." A few students (4%) spontaneously linked cowboys to smoking using words such as *cigarettes*.

The Marlboro cowboy (Figure 11.1) elicited completely different associations from the image of the generic cowboy (Figure 11.3). This is particularly noteworthy, given that the Marlboro cowboy had the same props as the photo of the cowboy, such as a horse, a hat, and a rope. Students failed to mention these words; instead, they focused on the Marlboro cowboy's link to smoking to the exclusion of other meanings.

Based on the comparisons between both of the cigarette characters and their generic counterparts, it appears that the core cultural meanings of the generic images (e.g., "clumsy"; "west") are not a part of the meaning of the cigarette characters. These findings suggest that any image that is associated with a cigarette brand over time may form such a tight connection to smoking that other associations are suppressed. If this is the case, any image, scene, or style that becomes associated with a cigarette brand over time may perform the same function as an ad character. Therefore, eliminating ad characters may have little effect on junior high school students.

Discussion and Future Research Directions

This study examines the cultural meanings of Joe Camel and the Marlboro cowboy for eighth grade students to understand the risk that cigarette characters pose in contributing to underage smoking. On one hand, this study shows that these characters do send positively identified messages and have some appeal regardless of an individual's smoking behavior. Therefore, eliminating these characters is likely to reduce, at least in a small way, adolescents' positive perceptions of smoking.

On the other hand, students are more skeptical and react more negatively to these characters than some advertising critics believe. Although they understand the ads' positive messages, students do not necessarily accept and believe them. In addition, the context and activities presented in the ad may have a more positive impact than the general use of a character. These findings suggest that replacing cigarette characters with other attractive images, such as a pool hall or baseball stadium, would do little to reduce these ads' attraction for eighth graders.

Finally, the appeal of the characters does not appear to have a large impact on students' brand choice. This finding does not imply, however, that advertising has no effect on youth's smoking behavior. Pollay et al. (1996) suggest that smoking behavior is linked to a brand's advertising share of voice; overall ad spending may be a more important factor than character appeal. Therefore, eliminating cigarette characters without decreasing overall ad spending may not reduce underage smoking as desired.

Several limitations of this study exist, the most important being the use of students at only one school, and the use of only one ad per cigarette character studied. Given that underage smoking behavior varies by region, generalizations to all eighth graders in the United States is not advised. In addition, the findings of this study suggest that the context in which a character is placed may be more important than the character itself; future research with a variety of character ads and situations can add insight into this proposition.

As cigarette advertising changes over the next few years, advertising researchers will be in a unique position to study the effect of characters on underage smoking. For example, Camel now features an ordinary camel in its advertising. In the future, researchers will be able to compare junior high school students' new cognitive map of a generic camel to the one described in this study. If our speculation is correct, themes such as "appearance" and "environment" will disappear from the camel's cognitive map and only a strong association with smoking will remain.

Alternatively, if cigarette ads stop using characters all together, new cigarette ads can be tested using the open-ended questions outlined in this study. Comparisons between old and new ad themes, relevance, and liking will be strong indicators of whether or not eliminating cigarette characters has changed the perceptions of junior high school students.

In conclusion, this study has given a voice to one of the most important constituents in the underage smoking debate—adolescents themselves. By viewing cigarette advertising through their eyes, one can begin to see cigarette characters as just one attractive tool used by cigarette companies. Continuing advertising research in this area will allow researchers to devise strategies to help young adults reject smoking regardless of the persuasive form of the communications message.

References

Beltrame, Julian (1997), "U.S. Begins Crackdown on Teenage Smoking," *The StarPhoenix* (March 1), B19.

Botvin, Gilbert J. (1993), "Smoking Behavior of Adolescents Exposed to Cigarette Advertising," *Public Health Reports*, 108 (2), 217-224.

Boush, David M., Marian Friestad, and Gregory M. Rose (1994), "Adolescent Skepticism Toward TV Advertising and Knowledge of Advertiser Tactics," *Journal of Consumer Research*, 21 (June), 165-175.

Brown, Stephen P. and Douglas M. Stayman (1992), "Antecedents and Consequences of Attitude Toward the Ad: A Meta-Analysis," *Journal of Consumer Research*, 19 (June), 34-51.

Feder, Barnaby J. (1997), *New York Times News Service* (April 20).

Foltz, Kim (1990), "Old Joe Is Paying Off for Camel," *New York Times* (August 7), D17.

Food and Drug Administration (FDA) Press Release (1996), August 23.

Freedman, Alix M. and Suein L. Hwang (1995), "Reynolds Marketing Strategy Sought to Get Young Adults to Smoke Camels," *Wall Street Journal* (November 2), B4.

Hastings, Gerald B. and Philip P. Aitken (1995), "Tobacco Advertising and Children's Smoking: A Review of the Evidence," *European Journal of Marketing*, 29 (11), 6-17.

Henke, Lucy L. (1995), "Young Children's Perceptions of Cigarette Brand Advertising Symbols: Awareness, Affect, and Target Market Identification," *Journal of Advertising*, 24 (4), 13-28.

Holt, Douglas B. and Michael Mulvey (1997), "The Reading Profile: An Interpretive Framework for Analyzing the Meaning of Ads," unpublished working paper (under review), Penn State University.

Horovitz, Bruce and Melanie Wells (1997), "Ads for Adult Vices Big Hit With Teens," *USA Today* (January 31), 1A.

Lohof, Bruce A. (1969), "The Higher Meaning of Marlboro Cigarettes," *Journal of Popular Culture,* 3 (3), 443-450.

Martin, Claude R., Jr. (1994), "Ethical Advertising Research Standards: Three Case Studies," *Journal of Advertising,* 23 (3), 17-29.

McDonald, Colin (1993), "Children, Smoking and Advertising: What Does the Research Really Tell Us?" *International Journal of Advertising,* 12, 279-287.

Mizerski, Richard (1995), "The Relationship Between Cartoon Trade Character Recognition and Attitude Toward Product Category in Young Children," *Journal of Marketing,* 59 (October), 58-70.

Moschis, George P. (1989), "Cigarette Advertising and Young Smokers," *Journal of Advertising Research,* 29 (April/May), 51-60.

Pechmann, Cornelia and S. Ratneshwar (1994), "The Effects of Antismoking and Cigarette Advertising on Young Adolescents' Perceptions of Peers Who Smoke," *Journal of Consumer Research,* 21 (September), 236-251.

Phillips, Barbara J. (1996a), "Advertising and the Cultural Meaning of Animals," *Advances in Consumer Research,* Kim Corfman and John Lynch, eds., Provo, UT: Association for Consumer Research, 23, 354-360.

⸻ (1996b), "The Role of Advertising Trade Characters in Forming Product Perceptions," *Proceedings of the 1996 Conference of the American Academy of Advertising,* Gary B. Wilcox, ed., Austin: University of Texas Press, 171-178.

Pollay, Richard W. (1997), "Hacks, Flacks, and Counter-Attacks: Cigarette Advertising, Sponsored Research, and Controversies," *Journal of Social Issues,* 53 (1), 53-74.

⸻, S. Siddarth, Michael Siegal, Anne Haddix, Robert K. Merritt, Gary A. Giovino, and Michael P. Eriksen (1996), "The Last Straw? Cigarette Advertising and Realized Market Shares Among Youths and Adults, 1979-1993," *Journal of Marketing,* 60 (April), 1-16.

Ramirez, Anthony (1990), "Times Change: The Man Rides On," *New York Times* (March 8), D1.

Scott, Jeffrey (1991), "Is Camel Too Cool With Kids?" *Atlanta Journal and Constitution* (December 11), A2.

Strauss, Anselm and Juliet Corbin (1990), *Basics of Qualitative Research: Grounded Theory Procedures and Techniques,* Newbury Park, CA: Sage.

Szalay, Lorand B. and James Deese (1978), *Subjective Meaning and Culture: An Assessment Through Word Associations,* Hillsdale, NJ: Lawrence Erlbaum.

CHAPTER

12

Adolescents' Attention to Beer and Cigarette Print Ads and Associated Product Warnings

RICHARD J. FOX
DEAN M. KRUGMAN
JAMES E. FLETCHER
PAUL M. FISCHER

Youth has its hazards. Cautioning adolescents about product dangers is a unique challenge for advertisers and policy makers. Given the current controversy surrounding the advertising and sale of tobacco and alcohol products to adolescents, it is important to understand how that audience attends to advertising for such products and associated cautionary statements. We report findings from an extensive eye tracking study conducted among adolescents that involved print ads and associated warning statements for tobacco and alcohol products.

AUTHORS' NOTE: Reprinted from *Journal of Advertising,* Vol. XXVII, Number 3, Fall 1998. Reprinted with permission.
The work was funded by the American Cancer Society, Grant PRB-55.

The teenage market in the United States is extremely lucrative. Teens are fashion and status conscious, and spend large amounts of money on clothing and entertainment. In addition to influencing household purchases, teenagers spend at least $95 billion a year (Peter and Olson 1996). Projections indicate that by 2010 the teenage population will have grown to approximately 31 million, exceeding their number in any of the baby boom years of the 1960s (Miller 1994). The fact that many brand loyalties begin during adolescence and last through adulthood makes the group even more important to marketers (Brandweek 1993; Raphel 1993).

As they age, adolescents depend increasingly on advertising as an information source (Assael 1992), and there is justifiable concern about the marketing appeals, particularly those relating to cigarettes and alcohol products, to which adolescents are exposed. Adolescence is a period of physical and mental maturation, a time of transition to adult roles and independence from parents (Institute of Medicine 1994, p. 106). The unique nature of adolescence renders teens more sensitive than other age groups to advertising imagery and promotional appeals. Young people are particularly susceptible to image-based advertising, which is used extensively in the advertising of alcohol and tobacco products (Strasburger 1995, ch. 4). When investigating cigarette brand market shares, Pollay et al. (1996) concluded that youths were much more sensitive to advertising than adults; Evans et al. (1995) and Hastings and Aitken (1995) found cigarette marketing to be important in encouraging young people to initiate smoking.

The tobacco unit of R. J. Reynolds, which markets Camel cigarettes, has been accused of deliberately developing the cartoon character Joe Camel as a spokesperson for the brand to stimulate interest in smoking among adolescents (see, e.g., DesRoches 1994). In fact, the FTC has charged R. J. Reynolds with unfair advertising practices for its use of the Joe Camel campaign and its appeal to young people (Neergaard 1997). The campaign has been tremendously successful among young people; Camel's share of the teenage market grew from .5% to 13% between 1988 and 1992 (U.S. Department of Health and Human Services 1994a). The recognizability of the cartoon character Joe Camel among very young children has fueled controversy about the advertising of tobacco products in general (Fischer et al. 1989; Mizerski 1995; Pollay et al.1996).

In 1997, because of legal and social pressure, R.J. Reynolds announced it would formally retire Joe Camel. The pressure stemmed in part from legal action initiated by 13 California cities and counties against R.J. Reynolds. The suit noted that sales of Camels to teenagers was $6 million when the Joe Camel campaign began in 1988 and rose to $476 million in 1992. Though not admitting wrongdoing, R.J. Reynolds retired Joe Camel as part of the settlement. The company also agreed to release internal documents and to pay the cities and counties $10 million to fund antismoking education.

Philip Morris has been similarly criticized for its introduction of Woman Thing Music in a promotion consisting of a new recording label featuring female vocalists who are particularly popular among female teenagers. The music can be purchased only with Virginia Slims proofs of purchase (Shane 1997). Virginia Slims originally gained popularity and acceptance among young women with its "you've come a long way, baby" campaign, which was launched in the late 1960s. Subsequent studies have linked a large increase in smoking among teenage girls to that campaign (Pierce, Lee, and Gilpin 1994).

Controversy also surrounds the marketing of alcohol products. Alcohol manufacturers have been accused of advertising in media whose audiences consist largely of underage consumers. Anheuser-Busch, and subsequently Miller Brewing Company (Teinowitz 1997c), ceased advertising on the MTV network after the FTC launched an investigation into the airing of a Schlitz Malt Liquor commercial during MTV programming targeted to teens (Ross 1996). That airing was in direct violation of the beer industry's own marketing code, which states that beer commercials should not be placed in a show whose audience consists mostly of underage viewers (Ross 1996). A sampling of MTV programming revealed numerous violations of the code (Ross and Teinowitz 1997).

Similar concerns have been raised about print media. Thirty percent of the readers of *Spin* magazine are under the age of 18, and almost one half are under 21. Yet, that magazine and others with large teen readership such as *Allure, Vibe,* and *Rolling Stone,* are filled with liquor ads despite insistence by industry spokespeople that they target consumers 21 to 35 years of age (Leonhardt 1997).

The content of beer commercials, which tends to portray beer drinkers as young, sexy, successful, and active (Strasburger 1995), has been criticized because that image is exactly the one many adolescents strive to project. Also, a survey found that nearly 60% of 5th and 6th graders could identify Spuds McKenzie, and more than 80% could match him with Budweiser beer (Wallack et al. 1990).

Unlike beer and wine products, liquor products are not advertised on radio or TV. Shortly after the repeal of Prohibition, to defuse social criticism of alcohol use, U.S. distillers agreed not to advertise on radio. The ban was extended to the new TV medium to avoid exposing children to liquor ads (Davidson 1997). However, distillers have since dropped their voluntary ban on TV advertising. In late 1996, House of Seagram announced that it would air TV ads for its liquor brands (Ross and McDowell 1996). Regulators have responded to the increasingly aggressive stance taken by alcohol marketers. The White House has publicly appealed to the industry to reinstate its self-imposed ban and has requested that the FCC investigate possible restrictions on liquor advertising on TV. Although no federal regulations apply to alcohol advertising, local governments are beginning to take action. In fact, alcohol and tobacco ads were recently banned from billboards in Baltimore, and other cities are planning similar actions (Teinowitz 1997b).

We are in an era of great concern about adolescents' use of cigarettes and alcohol, and the way those products are marketed. The research we report involved the use of eye tracking to monitor adolescents' viewing behavior for five selected print advertisements, including two ads for cigarettes and one ad for beer. After discussing the importance of warnings and the difficulty of warning adolescents, we describe the use of eye tracking to investigate warning effectiveness. We then report results on adolescents' viewing of ads for tobacco, beer, sunscreen, and a soft drink, and on attention to mandated warnings and voluntary disclosures within the context of print advertising. Finally, we discuss the implications of our findings.

Warnings and Adolescents

The Importance of Cigarette Warnings and Alcohol Warnings

Implemented in 1965, cigarette warnings are one of the most widely used disclosures mandated by federal policy, and have played a role in the government's policy to alert consumers to the dangers of smoking. The Comprehensive Smoking Education Act, passed by Congress in 1984, mandated that cigarette companies include specified warnings on cigarette packages and print advertisements. The warnings are ostensibly designed to make people aware of the adverse effects of smoking on health. However, information provision does not necessarily equate to information impact.

Recent agreements have elevated the role of warnings to a prominent position in the public policy debate over cigarettes. Plaintiffs in state health suits have contended that cigarette companies have not done enough to warn prospective users about the dangers of smoking. In June 1997, a group of state attorneys general reached a national agreement with all of the major tobacco companies about the reduction of smoking, particularly among teenagers, and the recovery of monies spent treating tobacco-related diseases. The agreement is being reviewed by branches of the federal government and major health organizations (Garland 1997).

A substantial part of the national agreement pertains to reducing teenage smoking rates and to the nature of warnings appearing on packages and in print advertising. A central aim is to achieve "dramatic and immediate reductions in the number of underage consumers of tobacco products" (*New York Times* 1997). The agreement notes that underage smoking must decrease 30% by the fifth year after enactment of the legislation. As part of the program to reduce consumption, a series of new warnings is to be implemented. The warnings would occupy 25% of the front panel of the package (including packs and cartons) and would appear in the upper portion thereof. In print advertising, warnings and, where relevant, "tar" and nicotine (or other constituent) content information would total 20% of the ad.

Warning adolescents about the dangers of smoking and reducing the rate of teenage smoking are important concerns, as 90% of smoking begins in adolescence (Institute of Medicine 1994; U.S. Department of Health and Human Services 1994b). The incidence of smoking has not declined among teenagers as it has among the U.S. adult population (U.S. Department of Health and Human Services 1994b). Further, exposure to advertising and other forms of marketing communication is believed to play a role in the initiation of use of tobacco products (Teinowitz 1997a). The addictive nature of tobacco makes breaking the smoking habit very difficult later in life. The cigarette industry had managed to avoid mentioning addiction in cigarette warnings until recently (Glantz et al. 1996). However, in 1997, Liggett Group, Inc., in exchange for release from liability for the cost of treating smokers' health problems, agreed to supplement current mandated warnings on its products with the statement, "Warning, Smoking is Addictive" (Broder 1997; Brownlee 1997).

Alcohol abuse has been well-documented as a problem of our society. Drinking and driving is a primary cause of traffic accidents and related fatalities. MADD (Mothers Against Drunk Driving) was formed to bring attention to the human toll, including innocent victims, resulting from driving while intoxicated (DWI). Many local governments have instituted stiff penalties for DWI violations in the hope of discouraging drinking and driving. The problems associated with this form of alcohol abuse are not restricted to adults. Teenagers are involved in the most automobile crashes and fatalities, with drinking and driving being a primary cause (Pertman 1997). In fact, alcohol use is involved in half of those automobile accidents, as well as approximately one third of all homicides and suicides among teens (Strasburger and Brown 1991). The public is demanding enforcement of the drinking age laws and considerable punishment for distributors who allow teenagers to obtain alcoholic beverages. Federal and local governments have been pushing for harsher penalties for teens who drink and drive (Moroney 1995; Shogren 1995).

In response, alcohol manufacturers have included cautionary statements in print advertising to encourage responsible use of alcohol. Unlike warnings appearing on alcohol beverage containers, which are mandatory, the cautionary statements included in advertising are voluntary. Further, some beer commercials include a moderation message, such as Budweiser's "know when to say when" slogan (Madden and Grube 1994). Beer companies have also sponsored TV segments that promote responsible drinking with slogans such as "friends don't let friends drive drunk."

Warning Adolescents

Warning young people can prove difficult because adolescence is characterized by experimentation and risk taking (U.S. Department of Health and Human Services 1994b). Adolescents tend to play down the risk of using hazardous products. Levanthal, Glynn, and Fleming (1987) found that adolescents tend to underestimate the dangers of smoking and overestimate smoking prevalence. Recent focus groups with adolescents confirm that adolescents perceive themselves to be invulnerable to the negative consequences of smoking (Fischer et al. 1993). Also, young people have difficulty relating to negative consequences that may occur in the distant future. Consequently, care must be taken to create a warning message that is meaningful.

Warnings that portray products as "forbidden fruit" may make them attractive to young people (Parker-Pope 1997). Snyder and Blood (1992) found that alcohol warnings had a reverse effect on young adults causing them to perceive more benefits than risks from alcohol consumption. Krugman et al. (1994) found that although many adolescents may be aware of the presence of a mandated warning, they usually do not remember the general concept or message. The research also showed that testing message concepts and designing new warnings could lead to warnings that are more germane to adolescents. Using the same size and location as mandated warnings, Fischer et al. (1993) found that new warnings containing simple, straightforward messages, with larger type and graphic devices, were more effective in communicating the dangers of smoking to adolescents. Other research on cigarette warnings indicates that they lack believability (Beltramini 1988) and require a high level of reading comprehension (Malouf 1992).

Clearly, mandated warnings for cigarettes and voluntary disclosures for alcohol products are being given an increasingly more important role in efforts to reduce the use of such products among adolescents. More work is needed to understand how adolescents react to both mandated warnings and voluntary disclosures in the context in which such messages are seen. We addressed that need by using eye tracking to provide an understanding of adolescents' attention to a variety of warnings and disclosures in the context of print advertising.

Method

We used eye tracking to monitor how subjects view prints ads. Eye tracking provides a moment-by-moment recording of what a subject sees in a print ad, and a record of what a subject looks at within the context of the whole ad. It is extremely useful in determining whether, and for how long, a subject actually looks at a feature of an ad. Eye movements during exposure provide a physiological assessment of attention that is linked directly to cognitive processing.

Fixations are short periods of no eye movement during which the subject is looking at a feature of the ad. Attention is linked to visual fixation or stopping long enough to actually look (Daffner et al. 1992). Fixation is linked to cognitive processing (Just and Carpenter 1980; Rayner 1978) because the eye fixates on a word or phrase as long as it is being cognitively processed. People interpret a word while they are fixating on it, and keep fixating until they have processed it as far as they can or want (Just and Carpenter 1980; Rayner 1977, 1978). The duration of fixations, in seconds, on any part of the ad is summarized as dwell time, the time spent looking at a particular feature of the ad (such as the warning message). Dwell time is a direct measure of the subject's cognitive processing of the feature.

The validity of dwell time as a measure of cognition is confirmed in two recent studies on warnings. For two different cigarette print ads, containing different warning statements, positive and significant relationships were found between the time spent looking at the warning and the ability to remember the warning's message, as measured in follow-up masked recall tests (Krugman et al. 1994). Fletcher et al. (1995) provided more compelling evidence of a positive association between dwell time and content recall by including print ads for two nontobacco products, which also contained cautionary statements, with the above-mentioned cigarette warnings in their analyses.

High school students, 14 to 18 years of age, were recruited in Augusta, Georgia, to participate in our eye tracking study. With some exceptions, such as the study by Janiszewski and Warlop (1993), most eye tracking studies have involved small base sizes and hence tend to be qualitative. Using a large sample of 143 students enabled us to do quantitative analyses.

The experiment was conducted with one student at a time in a quiet room of the high school. We used the Applied Science Laboratories Model 425OR eye tracker. Unlike older eye trackers that have chin rests, helmets, or headbands, it requires no attachment to the participant during recording. Each participant was seated in a comfortable chair facing a rear projection screen on which slides of the test ads were presented. In front of the participant was a box containing the cameras and light sources required by the eye tracker. The participants were instructed to relax and view the slides just as though they were looking at a magazine with which they were familiar. For each ad, they viewed what they chose to view for as long as they wanted to view it. They were also told how to advance to the next slide by using the control in the arm of the chair. The eye tracking apparatus recorded eye movement throughout the period of viewing. After presentations of the ads, the students were asked to complete a questionnaire that included demographic questions.

To examine warnings and disclosures in the context of print advertising, we selected a series of five frequently run print ads from popular magazines of interest to teens. Two cigarette ads were included. A Joe Camel ad was selected because of the controversy over its use and a Marlboro ad was selected because of the broad popularity of the brand. A Miller Lite ad and a Ban de Soleil ad, each containing a voluntary disclosure statement, were also chosen. The Diet Coke ad was selected because the brand appeals to youth, and the ad provided a potential benchmark in that it contained a logo/trademark in a location similar to that of the two cigarette warnings and the voluntary disclosure for beer (lower right corner). Each participant viewed the five full-page ads (Figures 12.1-12.5) in the following order:

- ✧ Diet Coke
- ✧ Marlboro cigarettes or Camel cigarettes
- ✧ Bain de Soleil
- ✧ Marlboro cigarettes or Camel cigarettes
- ✧ Miller Lite

Any effects associated with position in the presentation sequence were likely to be most pronounced for the two ads in the same product category. Hence, the order of presentation of the two cigarette ads, Marlboro and Camel, was rotated in the study. The two groups defined by order of presentation were compared by MANOVA in which the total time attending to each of the two rotated ads was the multivariate dependent measure. We found no significant difference ($p = .21$) between the two groups. Further, we found no significant difference between the percentages attending to the warning by group for either

(text continued on p. 262)

Figure 12.1. Test Exhibit 1

Figure 12.2. Test Exhibit 2

Figure 12.3. Test Exhibit 3

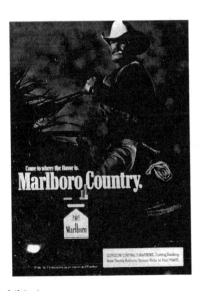

Figure 12.4. Test Exhibit 4

TABLE 12.2 Percent Attending to Mandated Warning for Cigarette Advertising

	Gender			Grade	
				9 and 10	11 and 12
	Total			(Under-	(Upper-
	Sample	Male	Female	Classmen)	Classmen)
Ad	(n = 143)	(62)	(81)	(92)	(51)
Camel	78	77	78	74	84
Marlboro	86[a]	81	90	83	92

a. Significantly higher ($p < .05$).

with the words SURGEON GENERAL'S WARNING—yet one attracted significantly more adolescents for a longer period of time.

Gender. For both ads, Camel and Marlboro, the percentages of participants fixating on the warning do not differ significantly by gender. Consistent with the findings for ads in general, the time spent dwelling on the warning was slightly higher for male respondents than for female respondents for both cigarette ads.

Grade in School. Cigarette warnings appear to be attended to more frequently by juniors and seniors (upperclassmen) in high school than by freshmen and sophomores (underclassmen). For both ads, about 10% more upperclassmen than underclassmen attended to the warning (Table 12.2). However, for our base sizes, the results are not statistically significant in either case at the .05 level.

Voluntary Cautionary Statements

The Miller Lite ad was analyzed to provide a *preliminary* understanding of how well adolescents attend to voluntary cautionary messages in alcohol ads. To date, very little, if any, research has investigated voluntary disclosures empirically. A Diet Coke ad was included to provide a point of reference. Though the products and creative elements were clearly different, both ads had limited graphic material placed on a plain white background and a small area in the lower right corner containing information in small print. In the Diet Coke ad, that area contained the Diet Coke trademark; in the Miller Lite ad, it contained a voluntary cautionary statement, "think when you drink." Thus, the Diet Coke ad provided a reasonable point of reference for simply establishing a benchmark for the impact and visibility of the Miller Lite cautionary statement. Again, by McNemar's test, the percentage of participants who fixated on the Miller Lite voluntary cautionary statement was significantly lower than the percentage who fixated in the comparable area in the Diet Coke ad, 84% versus 64% (Table 12.3). Hence, the cautionary statement attracted less attention than a miniature of a well-known trademark.

We found no significant difference in the percentage attending to the cautionary statement about drinking by gender or by grade in school, underclassmen (freshmen and sophomores) versus upperclassmen (juniors and seniors). However, the percentage attending to the warning was higher (67%) among underclassmen than among upperclassmen (59%).

Among those who fixated on the "drink responsibly" message, the average dwell time was 1.6 seconds (Table 12.3). That is less than the comparable means for the warning statements in the Camel and Marlboro cigarette ads, about 2.0 and 2.5 seconds, respectively (Krugman et al. 1994), and the trademark in the Diet Coke ad (2.0 seconds), as indicated in Table 12.3.

Discussion

____

Overall, the Camel ad received significantly more attention, as measured by dwell time, than any of the other print ads. In particular, the Joe Camel ad was looked at for almost twice as long as the Marlboro ad. Numerous factors that influence attention, such as amount of text, creative concept, execution, and product interest level, varied across the five ads. The Joe Camel ad contained a text section not present in the Marlboro ad. Hence, when comparing the Camel and Marlboro ads, we cannot unquestionably say that the difference between mean dwell times is due to the cartoon nature of the Joe Camel ad. However, if we adjust

TABLE 12.3 Results for Cautionary Statement in Miller Lite Ad

Ad	% Attending to Statement	Mean Dwell Time	
Miller Lite (n = 143)	64	1.6	(n = 92)
Diet Coke (n = 137)	84[a]	2.0	(n = 115)

a. Significantly higher (p < .01).

for the average dwell time on the text of the Camel ad (4.3 seconds), the mean viewing time for the Camel ad is still significantly and substantially longer than the mean viewing time for the Marlboro ad. We therefore can argue that the relatively high level of attention given to the Camel ad is due to the youth appeal of the Joe Camel campaign. That finding lends credibility to the arguments made by many groups, such as the 13 California cities and counties and the FTC, that the Joe Camel campaign appeals to adolescents. In fact, an R.J. Reynolds internal memo, recently made public as part of the California lawsuit, indicates that the use of "comic strip type copy" was a deliberate attempt to lure "younger smokers" away from Philip Morris' Marlboros (Neergaard 1998).

The internal validity of the experiment in the context of comparing the creative elements of the Camel and Marlboro ads, would have been greater if the ads had been more similar in their visible characteristics. In fact, if fictitious ads that were exactly the same in all elements other than Joe Camel and the Marlboro Man had been used, the results would clearly indicate that the creative element had an effect on dwell time in the experimental context. However, external validity would have been compromised and the results could be criticized as being an artifact of a contrived and artificial manipulation. Internal validity was compromised to a degree in our experiment, as is often the case (Cook and Campbell 1979, chap. 2), because we examined real ads appearing frequently in magazines of interest to adolescents.

Similar warnings differ significantly in effectiveness across print ads. Significantly more participants in our study attended to the warning in the Marlboro ad than attended to the warning in the Camel ad. Moreover, those who fixated on the warning spent more time on average viewing the Marlboro warning than viewing the Camel warning. The latter finding cannot be explained by amount of text (the Marlboro warning had 13 words and the Camel warning had 14 words). Therefore, at least for adolescents, it is critical that warnings be tested within the competitive environment of an ad, not in isolation. We clearly need an ongoing program to develop and evaluate warnings within the context in which they will be used.

Upperclassmen (eleventh and twelfth graders) appear to attend to cigarette warnings more often than underclassmen (ninth and tenth graders). Twice as many upperclassmen as underclassmen currently smoke (22% vs. 11%), which may explain the difference. However, the incidence of "ever smoking" among underclassmen is as high as it is among upperclassmen (48% and 49%, respectively). Hence, it seems to be just as important to warn underclassmen as upperclassmen. Indications that the currently mandated warnings are not effective suggest that different approaches may be needed for those two audiences.

The Miller Lite ad was viewed on average for a significantly longer period of time than the Diet Coke ad that was similar in appearance (about 14.5 seconds vs. about 10.0 seconds). Though the products, creative approaches, and executions differed for the two ads, which may explain the difference in dwell time, the fact remains that a print ad for a product whose purchase and public consumption by viewers is illegal was looked at substantially longer than an ad for a soft drink. It is also interesting that the cautionary warning in the Miller Lite ad was attended to by 64% of the adolescents, whereas the Diet Coke trademark, located in a similar position, was attended to by 84% of the adolescents. Though those two features are different, the comparison provides preliminary insight about the intrusiveness of the "drink responsibly" message.

The percentage of participants attending to the voluntary disclosure in the Miller Lite ad is also significantly ($p < .05$) less than the analogous percentages for the two mandated cigarette warnings (Table 12.2). Further, the mean time spent attending to the voluntary statement encouraging the reader to drink responsibly is considerably less than the analogous means for the two cigarette warnings. The cigarette warnings had slightly more words than the alcohol message, but the cigarette warnings used only text in sentence form (Figures 12.2 and 12.4), whereas the alcohol message integrated text into a symbol (Figure 12.5).

Hence, those measures of effectiveness suggest that the relatively novel voluntary cautionary statement is less effective than familiar mandated warnings, which have been found to have only limited impact among adolescents.

Conclusions

Adolescents have substantial interest in smoking and drinking. High school students spent more time viewing advertising for a beer brand than they spent viewing advertising for a popular soft drink brand, and as much time as they spent looking at an ad for a skin protection product. About one third of those students did not look at the cautionary statement "think when you drink." Adolescents viewed a Joe Camel cigarette ad on average for more than 16 seconds, longer than they viewed any other ad, and yet almost 25% of them never fixated on the warning message. Further, previous research has shown that the warning messages currently mandated by the government are not particularly effective in communicating health risks to the adolescent audience (Krugman et al. 1994)

Recognition of the lack of persuasive power of mandated tobacco warnings among teens has led to the inclusion of specific goals for reducing teen smoking in negotiations for a settlement of health-related claims against the tobacco industry. The pending agreement between the state attorneys general and the tobacco industry requires tobacco companies to pay a large sum of money per year for antismoking advertising and to cease marketing to teens. The proposed agreement further states specific goals for reducing underage smoking over time, which tobacco companies must meet to avoid large fines (*New York Times* 1997). No one knows what future regulations or agreements will emerge, but it appears certain that they will contain goals for reducing smoking among teens and warnings that are different from the ones currently used. The means of accomplishing the reduction goals will become the focus of much debate and research.

Drinking among adolescents is a major problem in our society. One survey found that two-thirds of eighth graders and almost 90% of high school seniors had experimented with alcohol (Johnston, Bachman, and O'Malley 1994). More troubling is the fact that 14% of the eighth graders and 28% of the high school seniors admitted that they had consumed five or more alcoholic drinks on at least one occasion in the two weeks prior to the survey. The beer industry has recognized the need to communicate to people that, if they drink, they should do so responsibly, and messages to that effect have been included in beer advertising on a voluntary basis. However, our results indicate that the disclosure used in the Miller Lite ad is less effective at attracting and holding adolescents' attention than currently mandated cigarette warnings, which have not been effective among adolescents.

Eye tracking is a useful approach for evaluating how individuals attend to print ads and can now be employed in an unobtrusive way. Less sophisticated methods can be used to measure time spent attending to an ad, but eye tracking is the only way to assess with certainty what features of an ad are actually viewed, how long specific aspects of the ad are viewed, elapsed time until a feature is viewed, and so forth. Those measures provide important indicators of how an ad is attended to. Researchers can develop a set of norms or communication standards for mandated warnings to assess effectiveness.

As the efforts to eliminate tobacco use and alcohol abuse by young people progress, more attention must be paid to the persuasiveness of antismoking and responsible drinking messages. Further, the intrusiveness and communication power of warnings included in product ads must be carefully assessed. Eye tracking can be a useful research method in related investigations among adolescents.

Our approach of investigating warnings within context of actual ads has limitations. In some cases, differences observed in our study can be attributed to more than one factor. Because we used real ads that appeared frequently in magazines read by adolescents, follow-up controlled experiments should be conducted to clarify possible ambiguities.

References

Assael, Henry (1992), *Consumer Behavior and Marketing Action,* Boston: PSW-Kent Publishing.

Beltramini, Richard F. (1988), "Perceived Believability of Warning Label Information Present in Cigarette Advertising," *Journal of Advertising,* 17 (2), 26-32.

Brandweek (1993), "Those Precocious 13-Year-Old Girls," 34 (4), 13.

Broder, John M. (1997), "Cigarette Maker Concedes Smoking Can Cause Cancer," *New York Times* (March 21), A1.

Brownlee, Lisa (1997), "Liggett's New Labels Lay It on the Line, Stating That Smoking Is Addictive," *Wall Street Journal* (May 15), B8.

Cook, Thomas D. and Donald T. Campbell (1979), *Quasi-Experimentation Design and Analysis Issues for Field Settings,* Boston: Houghton Mifflin.

Daffner, K. R., L. F. M. Scinto, S. Weintraup, J. E. Guinessey, and M. M. Mesulam (1992), "Diminished Curiosity in Patients with Probable Alzheimer's Disease as Measured by Exploratory Eye Movements," *Neurology,* 42, 2.

Davidson, Kirk (1997), "Look for Abundance of Opposition to TV Liquor Ads," *Marketing News,* 31 (1), 4, 30.

DesRoches, George (1994), "An Adman's Struggle With Joe Camel and Free Speech," *Advertising Age* (September 26), 23.

Evans, Nicola, Arthur Farkas, Elizabeth Gilpin, Charles Berry, and John P. Pierce (1995), "Influence of Tobacco Marketing and Exposure to Smokers on Adolescent Susceptibility to Smoking," *Journal of the National Cancer Institute,* 87 (20), 1538-1545.

Fischer, Paul M., Dean M. Krugman, James E. Fletcher, Richard J. Fox, and Tina H. Rojas (1993), "An Evaluation of Health Warnings in Cigarette Advertisements Using Standard Market Research Methods: What Does It Mean to Warn?" *Tobacco Control,* 2, 279-285.

———, John W. Richards, Earl J. Berman, and Dean M. Krugman (1989), "Recall and Eye Tracking Study of Adolescents Viewing Tobacco Advertisements," *Journal of the American Medical Association,* 261 (1), 84-89.

Fletcher, James E., Dean M. Krugman, Richard J. Fox, Paul Fischer, and Tina Rojas (1995), "Masked Recall and Eye Tracking of Adolescents Exposed to Cautionary Notices in Magazine Ads," *Marketing and Public Policy Conference Proceedings,* Vol. 5, P.S. Ellen and P. J. Kaufman, eds., Atlanta: Georgia State University, 128-135.

Garland, Susan B. (1997), "What May Stub Out the Settlement," *Business Week* (September 8), 83-88.

Glantz, Stanton A., John Slade, Lisa A. Bero, Peter Hanquer, and Deborah E. Barnes (1996), "The Cigarette Papers," Berkeley: University of California Press, 59-60.

Hastings, Gerald B. and Philip P. Aitken (1995), "Tobacco Advertising and Children's Smoking: A Review of the Evidence," *European Journal of Marketing,* 29 (11), 6-17.

Institute of Medicine (1994), "Growing Up Tobacco Free," Barbara S. Lynch and Richard J. Bonnie, eds., Washington, DC: National Academy Press.

Janiszewski, Chris and Luk Warlop (1993), "The Influence of Classical Conditioning Procedures on Subsequent Attention to the Conditioned Brand," *Journal of Consumer Research,* 20 (September), 171-189.

Johnston, L., J. Bachman, and P. O'Malley (1994), *1993 Monitoring the Future Survey,* Ann Arbor: University of Michigan.

Just, Marcel A. and Patricia Carpenter (1980), "A Theory of Reading: From Eye Fixations to Comprehension," *Psychological Review,* 87 (4), 329-354.

Krugman, Dean R., Richard J. Fox, James E. Fletcher, Paul M. Fischer, and Tina H. Rojas (1994), "Do Adolescents Attend to Warnings in Cigarette Advertising? An Eye

Tracking Approach," *Journal of Advertising Research,* 34 (6) (November/December), 39-52.

Lehmann, E. L. (1975), *Nonparametrics: Statistical Methods Based on Ranks,* San Francisco: Holden-Day.

Leonhardt, David (1997), "How Big Liquor Takes Aim at Teens," *Business Week* (May 19), 92.

Levanthal, Howard, Kathleen Glynn, and Raymond Fleming (1987), "Is the Smoking Decision an 'Informed Choice?' " *Journal of the American Medical Association,* 257 (24), 3373-3376.

Madden, Patricia A. and Joel W. Grube (1994), "The Frequency and Nature of Alcohol and Tobacco Advertising in Televised Sports, 1990 through 1992," *American Journal of Public Health,* 83, 585-587.

Malouf, John (1992), "Readability of Health Warnings on Alcohol and Tobacco Products," *American Journal of Public Health,* 82, 3.

Miller, Cyndee (1994), "That Is Where It's at for Today's Teen Market," *Marketing News* (August 15), 6-7.

Mizerski, Richard (1995), "The Relationship Between Cartoon Trade Character Recognition and Attitude Toward Product Category in Young Children," *Journal of Marketing,* 59 (4), 58-70.

Moroney, Tom (1995), "Teen-Age DWI Law Said To Be Little Used," *Boston Globe* (April 16), WW1.

Neergaard, Lauran (1997), "FTC Moves to Corral Joe Camel," *Atlanta Constitution* (May 29), A1.

———— (1998), "RJR Memo Targeted 'Young Adult Male Smoker,' " *Atlanta Journal* (January 15), A7.

New York Times (1997), "Excerpts from Agreement Between States and Tobacco Industry," (June 25), B8-B9.

Parker-Pope, Tara (1997), "Danger: Warning Labels May Backfire," *Wall Street Journal* (April 28), B1, B8.

Pertman, Adam (1997), "Teenage Crash-Rate is Highest," *Boston Globe* (April 4), A17.

Peter, J. Paul and Jerry C. Olson (1996), *Consumer Behavior and Marketing Strategy,* 4th ed., Chicago: Richard D. Irwin.

Pierce, J. P., L. Lee and E. A. Gilpin (1994), "Smoking Initiation by Adolescent Girls, 1944 through 1988: An Association with Targeted Advertising," *Journal of the American Medical Association,* 271 (8), 608-611.

Pollay, Richard W., S. Siddarth, M. Siegel, and A. Haddix (1996), "The Last Straw? Cigarette Advertising and Realized Market Shares Among Youths and Adults, 1979-1993," *Journal of Marketing,* 60 (2), 1-16.

Raphel, Murray (1993), "Are You Kidding?" *Direct Marketing,* 53 (3), 38-39.

Rayner, Keith (1977), "Visual Attention in Reading: Eye Movements Reflect Cognitive Processes," *Memory and Cognition,* 5 (4), 443-448.

———— (1978), "Eye Movements in Reading and Information Processing," *Psychological Bulletin,* 85 (78), 618-660.

Ross, Chuck (1996), "Anheuser-Busch Pulls Beer Ads Off MTV Network," *Advertising Age* (January 6), 4, 36.

———— and Bill McDowell (1996), "Seagram Prepares Barrage of TV Ads," *Advertising Age* (September 23), 1, 60.

———— and Ira Teinowitz (1997), "Beer Ads Had Wide Underage Reach on MTV," *Advertising Age* (January 6), 4, 36.

Shane, Scott (1997), "Pop Music Pitch Inflames Foes of Smoking: Virginia Slims Brings CD Offer to Baltimore," *Baltimore Sun* (May 5), 1A.

Shogren, Elizabeth (1995), "Clinton Seeks Strict Drunk Driving Laws," *Los Angeles Times* (June 11), A22.

Snyder, Leslie B. and Deborah J. Blood (1992), "Caution: Alcohol and The Surgeon General's Alcohol Warnings May Have Adverse Effects on Young Adults," *Journal of Applied Communication Research*, 20 (1) (February), 37-53.

Strasburger, Victor C. (1995), *Adolescents and the Media: Medical and Psychological Impact*, Thousand Oaks, CA: Sage Publications.

—— and R. T. Brown (1991), *Adolescent Medicine: A Practical Guide*, Boston: Little, Brown.

Teinowitz, Ira (1997a), "Justice Dept. Backs FDA, Sees Cig Ad/Kid Linkage," *Advertising Age* (January 20), 39.

—— (1997b), "Supreme Court's Inaction Opens Way for Outdoor Bans," *Advertising Age* (May 5), 58.

—— (1997c), "Miller Joins Exodus of Beer Ads From MTV," *Advertising Age* (May 26), 1, 44.

U. S. Department of Health and Human Services (1994a), *Morbidity and Mortality Weekly Report*, 43 (4), August 10.

—— (1994b), "Preventing Tobacco Use Among Young People: A Report of the Surgeon General," Atlanta, GA: U. S. Department of Health and Human Services et al.

Wallack, L., J. W. Grube, P. A. Madden, and W. Breed (1990), "Portrayals of Alcohol on Prime-Time Television," *Journal of Studies on Alcohol*, 51 (5), 428-437.

PART

IV

Future Directions for Research

CHAPTER

13

Advertising to Children in the Twenty-first Century

New Questions Within Familiar Themes

CHRISTINE WRIGHT-ISAK

Until recently, societal questions about advertising to children have been addressed primarily in the context of concern about the ability of television in general to influence and manipulate children. However, both academic and industry investigators have been accumulating more fundamental knowledge about this important consumer group for many years. Academic research has developed insights ranging from how children develop product understandings (Roedder John and Sujan 1990), to the different ways children process brand cues (Macklin 1996). Industry research over the past several decades has investigated how best to reach them and what products, brands, and advertising messages will appeal to them (McNeal 1992). These investigations have fallen into three areas: the impact of technology, controlling the influence advertising should be allowed to exert on children in a market-driven culture, and how we as a society should protect them from those

275

who would exploit them. As we move forward into the next century, industry phenomena are emerging that should prompt us to ask new questions within these familiar themes. The next century will raise three important issues:

✧ Scrutiny of how and why large organizations, universities, advertisers, ad agencies, and commercial research companies gather, manage, and use their accumulating information about children.

✧ The development of safeguards for children to ensure that their participation in new technologies expands their imaginations without making them vulnerable to unprecedented access to them by advertisers and others.

✧ Questions about how well and how appropriately advertisers are teaching, socializing, and entertaining children as they appeal to them on behalf of brands and products.

A Social Historical Perspective

As American society has changed, so has childhood. Children are more likely than not to live in households where both parents work; to experience the divorce of their parents and the formation of new, blended families; and to be more expert at new technologies at younger ages than previous generations. In particular, due to the rapid advance of the technologies of communications, children today truly inhabit a global village of diverse human customs and beliefs. What has not changed is that technology itself offers both benefits and dangers. Not only does the Internet allow children and others wider acquaintance with the world, it also allows the world to reach them in unexpected ways.

Technology is not the only changing aspect of society relevant to our inquiry. The interaction of advertising itself with society has become more complex. Its initial value to our individualist culture was that of bringing information to Americans about what their choices are in the marketplace (Marchand 1992). Since the penny press of the 18th and 19th centuries, advertising has become charged with greater social responsibility. Often it has volunteered to do good—most recently in campaigns like those of the Partnership for A Drug Free America or the numerous pro bono campaigns that agencies create for socially concerned corporations or institutions whose purpose is the social good. Advertising has always been accountable for factual accuracy, but more recently it is also being challenged to account for the outcomes of its efforts—especially where children are involved. However, criticism of specific advertisers is often expressed in ways that sound like criticism of the discipline of advertising in general. Closer inspection reveals that advertising is not separate from the debates and concerns of the rest of our culture, since its practitioners are members of the same society as its critics. Complicating this situation is the relatively low awareness of academic and industry researchers of each other's work and a growing need for new kinds of knowledge about children that could benefit from their collaboration. The issues that arise in the next century will require closer ties between the university and the marketplace if they are to be solved in ways that preserve democratic traditions while protecting our society's children and preparing them for the adult lives they will lead.

Fifty years ago the "new technology" of television itself had to show its capability as more than superficial by balancing its capacity for trivia with programming that was both useful and entertaining, such as The Children's Television Workshop productions. As programming for all ages was criticized in the 1960s and later, advertising itself came into sharper focus as a target for criticism, too. The issues raised paralleled the social changes occurring in American society at large.

Throughout the 1970s and 1980s advertisements were blamed for reinforcing a social status quo in which ethnic groups were negatively stereotyped, women were sex objects or servants, and a consumerist ethic threatened to trivialize social problems. Questions were raised about the effects of all this imagery on children, resulting in scrutiny of the commerce underlying the new technology. Critics questioned the products that advertisers were selling (Barbie and G.I. Joe), the way the messages were delivered (via Saturday morning programs for children), and scrutinizing who was endorsing these approaches to children (manufacturers or special interest groups). Today the Internet and cable TV are raising concerns about their influence on our society and our children.

Finally, as society's customs and conventions have become more complex, so has the definition of who is a child. Public expressions of the societal need to protect children today often assume a conception of childhood as a vulnerable time of innocence, but this assumption rarely includes specifics of when and under what circumstances childhood ends and adult individual responsibility begins. Maturation is a continuum with developmental checkpoints that vary in chronological age from one individual to the next. We necessarily use approximations in custom and law to take the real vulnerability of children into account in protecting them, and we also are often forced by circumstances to revise our conceptions. Compare our images of childhood innocence today to the Middle Ages when children were considered to be miniature adults with adult capacities for sin and virtue (Ariès 1965). Or contrast today's young consumers in the aisles of Toys R Us or learning to use the Internet to Victorian imagery of them as innocent angels, even though many as young as six years old were working in factories (Himmelfarb 1968; Mintz and Kellogg 1988). The past five years alone exemplify the difficulties of defining, much less protecting, children when we have enacted Megan's Law in many states, and are questioning the childhood status of high school shooters in several small towns around the nation.

The Next Century: New Technologies, Same Concerns

The specific issues that will preoccupy us in the next century stem from these earlier concerns. Academic research has delved into children's cognitive patterns, their socialization into sophisticated consumers, and how they process the commercial information they are given. At the same time, the marketing and advertising industries have invested in large, frequently updated, datasets that provide detailed information on the perceptions, attitudes, and behaviors of youth from toddler to teen. Today, industry conducts surveys with children and teens regarding a wide variety of their perceptions and behaviors. There are commercial datasets that tell advertisers which are the brands and products that already appeal most to children, as well as who are the most influential celebrities and other public figures; what are existing media habits; and extensive detail about why these entities are appealing, credible, and influential. Several recurrent surveys about teens, developed due to the recognition that they are the consumer group with the highest proportion of discretionary funds, explore how they purchase, what imagery influences them, and what life circumstances motivate them. Coupled with academic research that investigates how children learn, what their cognitive processing differences are from adults, and how they are socialized to make consumer choices, these data enable marketers and others to appeal more and more successfully to children's interests and to stimulate their desires with greater accuracy. Nevertheless, questions will arise over the proper use of these data to understand and influence children. They will include:

✧ Who is collecting the data and under what research circumstances?

✧ Who has access to the information?

✧ What purposes are being served by this knowledge—and how do they affect our conceptions of the need to protect children?

✧ Who are the children being investigated? What definition of *child* is being used?

✧ What are the appropriate guidelines for the questions raised above?

Those of us who conduct research about children, whether we work in the industry or in academia, will find ourselves challenged along the lines of these broad questions. We may discover that although research may inform these questions, the judgments that answer them will still fall to us as individual participants in a diverse and evolving society.

References

Ariès, Phillippe (1965), *Centuries of Childhood,* New York: McGraw-Hill.

Himmelfarb, Gertrude (1968), *Victorian Minds: A Study of Intellectuals in Crisis and Ideologies in Transition,* New York: Harper & Row.

John, Deborah Roedder and Mita Sujan (1990), "Children's Use of Perceptual Cues in Product Categorization," *Psychology and Marketing,* 7 (Winter), 452-460.

Macklin, M. Carole (1996), "Preschoolers' Learning of Brand Names From Visual Cues," *Journal of Consumer Research,* 23 (December), 251-261.

McNeal, James U. (1992), *Kids as Customers: A Handbook of Marketing to Children,* New York: Lexington.

Marchand, Roland (1992), *Advertising the American Dream: Making Way for Modernity, 1920–1940,* Berkeley: University of California Press.

Mintz, Stephen and Susan Kellogg (1988), *Domestic Revolutions: A Social History of American Family Life,* New York: Free Press.

14

The Future for Children and the Internet

CAROLE WALTERS

I have been in the media planning/buying business for almost 25 years now, and many exciting changes have occurred over that time. I have been challenged to explore and evaluate many options for clients, but the one that has presented the most dynamic opportunities to date, I believe, is the Internet.

In 1994, I began actively exploring ways to use this new tool. In October 1995, I began a pilot-project at Northlich Stolley LaWarre using a website as a testing area to determine whether it was possible to gain consumer insights from children/young teens (ages 8-14).

We confirmed previous learning about this age group—they are curious, they are early-adapters, they want to be entertained, they can be fickle, they are pushing for independence yet are still very susceptible to peer pressure.

The website experience allowed them to share their own consumer habits and practices—they were thrilled that we were asking them, not their moms. They felt empowered because we accepted them rather than bypassed them.

We ended up with a powerful consumer panel that could easily be accessed for any number of product testing or quantitative habits and practices research. Since much of our access to this audience was through cooperation with K-12 educators who had a vision for what the Internet could offer, we did some in-classroom research that served two purposes:

1. It provided a ready opportunity for teachers to include it as a classroom project.
2. We were able to access a more representative population of children because they did not have to have a computer in their household to participate.

There is much more detailed information that could be shared regarding what we implemented in the field and the interpretation of the data, but to me, the biggest insight (or blinding glimpse of the obvious) was the potential of this medium to be so much more than just another channel of distribution for static advertising communications and/or entertainment.

The key to unlocking this potential is to unleash the innate ability of children to multi-task.

Anyone under the age of 25 is not aware of a world without MTV, Nickelodeon, VCRs, and video games. Those under the age of 15 live in a world of cellular phones, pagers, Internet access, video and audio centers, and camcorders—all readily accessible if not owned personally. And, they can program a VCR in their sleep!

If you have a young teen in your home, you will have noticed that he or she often uses many of these at the same time! As a parent, you may not think of this a very good practice—but it is great! Fortune 500 companies are paying big money to train their executives to multi-task. We have a whole generation of individuals who already have this skill. We need to understand its value and develop new techniques for educating and communicating using it as a tool.

In our overregulated, paranoid society we are overlooking the potential that the Internet provides to enrich and improve children's learning experience. Government, parental control advocates, and parents with no personal working knowledge of the Internet are making decisions and lobbying for laws that could block all the "good" learning that this tool has to offer before we have even scratched the surface of its potential.

Consider an environment where children can "tour a country," learning its history, geography, and culture; they can hear the language spoken or learn it, while simultaneously teaching English to a another student who lives in that country.

Consider an environment where children participate in the organization of a mountain climbing expedition to Mt. Everest. They work with real climbers to get financial support; they assist in planning the type of food needed and determine quantities needed to sustain 25 people for three months; they design the travel itinerary for the climbers leaving from Seattle, Washington; Anchorage, Alaska; Cincinnati, Ohio; and London, England to meet in Katmandu within hours of one another.

Consider an environment where William Shakespeare is someone you can actually get to know and, ultimately, the idea of buying Cliff Notes doesn't even come to mind!

Think of any example that ties several subjects together or offers a subject in a more compelling way for a more involving and potentially more effective learning experience, and it can be done via the Internet.

Educators have told us time and again that while they appreciate corporate donations of computers or funding for computers and Internet access, if they do not have the necessary skills and tools, the equipment is seriously underutilized. Without proper training and ideas to incorporate computers in the classroom, many teachers are left frustrated. It is like giving a carpenter a hammer and nails but no blueprint for what he should be building.

Often, educators are only capable of teaching how to use e-mail and search engines because of their own personal lack of knowledge about the vast potential that the Internet offers. They should be exploring truly interactive assignments, live chats with experts, and shared learning with classrooms around the world.

There is a real opportunity for us, as communicators, to develop the blueprints that will enable educators to do a better job; enable our children to learn in a more involving and captivating environment; provide learning experiences to children who may never have the opportunity to explore the world beyond a few-block radius of their homes. By dedicating some of our effort to this, we will help ourselves in the long run. We will have aided in the development of a population of future employees whose creativity has been nurtured, not squelched. Consider an environment where individuals can think through, and understand, everything from transactional spreadsheets to an advertising concept!

In conclusion, I suggest that research be done against two objectives:

1. Determine what level of training K-12 educators need in order to optimize the Internet as a learning environment.
2. Measure the impact on media usage habits and advertising recall against varied levels of multi-tasking skills.

CHAPTER

15

Advertising's Effects

Juxtaposing Research With Older and Younger Youths

MARVIN E. GOLDBERG

A s with many literatures, the research examining advertising's effects on the young has tended to be somewhat insular. By convention, a somewhat arbitrary line has typically been set at age 12 to 13, such that there has been little cross-fertilization between those examining the responses of two- to 12-year-olds and those examining the responses of 13- to 18-year olds. While there may be meaningful developmental differences within each of these age groups, and while the goals of each subset of researchers may differ to some extent, there is likely much to be learned by juxtaposing their approaches, substantive findings, strengths, and weaknesses.

In recent years, society has evidenced as much or more concern for the vulnerability of 13- to 18-year-olds to advertising as for two- to 12-year-olds: witness the efforts to limit advertising for cigarettes because of their appeal for *all* young people under the legal (smoking) age of 18 and perhaps especially those in their teenage years. The literature on the effects of advertising on teenage smoking is one of the more extensive ones examining the reactions of youths to advertising (for an excellent summary, see U.S. Department of Health and Human Services 1994). Juxtaposing it with the literature examining advertising's effects on two- to 12-year-olds should be informative.

Is 12 to 13 a valid cutoff in examining young people's responses to advertising? Developmental psychologists typically differentiate on a number of dimensions between the developmental level associated with teenagers as distinct from younger children (cf. Kohlberg 1987). However, in terms of susceptibility to advertising targeted at them, consideration of just two studies suggests that the validity of drawing a clear line between the two age groups is more questionable. Roedder, Sternthal, and Calder (1983) did produce findings that contrasted the responses of nine- and 13-year-olds. Advertising induced the younger but not the older children to disregard their preestablished preference hierarchy. This would suggest that those 13 and above are better equipped than those younger than them to fend off advertising appeals and might be separately categorized. However, a study by Ross et al. (1981) found that 14-year-olds were no less influenced by the irrelevancies in an ad for a toy racing car than were younger children. These results would argue against categorizing at least 14-year-olds separately from younger children.

One of the strengths of the two- to 12-year-old literature is the accumulated weight of a large set of randomized experiments in which children are exposed or not exposed to a variety of advertising stimuli, typically for food or toys (for an excellent review, see Young 1990). The preponderance of evidence suggests that exposure to such advertising causally leads to a variety of effects among these youths, including attitudes favoring the advertised brands and related choice behavior. For obvious ethical reasons, parallel experiments exposing 13- to 18-year-olds (or still younger children) to cigarette advertising have not been conducted. To the extent the persuasion process for consumer goods such as candy, cereal, fast food, and toys is similar to that for cigarettes, one might also infer a causal linkage between advertising to youth and cigarette smoking. In this way, the literature on cigarettes and youth would gain considerably by a careful study of the two- to 12-year-old-advertising effects literature.

Conversely, consider the weaknesses inherent in the experimental paradigm favored by those studying two- to 12-year-olds, including the relative artificiality of the laboratory setting and the limited nature of the dependent measures utilized (for a related discussion, see Goldberg and Gorn 1983). Given these shortcomings, researchers in this domain might gain considerably from the approaches taken by those considering cigarette advertising and youth. Precluded from doing randomized experiments, researchers in this field have resorted to small- or large-scale lagged-time studies. Small-scale studies have documented how youths whose actual or ideal self-image more closely approximates their perception of a smoker (presumably gained in part as a result of exposure to cigarette advertising) are more likely to start smoking at a subsequent time (Aloise-Young, Hennigan, and Graham 1996).

Large-scale studies have used econometric methods to show that where countries (such as Norway) have stringently restricted cigarette advertising, total demand for cigarettes by youths has subsequently fallen (United Kingdom Department of Health 1992). What these studies lack in "air-tight" causal linkages, they make up for in mundane realism/external validity. Researchers examining advertising's effects on two- to 12-year-olds would benefit from a consideration of this literature. With worldwide sales of Barbie Dolls exceeding one billion dollars annually, econometric studies linking level of advertising to sales may well be possible, even with regard to this single product.

Another way the literature examining two- to 12-year-olds might benefit from the cigarette advertising and youth literature is with regard to the latter's focus on imagery, affect, and motives. Young (1990) suggests that future research with two- to 12-year-olds ought to incorporate more fully the affective dimension. Affect and motive have been relatively absent in the past, with research dominated by an information processing paradigm. The emphasis has been on what young people perceive, understand, and remember. Yet "knowing that advertisers want to sell you something in order to make a profit" is not necessarily a sufficient defense against advertising. In the short term, the hedonic value of a commercial, its emotional allure, and its ability to tap into powerful motives may be sufficient to eclipse momentarily any cognitive knowledge/defense. In the long term, low involvement learning operates such that the images of various brands "wash over" children and are internalized by them with little awareness of the process. The impact of affect and motive-linked imagery is something that seems to have been more intuitively appreciated by those studying cigarette advertising's effects on teens, perhaps because of the powerful images inherent in the Marlboro man and Joe Camel campaigns as well as attractive outdoor and interpersonal scenes in campaigns such as those for Newport and Salem cigarettes.

Our understanding of specific issues/concepts might benefit from a longer term consideration across age groups. For example, the study of family relationships between younger children and their parents (Carlson and Grossbart 1989) might lead to a better understanding of which children are later motivated as teenagers to smoke as a sign of rebellion and why this is the case. As a second example, children who are more heavily exposed to advertising at a young age appear to be more likely to develop stereotypes (such as those based on gender; Moschis and Moore 1982). It may be these children in particular who subsequently become more susceptible to media images of cigarettes such as the Marlboro man, which are themselves caricatures or stereotypes.

Dependent measures in one field may be borrowed and used to advantage in the other. As an example, consider the notion of the perceived prevalence of cigarette smoking by teenagers. Research has documented that teenagers who are more heavily exposed to cigarette advertising give higher estimates when asked for the percentage of their peers who smoke. In turn, a higher perceived prevalence of smoking is hypothesized to put teens at higher risk to begin smoking (Leventhal, Glynn, and Fleming 1987). Heavy advertising exposure by younger children may lead to the normative perception that many or even most children own a particular toy or go frequently to a specific fast food outlet. This in turn, may be a predictor of the child's subsequent behavior vis-à-vis that product/service.

One of the aspects of the effort to limit if not eliminate advertising for cigarettes to youths has been proposed restrictions on point-of-purchase advertising. This concern for the importance of the point of purchase in targeting youths appears to be well founded. Of the more than one billion dollars spent on advertising to children, about $200 million or 20% is spent on point-of-purchase advertising (McNeal 1992). It is clearly a gap in our research efforts that of all the advertising research done with children there is nothing close to 20% that has concerned itself with point-of-purchase influence. In the same vein, researchers will have to be alert to the new media that are highly likely to grow in importance. These include not just the omnipresent Internet, but also other experiments such as companies reaching children directly through pagers. To continue to focus research efforts largely on (network) television would be an error.

References

Aloise-Young, Patricia A., Karen M. Hennigan, and John W. Graham (1996), "Role of the Self-Image and Smoker Stereotype in Smoking Onset During Early Adolescence: A Longitudinal Study," *Health Psychology*, 15 (6), 494-497.

Carlson, Les and Sanford Grossbart (1988), "Parental Style and Consumer Socialization of Children," *Journal of Consumer Research*, 15 (June), 77-94.

Goldberg, Marvin E. and Gerald J. Gorn (1983), "Researching the Effects of TV Advertising on Children: A Methodological Critique," in *Learning From Television: Psychological and Educational Research*, M. Howe, ed., London: Academic Press.

Kohlberg, Lawrence (1987), *Childhood Psychology and Childhood Education*, New York: Longman.

Leventhal, Howard, Kathleen Glynn, and Raymond Fleming (1987), "Is the Smoking Decision an Informed Choice? Effect of Smoking Risk Factors on Smoking Beliefs," *Journal of the American Medical Association*, 257 (24), 3373-3376.

McNeal, James U. (1992), *Kids as Customers*. New York: Macmillan (Lexington).

Moschis George P. and R. L. Moore (1982), "A Longitudinal Study of Television Advertising Effects," *Journal of Consumer Research* 9 (3), 279-286.

Roedder, Debbie, Brian Sternthal, and Bobby J. Calder (1983), "Attitude-Behavior Consistency in Children's Responses to Television Advertising," *Journal of Marketing Research*, 20, 337-349.

Ross, R. P., T. Campbell, J. C. Wright, A. C. Huston, M. L. Rice, and P. Turk (1981), "When Celebrities Talk, Children Listen: An experimental Analysis of Children's Responses to TV Ads With Celebrity Endorsement," working paper, Lawrence: Center for Research on the Influence of Television on Children, University of Kansas.

United Kingdom Department of Health (1992), *Effect of Tobacco Advertising on Tobacco Consumption: A Discussion Document Reviewing the Evidence*, London: UK Department of Health, Economics and Operational Research Division.

U.S. Department of Health and Human Services (1994), *Preventing Tobacco Use Among Young People: A Report of the Surgeon General*, Washington, DC: Government Printing Office.

Young, Brian M. (1990), *Television Advertising and Children*, Oxford, UK: Oxford University Press.

CHAPTER

16

The Context of
Advertising and Children

Future Research Directions

JEFFREY J. STOLTMAN

Over the past several decades we have achieved a deeper and broader understanding of a number of different aspects of the relationship between advertising and children. Continuing interest in this topic reflects the assurance that children are influenced, by advertising and by all life experiences, in unique and important ways. There is a desire not only to understand what this influence might be, but also to provide appropriate safeguards against potentially negative influences. There is a continuing dialogue reflecting both more protective and more permissive points of view. Past and future research must be viewed in this context, and to the degree that this context ebbs and flows, future research would be expected to adapt accordingly.

The cognitive, emotional, social, and behavioral influence of advertising on children has been the subject of numerous studies reported across the disciplines of marketing, communications, psychology, and

291

sociology. What children understand about advertising representation, and the limitations and implications of their comprehension, has been the focus of most of the research in this arena. Another area of research has explored advertising's role in consumer socialization and in developing specific consumption habits. In recent years, we have been able to obtain a clearer understanding of the economic importance of advertising's influence. Aggregate spending by children is estimated to be more than $20 billion annually, and climbing. Children are a "primary market" for hundreds of companies and products. Children are also believed to exert significant direct and indirect influence on billions of dollars in other purchases each year. The moderating influence of caregivers—both in respect to socialization in general and with regard to the acquisition and application of specific product knowledge—represents a related though distinct area of research made all the more important by these figures.

In each of these areas, important work has been done—including efforts made by the authors contributing to this volume—and this research should certainly continue. Others have identified the nature of the most fruitful avenues to explore and the additional effort required. That exercise will not be repeated here. The purpose of this brief commentary is to present issues these future endeavors might wish to take into consideration.

Areas of Expanded Inquiry

Research regarding advertising and children will continue to expand because it is in the nature of scientific inquiry. New theories will be developed, applied from other fields, or both; there will be new constructs, measures, and procedures. Steady advances in the psychological literature regarding human abilities, developmental processes, perceptual learning, memory, and attitude formation would be the most productive areas to examine. Any recent review of these fields will provide a treasure trove of possibilities.

Our capability to observe, record, and conduct analysis will undoubtedly evolve further as well. The same basic issues—what do children need, want, feel, know, think, do, do repeatedly—and how does advertising influence each of these—will continue to capture our interest. Yet the basic approach to each question will likely change. Thus far, there has been little use/adaptation of the range of measures employed in educational settings. There is fertile ground to be plowed in the educational and school psychology literature, particularly with respect to learning assessment procedures involving icon-based measures and adaptive use of video games and board games. There have also been dramatic advances in the use of computing technology to present stimuli and to measure responses. These can be easily adapted and applied to the questions we have about advertising and children. A push in these directions will have practical applications as well, since the advertising research industry still lacks an adequate copy-testing system for use with child consumers.

In general, there has been little methodological variation observed in the research on advertising and children. Most studies deploy rather conventional experimental and survey research methods. These efforts have provided many important insights, but the one-shot approach should be complemented by research that allows us to observe the ways in which advertising influences children over time and across different contexts. In particular, it is high time we began to approach the study of advertising and children in the field—in the real world. A review of the quasi-experimental approaches advocated by Cook and Campbell (1979) will demonstrate how the appropriate level of scientific validity can be achieved as we begin to explore the richness of the boundary between advertising and children. The quasi-experimental approach will also provide a foundation for much needed longitudinal research.

Future researchers should also consider engaging in comparative studies. There should be replications of prior research with samples drawn from different ethnic and socioeconomic segments. Cross-sectional research is also needed because of the increased diversity of the U.S. population. This effort would complement the insights we have gained about the importance of factors such as age and gender, and help demonstrate the external validity of the findings previously reported. Similarities and differences across economic classes and cultures must be empirically demonstrated. Children appear to prefer national brands, probably the consequence of the amount of attention given to them by those who market national brands. Whether this is evident across all economic groups, and across all product categories, is less clear.

The tremendous growth in the size of the children's market is largely attributed to growth within different ethnic groups as a consequence of both immigration policy and birthrates. Thus, the practical importance of this research will also be considerable. Another confluence of practical concerns and scholarly research is the growth in the global economy. The emerging economies provide an unparalleled opportunity to observe the influence of advertising on children as it begins to take hold.

While similar future directions might be expected in just about every field of inquiry, the most dramatic expansion in the study of advertising and children will result because of the significant changes in advertising and, possibly, in children. The explosion of new technologies has led many scholars and commentators to conclude that we are witnessing the emergence of a new economic and social structure. Whether one accepts such speculation or not, the Internet and the near omnipresence of the computer have certainly altered the nature of the boundary between advertising and children. Likewise, what we know about children may be changing as a consequence of the significant demographic and lifestyle changes occurring over the past 25 years or more. The economic magnitude of the child market reflects these changes.

Many children now grow up in ways and in households dramatically different from the household of decades past. It is plausible to assume that the way in which children cognitively filter advertising has changed, and that a more direct link between advertising and purchase would be readily observable. Children are spending time and money in ways previously unseen; the amount of parental "control" exercised may be changing as well.

Many households are now led by a single parent, and, regardless of the number of control agents, many have less opportunity to exercise control because the demands of work often require a great deal more time away from one's children. "Parents who work longer hours have less time, and so do the kids. Between tutoring, after-school activities, organized sports programs and homework at lower grade levels; children have less time to do what they want. They are even watching less television than they were five years ago" (Pereira and Bulkeley 1998). If the "nurture" factor has been transformed, then our understanding of this moderating influence needs to be reexamined. And if children are watching less television, perhaps our preoccupation with this particular form of advertising should be reconsidered. In general, there is a need for research focused on advertising presented in other media—this shift in time use would make the case more compelling.

A related area of importance involves the well-documented age-related differences in the influence of advertising. There has been the suggestion that, as a result of the changes occurring around them, children are growing up faster. This so-called age compression—attributed to factors such as caregiver work habits and exposure to a broader portion of the adult advertising, entertainment, and life experience bandwidth—must be empirically demonstrated. Yet if it is occurring, and many in the education system accept that it is, it could very well alter what we believe about the influence of advertising at various ages. It could also begin to alter the public policy debate and the research focused on public policy issues.

For example, the policies and guidelines advanced by the Children's Advertising Review Unit (CARU) of the Better Business Bureau are based on the premise that children lack the sophistication and maturity needed to deal appropriately with advertising. The implicit notion of a vulnerable child stands in contrast to the view of children as hardened realists. Research can make significant contributions in this context, and we might expect an invigorated round of research on the capabilities of the child consumer.

Whether or not one accepts the view of a "hardened" child consumer, one cannot easily dismiss the reality surrounding children of today and tomorrow. The recent announcement of an effort to address the problem of drug use by focusing a multimillion dollar advertising campaign at children, and similarly targeted campaigns regarding tobacco, alcohol, and sexual conduct, serve as reminders of the realities that children must learn to navigate. Researchers can be expected to contribute to our understanding of the effectiveness of these campaigns.

Another area deserving of attention involves the short- and long-term effects of exposure to communications intended for adult audiences. The fact that many of these "misdirected" communications send contrary signals, signals that may overwhelm messages advocating abstinence and moderation, should be examined. It is hard to watch a sporting event where entertaining ads promoting alcoholic beverages are not prominently displayed, and hard to find even a PG movie where matters of sexual conduct aren't portrayed in a conflicting manner. So-called family programming is frequently accompanied by advertising breaks containing trailers for feature films that portray scenes objectionable to many parents. Which message stream has the greater impact? Do children process these communications in the same way, and with the same effect, or does the adult fare have a different type and degree of influence on children—perhaps because it is meant for adults? Is the influence heightened by the diminished parental control presented to many children? Research can make important contributions to the understanding of the effects of various attempts to intervene and shape future behavior. By its very nature, such research calls out for the application of longitudinal, comparative, and field methods noted above.

The antidrug campaign is noteworthy in another respect. This government effort includes a significant arrangement with the Walt Disney Co.—now a media and entertainment conglomerate. Disney will place advertisements in its various broadcast and print outlets, along with promotions on the property of its entertainment venues (Teinowitz 1998). The context of advertising and children has changed because of the emergence of such highly integrated, multimedia enterprises.

The CARU guidelines address the tremendous transformation of the advertising industry in the past decade. Thus far, these changes have scarcely affected scholarly research focused on advertising and children. CARU guidelines have been developed covering videos, films, software, and interactive media such as the Internet and on-line services. There are also guidelines pertaining to premiums and promotions targeting children. The influence of these various "media" is not well understood, and the cumulative effect of a so-called integrated marketing effort— one that bears down on a target market coordinating and using all media and promotions as are appropriate—is even less understood.

From one perspective, the lines separating advertising from other forms of market influence have blurred to the point where a distinct boundary may no longer exist. The promotions and merchandising of marketers both transcend and transform advertising. Cable channels, such as Nickelodeon, Cartoon Network, and Fox Kids, now focus squarely on the youth market. No longer is the action confined to Saturday morning television. Enterprise systems, such as Disney, and even the Children's Television Workshop, have reached beyond television and advertising. These conglomerates are developing and merchandising products and services, ranging from performing troupes to theme parks, to theatrical releases complete with complete lines of licensed toys, clothing, and school supplies. Brands such as Nike, Reebok, Powerade, and Chevrolet have entire advertising campaigns— intended for adults—built around sponsorship of youth athletic federations. Magazines—such as *Barbie Magazine*—serve as printed "infomercials."

Sports Illustrated recently introduced a magazine for children, along with a Saturday morning television show and web site extending this effort. The LEGO company has used a catalog marketing program, and in its recent CD-rom product provided inserts that "advertised" various product lines, offered an inducement to join the "Lego Kids Club," and the CD itself provided links to the Lego web site, which provided more of the same. Other marketing firms are hard at work compiling and "scoring" lists of children's names—lists obtained from Little League rosters, responses to Burger King promotions, and purchases of postage stamps from the U.S. Postal Service. The name lists are then used to mail "advertising" directly into the home. There is ample room for future researchers to make a contribution because there has been little research focused on the influence of many of the media options that marketers are learning to harness.

Computer technology has further extended the shape of advertising, such that its reach is now directly to children, often with little chance that parental intervention will occur. Some have observed that this technology is to the current and next generation what television has been to the baby boomer generation (Crispell 1998).

Children can now seek out information, rather than wait to be exposed. Following ad exposure, children can use the computer to actively seek additional information, thus transforming the influence of the advertising. There has been a good deal of discussion about the need to "protect" children who are exposed to advertising via the Internet, but so far there hasn't been a demonstration of the influence of this form of advertising. Information is also being provided more quickly; and advertisers have a more engaging repertoire of techniques at their disposal thanks to technological advances. Children may be acquiring a limited "attention span"—that needs to be demonstrated, and the implication needs to be explored. At a minimum, it seems important to find out how children are integrating all of this.

Surely the influence of advertising on children is taking on new meaning as the context continues to evolve at a rapid pace. It will be far easier to identify uncharted waters than it will be to isolate the influence of advertising. Researchers have plenty to do, and the subject matter is arguably of greater importance than ever before.

References

Cook, Thomas D. and Donald T. Campbell (1979), *Quasi-Experimentation: Design and Analysis Issues for Field Settings,* Chicago: Rand McNally.

Crispell, Diane (1998), "Fruit of the Boom: What's the Difference Between Baby Boomers and Their Children?" *Marketing Tools* (April), 38-43.

Pereira, Joseph and William Bulkeley (1998), "Toy-Buying Patterns Are Changing and That Is Shaking the Industry," *Wall Street Journal* (June 16), A1, A8.

Teinowitz, Ira (1998), "Disney Leads Media Pack in Deals for Anti-Drug Ads," *Advertising Age* (July 13), 39.

Index

299

About the Editors

Les Carlson is Professor of Marketing, Clemson University, Clemson, South Carolina. He received his Ph.D. in Business (Marketing) from the University of Nebraska–Lincoln. His work on advertising and socialization effects has been widely published in such journals as *Journal of Advertising, Journal of Consumer Research, Journal of Public Policy & Marketing, Journal of Consumer Affairs, Journal of the Academy of Marketing Science,* and *Journal of Business Research.* He has served as the editor of the *Journal of Advertising.*

M. Carole Macklin is Professor of Marketing, University of Cincinnati, Cincinnati, Ohio. She received her Ph.D. in Business Administration from The Ohio State University in 1981. Her research on issues of advertising and marketing to children have appeared in such journals as *Journal of Advertising, Journal of Consumer Research, Journal of Advertising Research, Journal of Consumer Affairs, Marketing Letters,* and *Psychology & Marketing.* She is an active member of the American Academy of Advertising, serving as President (1999).

311

About the Authors

Robert Abelman (Ph.D., University of Texas-Austin, 1982; M.A., Michigan State University) is Distinguished Professor of Communication and Assistant Dean of Arts & Sciences at Cleveland State University. His research interests include media literacy and media literacy education, particularly among exceptional child populations. He serves as a consultant to the children's television industry and children's advocacy organizations.

Alison Alexander (Ph.D., Ohio State University) is a Professor and Department Head of the Department of Telecommunications, Grady College of Journalism & Mass Communication, University of Georgia. She works in the area of audience research, with a focus on children and the family.

David Atkin (Ph.D., M.A., Michigan State University) is Professor of Communication at Cleveland State University. His research interests include past and present diffusion of new media, and the access opportunities they create for underrepresented groups.

Louise M. Benjamin is Associate Professor, Department of Telecommunications, Grady College of Journalism and Mass Communication, University of Georgia. Her research areas are media history, telecommunications policy history, and contemporary media law and policy. She has published numerous scholarly book chapters and journal articles in communication publications.

Terry Bristol (Ph.D., Virginia Polytechnic Institute and State University, 1992) is Assistant Professor of Marketing & Advertising at the University of Arkansas at Little Rock. His research interests include the acquisition of skills by younger consumers through socialization and those factors researchers can control that impact focus group output.

Cindy Dell Clark (Ph.D., University of Chicago) has done research with children on a consulting basis for prominent national clients (including McDonald's, Nestle, Oscar Mayer, Kraft, Nike, Frito Lay, Coca Cola Foods Division, and others), and has been a researcher at a national advertising agency (Leo Burnett). In addition, she has taught numerous college and graduate level courses, including both social sciences and consumer behavior, and has authored several academic publications. She current teaches at Rutgers University Camden. She holds an interdisciplinary doctorate, a Ph.D. from the University of Chicago Committee on Human Development.

Paul M. Fischer (M.D., University of Connecticut), was one of the first researchers in the areas of the influence of tobacco advertising on children, and the limitations of in-ad warnings for tobacco products. His research identified the widespread recognition of "Old Joe," the Camel cartoon character, by very young children. He served as an expert witness to the state Attorneys General in their now-settled suits against the tobacco industry. He currently serves as CEO of Center for Primary Care, a multisite health care provider in Augusta, Georgia.

James E. Fletcher (Ph.D., University of Utah) is Professor of Telecommunications and Associate Vice President for Academic Affairs at the University of Georgia. He is Editor of *Journal of Broadcasting and Electronic Media,* a refereed journal of the Broadcast Education Association. He is known for research on physiological effects of communication messages and commercial testing, as well as audience measurement for the electronic media. His latest work addresses higher education curricula for the 21st century.

Richard J. Fox (Ph.D., Michigan State University), is Associate Professor, Department of Marketing and Distribution, University of Georgia. Before joining academia, he worked in consumer research for over 10 years at Procter & Gamble. His publications have appeared in numerous academic journals, including the *Journal of the Academy of Marketing Science, Public Opinion Quarterly, Journal of Advertising Research,* and the *Journal of Advertising.* He is coauthor of a marketing research textbook, *Marketing Research Principles and Applications.*

James W. Gentry (Ph.D., Indiana University) is a Professor in the Department of Marketing at the University of Nebraska-Lincoln. He has served on the marketing faculty at Kansas State University, Oklahoma State University, and the University of Wisconsin-Madison. His current research interests focus on issues in cross-cultural consumer behavior and in family decision making.

Marvin E. Goldberg is the Irving and Irene Bard Professor of Marketing at Penn State University. He is a past president of the Society for Consumer Psychology. Among the editorial boards on which he serves are the *Journal of Consumer Research, Journal of Consumer Psychology,* and *Journal of Public Policy and Marketing.* His current research involves theory-based interventions aimed at inhibiting alcohol and cigarette usage among adolescents. His research has been published in a wide variety of scholarly journals.

Ronald Paul Hill (Ph.D., University of Maryland) is a Professor in and Dean of the School of Business Administration at the University of Portland, Oregon. He holds B.S., MBA, and Ph.D. degrees in business administration from the University of Maryland at College Park. Previously, he served on the faculties at Villanova, Cornell, American University, George Washington, and University of Maryland at College Park. He has published over 80 scholarly works in major journals and professional proceedings on topics including marketing management, advertising, health care, consumer behavior, and ethics.

Keisha Hoerrner (Ph.D., University of Georgia, 1998) is an Assistant Professor in the Manship School of Mass Communication at Louisiana State University. Her research interests include pedagogical training in graduate programs, children and television issues, and electronic media regulation. She teaches media law, electronic media law and policy, research methods, and mass media industries and behavior, and is currently developing a special topics course on children and television.

Deborah Roedder John (Ph.D., Northwestern University) is the Curtis L. Carlson Chair in Marketing, Carlson School of Management, University of Minnesota, Minneapolis. She served on the faculties of UCLA and the University of Wisconsin prior to her appointment at Minnesota. She has published widely in major marketing journals, including the *Journal of Marketing Research,* the *Journal of Consumer Reseach,* and the *Journal of Marketing.* She is a member of the editorial boards of these three journals as well as the *Journal of Consumer Psychology* and the *Journal of Public Policy & Marketing.* She has served as an associate editor for the *Journal of Consumer Research* and is currently the founding editor of the Monographs of the *Journal of Consumer Research.* She has also served as president and treasurer of the Association for Consumer Research. Her current research interests focus on children and consumer brands, especially the measurement of brand equity in children and the meanings of brands to children of different ages.

Richard H. Kolbe (Ph.D., University of Cincinnati), is an Associate Professor of Marketing at Kent State University. His research involves issues related to children and advertising, fine print in advertising, fan loyalty in professional sports, and the use of content analysis data collection methods. His publications have appeared in the *Journal of Consumer Research, Journal of Advertising, Journal of Current Issues and Research in Advertising, Sex Roles,* and other academic journals and proceedings. He is a member of the editorial review board of the *Journal of Advertising* and the *Journal of Current Issues and Research in Advertising.*

Dean M. Krugman (Ph.D., University of Illinois) is Professor and Department Head, Department of Advertising and Public Relations at the University of Georgia. His Ph.D. in communications research (1977) and M.S. in advertising (1972) are both from the University of Illinois at Urbana. He holds a B.S. in journalism from Southern Illinois University (1970). His expertise is in the areas of marketing communication research, how people deal with media change, and how people process warning information. One of his recent studies on audiences and advertising received the 1995 outstanding research article award from the *Journal of Advertising.* He has published articles in several other leading academic journals (e.g., *Journal of Advertising Research, Journal of Broadcasting & Electronic Media, Journalism Quarterly, Journal of The American Medical Association,* and *Health Communication*).

Russell N. Laczniak (Ph.D., University of Nebraska) is Associate Professor of Marketing, College of Business, Iowa State University. His research foci include the effects of advertising targeted at children and consumers' processing of marketing communication. He has published in numerous journals and proceedings, including the *Journal of Advertising, Journal of Current Issues and Research in Advertising, Journal of Public Policy and Marketing, Journal of Consumer Affairs, Journal of Marketing Communication,* and *Journal of Business Research.*

David Luna (Ph.D., University of Wisconsin-Milwaukee) is Assistant Professor of Marketing at Chapman University, Orange, California. His research interests include marketing to children, cross-cultural consumer behavior, and the application of psycholinguistics theories to advertising. His research has appeared in the *Journal of Advertising, Advances in Consumer Research,* and the proceedings of a number of national and international conferences.

Tamara F. Mangleburg (Ph.D., Virginia Polytechnic Institute and State University) is Associate Professor of Marketing at Florida Atlantic University. Her research interests include the consumer socialization and behavior of children, family decision making, and self-concept effects on persuasion. She has published articles on these topics in the *Journal of Advertising, Journal of Consumer Affairs, Journal of the Academy of Marketing Science,* and *Advances in Consumer Research.* She is a member of the editorial review board for the *Journal of Macromarketing.*

Mary C. Martin (Ph.D., University of Nebraska–Lincoln) is Vice President of Sun Global, Charlotte, North Carolina. Her work has been published, among other places, in the *Journal of Advertising, Journal of Public Policy & Marketing,* and *Psychology and Marketing.*

Darrel D. Muehling (Ph.D., University of Nebraska) is Professor and Chair of the Department of Marketing, Washington State University,

Pullman. His research on consumer responses to advertising has been published in numerous advertising/marketing journals, including the *Journal of Advertising, Journal of Current Issues & Research in Advertising, Journal of Advertising Research,* and *Journal of Public Policy & Marketing,* among others. He currently serves on the editorial review boards of the *Journal of Current Issues & Research in Advertising* and the *Journal of Marketing Communications,* and is President-Elect of the American Academy of Advertising.

Laura Peracchio (Ph.D., Northwestern University) is a Professor of Marketing at the University of Wisconsin-Milwaukee. She also has degrees in marketing and psychology from the Wharton School and the College of Arts and Sciences of the University of Pennsylvania. Her research focuses on how marketing information impacts young children and how visual information impacts consumers of all ages. Her research has been published in the *Journal of Consumer Research* and the *Journal of Marketing Research.* She has received awards from the Marketing Science Institute and the American Marketing Association for research excellence.

Barbara J. Phillips (Ph.D., University of Texas at Austin) is an Associate Professor of Marketing at the University of Saskatchewan. She received her M.A. and Ph.D. in Advertising from the University of Texas at Austin, and her undergraduate degree in Marketing from the University of Manitoba (Canada). Her research interests include spokes-characters, rhetoric in advertising images, and popular culture. She has published papers in such journals as the *Journal of Advertising, Journal of Advertising Research,* and the *Journal of Business Ethics.*

Bonnie B. Reece (Ph.D., University of Michigan) is a Professor and the Chairperson of the Department of Advertising at Michigan State University, East Lansing, Michigan. She teaches Advertising and Promotion

Management as well as Quantitative Research Design, both graduate-level courses. Her research interests have focused primarily on children as consumers, nutrition claims in food advertising, and the advertising of prescription drugs directly to consumers.

Nora J. Rifon (Ph.D., City University of New York) is an associate professor in the Department of Advertising at Michigan State University. She holds degrees in psychology from the University of Rochester (B.A.) and the State University of New York at Binghamton (M.A.). Her Ph.D. in Business is from the City Unversity of New York Graduate Center. She is interested in all areas of consumer behavior and advertising, but has focused much of her research in the area of consumer health decisions and related advertising and promotions. She has coauthored a textbook, two book chapters, several journal articles, and conference proceedings.

Kimberly Rodriguez (M.A., Michigan State University) is an Assistant Account Representative at J. Walter Thompson in Chicago, on Oscar Mayer Lunchables. She previously worked on the Kraft Macaroni & Cheese account at Foote, Cone & Belding Chicago after graduating with a master's degree in advertising account management from Michigan State University.

Darrell Roe (Ph.D., University of Georgia) is currently an Assistant Professor in Media Arts at Marist College. He has taught at the University of Georgia, Sam Houston State University, and Cameron University. Professionally, he has worked in radio and TV. His research interests include: telecommunications history, production aesthetics effects, and educational television. He recently presented a paper critically analyzing the portrayal of women in a TV western miniseries. Another paper explored visual intensity effects on cognitive resource shifting. Currently, he is working on two books: *Telecommunications Revolutions* and *Legislation of Maritime Wireless Telegraphy (1903-1912)*.

Liza Stavchansky is a doctoral candidate in advertising at The University of Texas at Austin; she expects to finish her dissertation in December 1999. She received both her M.A. in Advertising and her undergraduate degree in Marketing from the University of Texas at Austin. Her research interests include direct-to-consumer (DTC) prescription drug advertising and marketing. Recently, she presented a special topics session regarding DTC advertising and marketing at the 1999 American Academy of Advertising Conference in Albuquerque, New Mexico.

Jeffrey J. Stoltman (Ph.D., Syracuse University) is a Professor of Marketing at Wayne State University. His academic interests are focused on aspects of promotion and marketing strategy, consumer research, and public policy. He has worked in academia for over 20 years, has served as a consultant to several Fortune 500 firms, and is currently serving as University Vice President for Marketing and Communications.

Ann D. Walsh (Ph.D., University of Nebraska) is Assistant Professor of Marketing, College of Business and Technology, Western Illinois University.

Carole Walters (Bachelor of Commerce, University of Alberta) joined NSL in 1984 as Media Director. Prior to NSL she was Broadcast Supervisor at J. Walter Thompson, Vancouver, B.C., and Associate Media Director at McKim Advertising, Vancouver, B.C. She currently serves on the American Association of Advertising Agencies Interactive Marketing and New Media Committee, and consults on the development of an Interactive Media Studies curriculum for Miami University.

Christine Wright-Isak (Ph.D., University of Chicago) is former Senior Vice-President, Account Planning Director, Young & Rubicam New York. She is now president of her own marketing consulting firm, Northlight

Marketing, Inc. She is a member of the American Academy of Advertising, the AAA Publications Committee, and is Chair of the AAA Industry Relations Committee. She is also a member of the Association for Consumer Research, The Market Research Council, and Chief Judge of the Advertising Effectiveness Awards (The "EFFIES") from 1992-1997. She served on the Policy Board of ACR and Chaired its special Academia-Industry Relations Task Force in 1994. She served as Chairperson of the Advertising Research Foundation Qualitative Workshop, October 1998.